Along The Tracks:
A Directory of Named Places
on
Michigan Railroads

A
Clarke Historical Library
Sesquicentennial Publication

Along The Tracks:
A Directory of Named Places
on
Michigan Railroads

Graydon M. Meints

Mount Pleasant

Clarke Historical Library
Central Michigan University
1987

Publication of this book supported by a grant from the ANR Pipeline Company—a subsidiary of the Coastal Corporation.

Cover photographs courtesy of Sam Breck.

This book has been endorsed by the Michigan Sesquicentennial Commission as a Sesquicentennial project.

ISBN 0-916699-11-0
0-916699-12-9 (paper)

For my wife Gerlinde,
who always knew where I was.

TABLE OF CONTENTS

INTRODUCTION

A station, by railroad definition, is "a place designated on the time-table by name, at which a train may stop for traffic; or to enter or leave the main track; or from which fixed signals are operated." The first part of this definition describes places for public traffic — passenger depots, freight houses, country flag stops, and any other places where passengers or freight are received or delivered. These types of places comprise the great majority of the entries herein. The remainder of the definition identifies locations of railroad operations — sidings, yards, junctions, railroad crossings, and signal towers.

This directory is a comprehensive listing of named railroad locations in the state of Michigan. It includes named places on the common carrier railroads only, and does not include privately-owned industrial, mining, logging, tourist, and such type railroads. Also it does not include electric interurban or street railway lines. There have been very few communities of any size that have not been served at some time by a common carrier railroad.

Part 1 of this directory is an alphabetical listing of all named places and gives the county in which it is located. Part 2 has an alphabetical list of Lower Peninsula railroads followed by a listing, by county, of the named places in each Lower Peninsula county. Part 3 is similarly arranged for the Upper Peninsula.

Three added data accompany each railroad place name entry in Parts 2 and 3. A number symbol (#) is to the left of the name if the location has not been determined with some precision. To the right of the name are given, when determinable, the section, the township, and the range number of the named place. Michigan was surveyed by the Congressional township method, laying out the state in a grid of townships six miles square, with thirty-six one-square-mile sections in each township. Section numbers, with township numbers, are readily available on Michigan Department of Natural Resources maps, U.S. topographic maps, and Rockford Map Publishers' county plat atlases. The eastern parts of the counties of Monroe, Wayne, Macomb, and St. Clair were not surveyed by this method; the absence of this data is indicated by a dash.

The right side of the page identifies the railroad line or lines at that place together with mileage shown to one decimal place, if the location has been determined with accuracy. The mileage given is the distance from the initial station on that line — most often the place at which original construction began. Usually construction progressed east-to-west or south-to-north in Michigan. On existing lines the distances coincide with current mile posts (mileage markers). Mileages without decimals or with fractions indicate approximate locations. When two rail lines are joined by a dash, the same site served both lines. A semicolon separating two lines indicates a separate site for each railroad line. The railroad name abbreviations and main line and branch line designations at the beginning of Parts 2 and 3 are those of the compiler and have been developed in his unpublished research. Some familiarity is presumed as to corporate names and the succession of changes of them. In general the ownership of property is as it existed about the 1940s.

No attempt has been made in this compilation to show the date when the location was first named, or when the name ceased to be used. It was planned initially to do this but the task soon proved impractical if not impossible. Names appeared and disappeared very casually; others were dropped from the record and reinstated later. The railroad station and the post office sometimes had different names, and one of them might eventually change its name formally to conform to the other's. If, however, a location has had more than one name, the earlier name has a reference to the newer name with the word "now". If a name has been assigned to two locations a quarter-mile or more distant from each other, "old" and "new" identify the sequence.

Spelling presented its own particular problem. Orthography a hundred years ago was not better than it is today. The spelling used herein is that used by the railroad, so far as possible. When an alternate spelling was used occasionally it is also shown. Also, the use of the apostrophe has been a problem. A station that was first named, say, Smith's Siding, in time became Smith's, and today is known as Smiths or Smith. is an example. For the sake of consistency the apostrophe has been omitted and the plural or possessive or extended form is shown with the additional letters or word enclosed in parentheses: Smith(s) (Siding).

Nearly ten years of research have gone into the compilation of the information included in this work. The compiler accepts full responsibility for any errors or omissions. Readers are invited to forward any corrections or additional information to the compiler at 5220 Texas Drive, Kalamazoo, Mich. 49009.

PART ONE:

NAMED PLACES IN MICHIGAN

A	Calhoun
A	Jackson
Aabee	Antrim
Aarwood	Kalkaska
Abbott	Lenawee
Abbottsford	St. Clair
Abitosse	Gogebic
Abke	Tuscola
Abronia	Allegan
Achas	Benzie
Achill	Roscommon
Acker Mill	Alger
Ackers	Alger
Ackers Point	Barry
Ackerson Lake	Jackson
Ackley	Schoolcraft
Acme	Grand Traverse
Ada	Kent
Adair	St. Clair
Adams	Calhoun
Adams Corners	Huron
Adams Mine	Marquette
Adamsville	Mason
Addis	Alger
Addison	Lenawee
Addison Jct.	Lenawee
Adrian	Lenawee
Adventure	Ontonagon
Afton	Cheboygan
Agate	Ontonagon
Agnew	Ottawa
Ahmeek	Keweenaw
Ahmeek Jct.	Keweenaw
Ahmeek Mill	Houghton
Ainger	Eaton
Air Line Jct.	Cass

Akron	Tuscola
Akron Coal Mine	Tuscola
Alabaster	Iosco
Alabaster Jct.	Iosco
Alamando	Midland
Alamo	Kalamazoo
Alanson	Emmet
Alba	Antrim
Alberta	Chippewa
Albion	Calhoun
Albion Mine	Marquette
Alcock	Monroe
Alcona	Alcona
Alden	Antrim
Alder	Alger
Alder	Marquette
Alderson	Newaygo
Alecto	Delta
Alexander	Chippewa
Alexander	Crawford
Alfred	Berrien
Alfred	Dickinson
Alger	Arenac
Algonac	St. Clair
Alicia	Saginaw
Allegan	Allegan
Allen	Hillsdale
Allen Mine	Marquette
Allen Park	Wayne
Allen Road	Wayne
Allens	Osceola
Allenton	St. Clair
Allenville	Mackinac
Alleyton	Newaygo
Allouez Mine	Houghton
Allyn	Benzie
Alma	Gratiot
Almont	Lapeer
Almont Jct.	St. Clair
Aloha	Cheboygan
Alpena	Alpena

Alpena Jct.	Alpena
Alperos	Eaton
Alpha	Benzie
Alpha	Iron
Alpine	Kent
Alston	Houghton
Alto	Kent
Alyn	Lake
Amadore	Sanilac
Amasa	Iron
Amasa Porter Mine	Iron
Amasa Porter Mine Jct.	Iron
Amber	Mason
American Mine	Marquette
American Mine Jct.	Marquette
Ambroses	Ogemaw
Amble	Montcalm
Ames	Alger
Ames	Menominee
Amy	Oakland
Anderson	Livingston
Anderson	Marquette
Anderson	Menominee
Anderson	Midland
Anderson	Montmorency
Anderson	Osceola
Anderson	Otsego
Anderson	Sanilac
Andersons Siding	Huron
Andersons Spur	Iron
Andersonville	Oakland
Angell	Grand Traverse
Angling	Kalkaska
Ann Arbor	Washtenaw
Anna River	Alger
Ann Pere	Livingston
Anthony	Houghton
Antlers	Marquette
Antoine	Dickinson
Antoine Mine	Dickinson
Antrim	Antrim

Anvil Mine	Gogebic
Applegate	Sanilac
Appleton Mine	Dickinson
Aragon Jct.	Dickinson
Aragon Mine	Dickinson
Arbutus Beach	Otsego
Arcadia	Manistee
Arcadia	Wexford
Arcadian Jct.	Houghton
Arcadian Mine	Houghton
Archibald Mine	Marquette
Ardis	Missaukee
Ardis Jct.	Missaukee
Arenac Spur	Arenac
Arendal	Manistee
Argenta	Kalamazoo
Arland	Jackson
Armada	Macomb
Armenia Mine	Iron
Armstrong	Iron
Arn	Bay
Arn	Iosco
Arndt	Saginaw
Arnheim	Baraga
Arnold	Bay
Arnold	Marquette
Arnold	Menominee
Arnold Lake	Clare
Arrow	Bay
Arthur	Saginaw
Ash	Marquette
Ash	Wayne
Ash	Wexford
Ashland	Newaygo
Ashland Mine	Gogebic
Ashley	Gratiot
Ashmore	Tuscola
Ashton	Osceola
Aspinwall	Jackson
Assinins	Baraga
Asteroid Mine	Gogebic

Athens	Calhoun
Athens Mine	Marquette
Atherton	Huron
Atkins	St. Clair
Atkinson	Iron
Atlanta	Montmorency
Atlantic	Houghton
Atlas	Houghton
Attica	Lapeer
Atwater	Huron
Atwood	Tuscola
Atwood Jct.	Genesee
Atwoods Siding	Clare
Auburn	Bay
Auburn	Oakland
Auburn Heights	Oakland
AuGres	Arenac
Augusta	Kalamazoo
Augusta Coal Chutes	Kalamazoo
Aurora Mine	Gogebic
AuSable	Iosco
AuSable River	Crawford
AuSable River	Mason
AuSable River Jct.	Iosco
Austin	Kalamazoo
Austin	Marquette
Austin Jct.	Marquette
Austin Lake	Kalamazoo
Austins Siding	Presque Isle
AuTrain	Alger
Avenue Jct.	Kent
Averill(s)	Midland
Avery(s)	Berrien
Avery Avenue	Wayne
Avery Track Pan	Berrien
Avoca	St. Clair
Azalia	Monroe

-B-

Babcocks Wye	Arenac
Bach	Huron

Bacon	Antrim
Bad Axe	Huron
Bagdad	Marquette
Bagdad Jct.	Marquette
Bagley	Menominee
Bagley	Otsego
Bagnall	Wexford
Bahles Switch	Leelanau
Bailey	Muskegon
Baileys Wye	Oakland
Bailies	Newaygo
Bainton	Berrien
Baird	St. Clair
Baker	Kalamazoo
Baker Mine	Iron
Bakers	Hillsdale
Bakers	Newaygo
Bakers	Ottawa
Bakertown	Berrien
Balch	Kalamazoo
Balch	Lenawee
Baldwin	Lake
Baldwin Mills	Jackson
Baldwins Crossing	Lenawee
Baldy	Alger
Balkan Mine	Iron
Balkwell	St. Clair
Ball Creek	Kent
Ballous	Menominee
Ballous Siding	Charlevoix
Balmers	St. Clair
Balsam	Iron
Baltic	Houghton
Baltic Jct.	Houghton
Baltic Mine	Iron
Baltimore	Ontonagon
Bamfield	Alcona
Banat	Menominee
Bancroft	Marquette
Bancroft	Shiawassee
Bangor	Bay

Bangor	Van Buren
Bank 6	Otsego
Bankers	Berrien
Bankers	Hillsdale
Banks	Bay
Bank Sand	Tuscola
Bannister	Gratiot
Baraga	Baraga
Barclay	Ontonagon
Bark	Manistee
Barker City	Roscommon
Barker Creek	Kalkaska
Bark River	Delta
Barkville	Delta
Barnards	Antrim
Barn Branch	Otsego
Barnes	Kalkaska
Barnes	Marquette
Barnes-Hecker Mine	Marquette
Barnett	Oceana
Barnetts Siding	Berrien
Barnum Mine	Marquette
Barnum Siding	Marquette
Baroda	Berrien
Barrett Track	Wayne
Barrison	Van Buren
Barron Lake	Cass
Barry	Jackson
Barryton	Mecosta
Bart	Huron
Bartlett Street	Kent
Barton	Washtenaw
Bashore	Baraga
Basil	Marquette
Basswood	Iron
Batavia	Branch
Batchellor	Mason
Bates	Grand Traverse
Bates Interchange	Iron
Bates Jct.	Iron
Bates Mine	Iron

Bath	Clinton
Bath Mills	Jackson
Battle Creek	Calhoun
Batton	Alcona
Baw Beese	Hillsdale
Baxter	Wexford
Bay City	Bay
Bay City Crossing	Oakland
Bay City E. S.	Bay
Bay City Jct.	Wayne
Bay City Road	Midland
Bay City W.S.	Bay
Bay Jct.	Bay
Bay Mills	Chippewa
Bay Point	Benzie
Bay Port	Huron
Bay Port Jct.	Huron
Bayshore	Charlevoix
Bayshore	Marquette
Bay Siding	Delta
Bay View	Emmet
B.C. & B.C. Jct.	Bay
B. & D. Camp 1	Manistee
B. & D. Camp 2	Manistee
Beacon Hill	Houghton
Beadle	Iosco
Beadle Lake	Calhoun
Beahan	Emmet
Bear Creek	Manistee
Bear Creek	Schoolcraft
Beardsleys	Bay
Bear Lake	Otsego
Bear Lake Jct.	Charlevoix
Bear Lake Mills	Van Buren
Beaton	Gogebic
Beaubien Street	Wayne
Beaufait Station	Wayne
Beaufort	Baraga
Beaufort Mine	Baraga
Beaver	Alger
Beaver	Delta

Beaver	Marquette
Beaver Lake	Ogemaw
Beaver Mine	Bay
Beaverton	Gladwin
Beck	Wayne
Becketts Crossing	Missaukee
Beckwith Siding	Kalamazoo
Bedford	Calhoun
Bedford	Wayne
Beebe	Bay
Beebe	Cass
Beebes	Macomb
Beebe Spur	Alpena
Beech Tree	Ottawa
Beechwood	Iron
Beehan	Otsego
Beesons (Spur)	Schoolcraft
Beet	Gratiot
Beever(s)	Alcona
Beitners	Grand Traverse
Belden	Wayne
Belding	Ionia
Belford	Oakland
Bell	Presque Isle
Bell	Washtenaw
Bellaire	Antrim
Bellaire	Baraga
Belle River	St. Clair
Belleville	Wayne
Bellevue	Eaton
Bell Siding	Mecosta
Bells Landing	Emmet
Belmont	Kent
Belsay	Genesee
Belsay Yard	Genesee
Belt	Ontonagon
Belt Line	Oakland
Belt Line Jct.	Houghton
Belt Line Jct.	Wayne
Belvedere	Charlevoix
Belvidere	Montcalm

Bender	Oceana
Bendon	Benzie
Bengal Mine	Iron
Benham	Emmet
Bennett	Alger
Bennett	Lake
Bennett	Wayne
Bennett Mine	Marquette
Bennington	Shiawassee
Benson Yard	Wayne
Bentley	Bay
Benton Harbor	Berrien
Benway	Van Buren
Benzonia	Benzie
Bergam	Dickinson
Bergland	Ontonagon
Bergland Mills	Ontonagon
Berglands Mill Trk.	Houghton
Berkshire	Sanilac
Berkshire Mine	Iron
Berlamont	Van Buren
Berlin	Ottawa
Berlin	Tuscola
Berlin Yard	Wayne
Bernard	Gogebic
Berne Jct.	Huron
Berrien Center	Berrien
Berrien Springs	Berrien
Berry	Muskegon
Berta	Menominee
Bertrand	Berrien
Berville	St. Clair
Bess	Baraga
Bessemer	Gogebic
Bessemer Jct.	Gogebic
Bessie Mine	Marquette
Bessie Mine Jct.	Marquette
Beta Mine	Iron
Betsey	Benzie
Beulah	Benzie
Beyersdorf Spur	Iron

Bichler	Delta
Big Bay	Marquette
Big Creek	Marquette
Big Creek	Oscoda
Big Cut	Presque Isle
Bigelow	Montmorency
Bigelows	Mecosta
Big Rapids	Mecosta
Big Rapids Jct.	Muskegon
Big Rock	Montmorency
Bills	Crawford
Bimo	Lenawee
Bing	Alger
Bingham	Leelanau
Birch	Baraga
Birch	Marquette
Birch Creek	Menominee
Birch Run	Saginaw
Birchwood	Cheboygan
Bird	Menominee
Birdsall	Lenawee
Birdseye	Alger
Birmingham	Oakland
Birrell	Wayne
Bisonette	Iosco
Bissell	Mackinac
Bitely	Newaygo
Bjorkman	Dickinson
Black Creek	Mason
Black Lake	Muskegon
Black Lake	Presque Isle
Black Lake Jct.	Presque Isle
Blackmar	Saginaw
Blackmarrs	Oceana
Black River	Alcona
Black River	Allegan
Black Siding	Gogebic
Blaine	St. Clair
Blair	Grand Traverse
Blake	Benzie
Blakes	Berrien

Blanchard	Isabella
Blanchards	Montcalm
Blanchards New Spur	Antrim
Blaney	Schoolcraft
Blaney Jct.	Schoolcraft
Blemers	Gogebic
Blendon	Ottawa
Bliss Branch	Gladwin
Blissfield	Lenawee
Blissfield Jct.	Lenawee
Block	Alger
Blodgett	Missaukee
Blodgett	Wexford
Bloomfield	Tuscola
Bloomfield Hills	Oakland
Bloomingdale	Van Buren
Blond	Presque Isle
Blosser	Antrim
Blount	Menominee
Blueberry	Alger
Blueberry Mine	Marquette
Blueberry Mine Jct.	Marquette
Blue Lake	Kalkaska
Blue Lake Jct.	Antrim
Bluffs	Midland
Blum	Menominee
Bly	Kalamazoo
BO	Kalamazoo
Boardman	Grand Traverse
Boardman Jct.	Grand Traverse
Boat Landing	Benzie
Bodus	Leelanau
Bogardus	Emmet
Bohnet	Ogemaw
Bolton	Alpena
Bonds	Wexford
Bonds Mill	Wexford
Bonifas	Luce
Book Mine	Iron
Boomers	Oakland
Boon	Wexford

Borland	Mecosta
Boston	Houghton
Boston Jct.	Houghton
Boston Jct.	Marquette
Boston Mine	Marquette
Botsford	Kalamazoo
Bottje	Ottawa
Boucha	Alger
Boulevard	Wayne
Boulevard Switch	Wayne
Bovee	Mackinac
Boven	Alger
Bovine Siding	Baraga
Bowen	Kent
Bowens	Allegan
Bowles Spur	Ontonagon
Boyd	Allegan
Boyds	Houghton
Boyces	Roscommon
Boyers	Gratiot
Boyne	Charlevoix
Boyne City	Charlevoix
Boyne Falls	Charlevoix
Brabant	Alger
Bradford (Lake)	Otsego
Bradkins	Chippewa
Bradley	Allegan
Bradley (Farm)	Tuscola
Bradley Mine	Dickinson
Bradleyville	Tuscola
Brady	Kalamazoo
Brady	Ontonagon
Brampton	Delta
Branch	Mason
Branch Lake	Charlevoix
Branch Siding	Genesee
Brannin	Kent
Brasted Mine	Marquette
Bravo	Allegan
Brazil	Osceola
Breckenridge	Gratiot

Breedsville	Van Buren
Breen Mine	Dickinson
Breitung Mine	Marquette
Breitung-Hematite Mine	Marquette
Brennan	Antrim
Brent Creek	Genesee
Breshme	Chippewa
Brethren	Manistee
Brewer	Saginaw
Brewster Siding	Saginaw
Briar Hill	Monroe
Brickerville	Antrim
Bricks	Gladwin
Brickton	Muskegon
Brick Yard Siding	Calhoun
Bridgehampton	Sanilac
Bridge Jct.	Bay
Bridgeport	Saginaw
Bridge Street	Kent
Bridgewater	Washtenaw
Bridges	Benzie
Bridgman	Berrien
Brier Hill Mine	Dickinson
Brighton	Kalamazoo
Brighton	Livingston
Briley	Montmorency
Brimley	Chippewa
Bristol	Iosco
Bristol	Kent
Bristol Mine	Iron
Britton	Lenawee
Britton Spur	Houghton
Broadbridge	St. Clair
Brockton	Sanilac
Brockway	Eaton
Brockway Center	St. Clair
Brodie	Isabella
Brohman	Newaygo
Bronson	Branch
Brookfield	Manistee
Brookings (Lake)	Newaygo

Brooklyn	Jackson
Brooks	Bay
Brooks	Menominee
Brooks	Newaygo
Brothers	Otsego
Brotherton	Houghton
Brotherton	Sanilac
Brotherton Mine	Gogebic
Brotherton Mine	Marquette
Brown	Charlevoix
Brown	Gratiot
Brown	Missaukee
Brown City	Sanilac
Brownell	Kalamazoo
Browns	Berrien
Browns Crossing	Marquette
Browns Mills	Van Buren
Browns Siding	Calhoun
Browns Siding	Marquette
Brownstone	Alger
Brownstown	Wayne
Bruce	Marquette
Bruce	St. Clair
Bruce	Tuscola
Bruces Crossing	Ontonagon
Brundage Spur	Bay
Brunswick	Muskegon
Brutus	Emmet
Bryant	Alcona
Bryar Hill	Monroe
Bryden	Dickinson
Buchanan	Berrien
Buchholz Mine	Iron
Buchtel	Isabella
Buckley	Wexford
Buckley & Douglas Spur	Antrim
Buckroe	Marquette
Bucks	Crawford
Buells	Otsego
Buena Vista	Saginaw
Buffalo Mine	Marquette

Bundy	Isabella
Bunker Lake	Oceana
Bunns	Marquette
Bunton	Presque Isle
Bunyea	Wexford
Burchs Mill	Kent
Burdick	Isabella
Burgess	Charlevoix
Burlington	Calhoun
Burnham	Isabella
Burns	St. Clair
Burns Siding	Monroe
Burr Oak	St. Joseph
Burt	Saginaw
Burtis	Marquette
Burton	Shiawassee
Bushkill	Ottawa
Bush Lake	Ogemaw
Bushnell	Montcalm
Bushs	Kent
Bushville	Cheboygan
Butcher	Kalkaska
Butlins	St. Clair
Butternut	Montcalm
Buttersville	Mason
Butwell	Manistee
Byers	Alcona
Byers	Mecosta
Byron	Kent
Byron	Shiawassee
Byron Center	Kent

-C-

Cableton	Van Buren
Cadillac	Wexford
Cadiz	Iron
Cadmus	Lenawee
Caffey	Mackinac
Cahoon(s)	Montmorency
Cairns	Clare
Calciferous	Alger

Calcite	Presque Isle
Caledonia	Kent
Califf	Muskegon
Calkinsville	Isabella
Callan	Dickinson
Calumet	Houghton
Calumet Jct.	Houghton
Calumet Mine	Dickinson
Calvin	Saginaw
Camden	Hillsdale
Cambria Mine	Marquette
Cambria-Jackson Mine	Marquette
Cambridge	Lenawee
Cameron	Antrim
Cameron	Otsego
Campbell	Charlevoix
Campbell	Clare
Campbell	Delta
Camp Frances	Gogebic
Camp Lake	Kent
Camp 1	Charlevoix
Camp 2	Charlevoix
Camp 3	Charlevoix
Camp 4	Charlevoix
Camp 4	Marquette
Camp 4	Menominee
Camp 5	Charlevoix
Camp 5	Ontonagon
Camp 6	Charlevoix
Camp 6	Menominee
Camp Seven Hill	Schoolcraft
Camp 7	Marquette
Camp 8	Charlevoix
Camp 8	Marquette
Camp 8	Newaygo
Camp 9	Charlevoix
Camp 10	Antrim
Camp 10	Charlevoix
Camp 10	Schoolcraft
Camp 11	Antrim
Camp 14	Schoolcraft

Camp 15	Alger
Camp 21	Montmorency
Camp 21	Otsego
Camp 22	Otsego
Camp 25	Montmorency
Camp 29	Montmorency
Camp 30	Montmorency
Camp 31	Menominee
Camp 34	Schoolcraft
Camp 35	Schoolcraft
Camp 65	Schoolcraft
Camp 74	Schoolcraft
Camp 85	Schoolcraft
Camp 86	Schoolcraft
Camp St. Louis	Kalamazoo
Camp Tolfree	Ontonagon
Cana	Chippewa
Canal Bridge	St. Clair
Canfield	Alpena
Canfield Camp	Mason
Canfields	Lake
Canfields "Y"	Lake
Canton	Wayne
Canwell	Livingston
Capac	St. Clair
Carbondale	Menominee
Cardiff Mine	Iron
Cardinal Jct.	Newaygo
Carey(ville)	Lake
Carl	Berrien
Carland	Shiawassee
Carleton	Monroe
Carlisle	Kent
Carlshend	Marquette
Carlson	Gogebic
Carlton	St. Clair
Carney	Menominee
Caro	Tuscola
Caro Jct.	Tuscola
Carons	Alger
Carp	Marquette

Carpenter	Emmet
Carpenter	Lapeer
Carpenter Jct.	Iron
Carpenter Mine	Iron
Carp Furnace	Marquette
Carp Lake	Emmet
Carp Lake	Leelanau
Carrolls	Kalamazoo
Carrollton	Saginaw
Carruthers Spur	Mackinac
Carson City	Montcalm
Carsonville	Sanilac
Carters	Benzie
Carys Spur	Dickinson
Cascade	Antrim
Cascade	Kent
Cascade Jct.	Marquette
Cascade Mine	Marquette
Case	Benzie
Case	Presque Isle
Casemore	Schoolcraft
Cases	Benzie
Caseville	Huron
Cash	Sanilac
Casnovia	Muskegon
Caspian	Iron
Caspian Mine	Iron
Cass City	Tuscola
Cassopolis	Cass
Castile Mine	Gogebic
Cathro	Alpena
Cavite	Alger
C. B. Jct.	Otsego
Cedar	Leelanau
Cedar	Menominee
Cedar	Presque Isle
Cedar Bank	Marquette
Cedar City	Leelanau
Cedardale	Sanilac
Cedar Lake	Montcalm
Cedarmere	Alcona

Cedar Run	Grand Traverse
Cedar Springs	Kent
Cedar Spur	Alpena
Cedar Street	Ingham
Cement City	Lenawee
Cemetery	Mason
Cemetery Crossing	Ottawa
Center Line	Macomb
Center Street	Bay
Centerville	Delta
Centerville	St. Joseph
Central	Keweenaw
Central Lake	Antrim
Centre Street	Saginaw
Ceresco	Calhoun
Chadwick	Ionia
Chairson	Delta
Chamberlains	St. Joseph
Chamberlin	Otsego
Chamberlins	Berrien
Champion	Marquette
Champion Jct.	Marquette
Champion Mine	Marquette
Champlain St.	Wayne
Chandler	Clinton
Chandler	Delta
Chandler	Wayne
Chandler Falls	Delta
Channing	Dickinson
Chapin Mine	Dickinson
Chapins	Ingham
Chapman	Alger
Chapman	Monroe
Charcoal Kilns	Oceana
Charing Cross	Oakland
Charlesworth	Eaton
Charlevoix	Charlevoix
Charlotte	Eaton
Charltons	Charlevoix
Chase	Lake
Chase Mine	Marquette

Chases	Lenawee
Chassell	Houghton
Chatham	Alger
Chatham Mine	Iron
Chatterton	Mecosta
Cheboygan	Cheboygan
Cheboygan Dock	Cheboygan
Cheboyganing	Bay
Chelsea	Washtenaw
Chelsea Track Pan	Washtenaw
Chene St.	Wayne
Cheney	Crawford
Cherrie	Charlevoix
Cherry Valley	Schoolcraft
Chesaning	Saginaw
Chesebrough	Chippewa
Cheshire Jct.	Marquette
Cheshire Mine	Marquette
Chester	Eaton
Chesterfield	Macomb
Chestonia	Antrim
Chevriers	Alcona
Chicago Jct.	Ingham
Chicago Mine	Gogebic
Chicago Mine	Marquette
Chicago Siding	Ogemaw
Chicagon	Iron
Chicagon Mine	Iron
Chickaming	Berrien
Chief Lake	Manistee
Childsdale	Kent
Childs Mill	Kent
Chilson	Livingston
Chippewa	Osceola
Chippewa Lake	Mecosta
Choate	Ontonagon
Chocolay	Marquette
Church	Oscoda
Churchill	Antrim
Churchill	Cheboygan
Churchills	Manistee

Cicotte St.	Wayne
Cisco	Mackinac
Cisco Lake	Gogebic
Claggetts	Wexford
Claire Mine	Iron
Clam Lake	Wexford
Clano	Dickinson
Clare	Clare
Clarence	Clare
Clarence	Livingston
Clarendon	Calhoun
Clarion	Charlevoix
Clark	Houghton
Clarkesville	Monroe
Clark Lake	Jackson
Clarks	Huron
Clarks	Wexford
Clarksburg	Marquette
Clarkston	Oakland
Clarksville	Ionia
Clary	Benzie
Clay	Eaton
Clay	Lenawee
Clay Avenue	Wayne
Clay Track	Genesee
Clayton	Lenawee
Clear Lake	Hillsdale
Clear Lake Jct.	Crawford
Clearwater	Kalkaska
Cleeremans	Menominee
Clement	Kalkaska
Cleveland	Cheboygan
Cleveland Mine	Marquette
Cleveland Hematite Mine	Marquette
Cliff	Keweenaw
Clifford	Lapeer
Clifford Mine	Dickinson
Cliffs	Delta
Cliffs Mine	Marquette
Cliffs Siding	Baraga
Climax	Kalamazoo

Clinton	Lenawee
Clintons	Clare
Clio	Genesee
Cloverdale	Barry
Clovers	Leelanau
Cloverville	Muskegon
Clowry	Marquette
Clyde	Allegan
Clyde	Oakland
Clydes	Arenac
Clytie	Menominee
CN	Wexford
Coal Dock	Marquette
Coal Kiln	Midland
Coalville	Jackson
Coalwood	Alger
Coats Grove	Barry
Cobb Jct.	Grand Traverse
Cockell	Oceana
Code	Alcona
Cohoctah	Livingston
Colby	Montcalm
Colby Mine	Gogebic
Colden	Bay
Coldwater	Branch
Cole	Oakland
Cole Creek	Houghton
Coleman	Midland
Colerain	Oakland
Coles	Chippewa
Colfax	Bay
Colfax	Mecosta
College Farm	Ingham
Colling	Tuscola
Collins	Ionia
Collins	Oceana
Coloma	Berrien
Colon	St. Joseph
Colon Jct.	St. Joseph
Columbia	Van Buren
Columbia Mine	Marquette

Columbiaville	Lapeer
Columbus	St. Clair
Columbus Avenue	Bay
Colwell	Montcalm
Comfort	Antrim
Comfort Siding	Kalamazoo
Comins	Oscoda
Compton	Osceola
Comstock	Kalamazoo
Comstock Park	Kent
Comus	Menominee
Concord	Jackson
Condit	Calhoun
Cone	Monroe
Conger	Manistee
Conger	Montcalm
Congo	Menominee
Conklin	Ottawa
Conley	Lake
Connor(s)	Montmorency
Connors Camp 2	Montmorency
Connors Grove	Wayne
Connors Spur	Mackinac
Connorville	Gogebic
Conrad	Mason
Constantine	St. Joseph
Conway	Emmet
Cooke Dam	Iosco
Cooks	Sanilac
Cooks	Schoolcraft
Cooks Mill	Schoolcraft
Cooks Switch	Oceana
Cooley Road	Sanilac
Coolidge	Wayne
Cooper	Kalamazoo
Cooper	Schoolcraft
Coopers Corner	Iosco
Coopersville	Ottawa
Copemish	Manistee
Copper City	Houghton
Copps Spur	Marquette

Coral	Montcalm
Corbett	Houghton
Corbin	Otsego
Corbus	Lenawee
Cordell	Chippewa
Corey	Cass
Corfu	Manistee
Corinne	Mackinac
Cornell	Delta
Cornell	St. Clair
Cornwells	Otsego
Corsan	Tuscola
Cortland Mine	Iron
Corunna	Shiawassee
Corunna Coal Mine	Shiawassee
Coryell	Bay
Corymbo	Berrien
Cottage Park	Chippewa
County Line	Muskegon
County Line	Saginaw
County Line	Tuscola
County Spur	Kalamazoo
Court Street	Saginaw
Court St. W. S.	Saginaw
Cousin	Ontonagon
Cousino	Monroe
Covert	Van Buren
Covington	Baraga
Cowdens	Isabella
Cowham	Lenawee
Cowley(s Spur)	Iosco
Craigsmere	Ontonagon
Crampton	Charlevoix
Cramptons	Tuscola
Cranage	Bay
Cranage	Ogemaw
Cranberry Jct.	Ontonagon
Cranberry Spur	Alpena
Cranes	Benzie
Cranmer	Missaukee
Crapo	Genesee

Crapo	Mecosta
Crapo Farm	Genesee
Crapo Street	Genesee
Crawford	Crawford
Crawford (Quarry)	Presque Isle
Creen	Saginaw
Creevy Siding	Huron
Creighton	Schoolcraft
Crescent	Marquette
Cressey	Barry
Crestview	Keweenaw
Crestview Jct.	Keweenaw
Crocker	Osceola
Crofton	Kalkaska
Cronje	Ottawa
Crooked Lake	Barry
Crooked Lake	Clare
Crooked Lake Jct.	Alcona
Cross Bank	Cass
Crossman	Tuscola
Crossmans	Oceana
Croswell	Sanilac
Croton	Newaygo
Crow Island	Saginaw
Crowley	Otsego
Crozer	Gogebic
Croziers Mill	Gogebic
Cruse	Benzie
Crystal City	Benzie
Crystal Falls	Iron
Crystal Falls Jct.	Iron
Crystal Lake	Benzie
Crystal Lake	Houghton
Cuff Siding	Dickinson
Culver	Kalkaska
Culvers	Arenac
Cummer	Missaukee
Cunard	Menominee
Cundy (Mine)	Dickinson
Curfew	Charlevoix
Curran	Alcona

Curry (Mine)	Dickinson
Curtis	Emmet
Curtis	Mackinac
Curtis Siding	Wayne
Cushman	Charlevoix
Cusino	Schoolcraft
Custer	Mason
Cutlers	Wexford
Cyclops Mine	Dickinson
Cyre	Marquette
Cyr Mine	Marquette

-D-

D&I Jct.	Wayne
D&M Jct.	Wayne
Dafter	Chippewa
Daggett	Menominee
Dailey	Cass
Dakes Mill	Wexford
Dale Branch	Crawford
Dallas	Clinton
Dalton	Muskegon
Damon	Ogemaw
Dana	Ingham
Dana	Montmorency
Danaher	Lake
Danaher	Luce
Danby	Ionia
Danford	Antrim
Daniels	Clinton
Danielson	Houghton
Dault Spur	Alcona
Daust	Presque Isle
Davidson	Arenac
Davidson	Alcona
Davidson	Washtenaw
Davidson No. 1 Mine	Iron
Davidson No. 2 Mine	Iron
Davidson No. 3 Mine	Iron
Davidson Wye Branch Jct.	Montmorency
Davisburg	Oakland

Davis Mine	Gogebic
Davis Mine	Marquette
Davison	Genesee
Dawson	Genesee
Days River	Delta
Dayton	Berrien
Dayton	Tuscola
Dead River	Marquette
Dean	Midland
Dearborn	Wayne
Dearborn Jct.	Wayne
Dearoad	Wayne
Decatur	Van Buren
Decker	Sanilac
Deckerville	Sanilac
Deep River	Arenac
Deerfield	Lenawee
Deerfield	Van Buren
Deer Lake	Charlevoix
Deer Lake	Lake
Deer Lake	Marquette
Deer Park	Luce
Deerton	Alger
Defer	Gogebic
Deford	Tuscola
DeGrass Mine	Iron
Dehoco	Wayne
Deiberts	Kalkaska
Deisinger Siding	Sanilac
Delaware	Keweenaw
Delhi	Ingham
Delhi	Washtenaw
Delhi Mills	Washtenaw
Dell	Chippewa
Della	Marquette
Delray	Wayne
Delta	Clinton
Delta (Jct.)	Schoolcraft
Delta Switch	Wayne
Delta Yard	Wayne
Delton	Barry

Delwin	Isabella
Dempsey	Kalkaska
Denmark Jct.	Tuscola
Dennis	Antrim
Dennis	Grand Traverse
Dennis	Osceola
Dennison(s)	Ottawa
Denton	Wayne
Denver	Isabella
Depews Siding	Macomb
Dequindre St.	Wayne
Derby	Berrien
Derry(s)	Wexford
Desmond	Manistee
Detroit	Wayne
Detroiter Mobile	Gratiot
Detroit Mine	Marquette
Devereaux	Jackson
Dew	Oscoda
Dewar	Tuscola
Deward	Crawford
Dewey	Alger
Dewey	Kent
Dewey	Marquette
Dewey	Shiawassee
Dewings	Osceola
Dexter	Washtenaw
Dexter Jct.	Marquette
Dey Mine	Marquette
Diamond Lake	Cass
Diamond Loch	Newaygo
Diana	Iron
Diann	Monroe
Dibble	Midland
Dick	Chippewa
Dickinson	Newaygo
Dickinsons	Montcalm
Dickson	Kent
Dicksons	Washtenaw
Dieming	Alger
Diffin	Alger

Diggins	Wexford
Dighton	Osceola
Diller	Mackinac
Dimondale	Eaton
Dingmans	Antrim
Dingmans	Isabella
Diorite	Marquette
Dishneau	Marquette
Dishno	Marquette
Diver	Cheboygan
Dix	Antrim
Dixon	Alger
Doane	Iosco
Dober No. 2 Mine	Iron
Dobbins	Montmorency
Dock	Kalamazoo
Dodge	Clare
Doherty	Isabella
Dollar Bay	Houghton
Dollar Bay Dock	Houghton
Dollarville	Luce
Donald	Saginaw
Donken	Houghton
Donnelly Branch Jct.	Montmorency
Dorgans	Chippewa
Dorias	Marquette
Dorr	Allegan
Dorr	Midland
Dorsey	Alger
Doster	Allegan
Doty	Alger
Double Track Switch	Macomb
Doubling	Alger
Doubling	Manistee
Doubling Track	Kalamazoo
Dougherty	Menominee
Douglas	Manistee
Douglass	St. Joseph
Dover	Lenawee
Dow	Antrim
Dow	Houghton

Dow	Marquette
Dowagiac	Cass
Downing	Sanilac
Downing	Tuscola
Downington	Sanilac
Doyle	Gratiot
Doyle	Mecosta
Doyle	St. Clair
Doyles	Charlevoix
Doyles	Schoolcraft
Doyles Wye	Schoolcraft
Drayton Plains	Oakland
Drew	Isabella
Drew	Newaygo
Driggs	Schoolcraft
Drissel(s)	Saginaw
Dryads	Menominee
Dryburg	Chippewa
Dryden	Lapeer
Dublin	Manistee
Ducettes Spur	Delta
Ducey	Alger
Dudley	Missaukee
Dufeck Spur	Iron
Duffield	Genesee
Duforts	Wexford
Duke	Gogebic
Dukes	Marquette
Dunbars	Berrien
Duncan	Marquette
Dundee	Monroe
Dunham	Arenac
Dunham	Gogebic
Dunleith	Mackinac
Dunning	Allegan
Dunningville	Allegan
Dunn Mine	Iron
Dupont Jct.	Houghton
Durand	Shiawassee
Durban	Monroe
Durham	Charlevoix

Duro	Tuscola
Duroy	Osceola
Dutton	Kent
Dwight	Huron
Dyer	Cass

-E-

Eagle	Clinton
Eagle Bay	Huron
Eagle Mills	Kent
Eagle Mills	Marquette
Eagle Mills Transfer	Marquette
Eames	Oakland
Eassom	Kalamazoo
East Avenue	Jackson
East Avenue	Kalamazoo
East Bay	Alger
East Bay	Grand Traverse
East Branch	Luce
East Branch Jct.	Schoolcraft
East Cambria Mine	Marquette
East Champion Mine	Marquette
East Chicago Mine	Marquette
East Cohoctah	Livingston
East Cooper	Kalamazoo
East Detroit	Macomb
East Durand	Shiawassee
East Empire	Leelanau
East End	Antrim
East End	Cass
East Flint	Genesee
East Golden	Oceana
East Grand Rapids	Kent
East Houghton	Houghton
East Jordan	Charlevoix
East Lake	Manistee
Eastlake	Schoolcraft
East Lansing	Ingham
East Leroy	Calhoun
Eastman	Kalkaska
Eastman	Newaygo

East Mosherville	Hillsdale
East New York Mine	Marquette
East Norrie Mine	Gogebic
East Norway	Dickinson
Easton	Charlevoix
East Paris	Kent
East Saginaw	Saginaw
East Saugatuck	Allegan
East Tawas	Iosco
East Vulcan Mine	Dickinson
East Wequetonsing	Emmet
East Yard	Jackson
East Yard	Marquette
East Yard	Wayne
Eaton	Antrim
Eaton	Gratiot
Eaton Rapids	Eaton
Eaton Rapids Jct.	Jackson
Eau Claire	Berrien
Eben Jct.	Alger
Eckerman	Chippewa
Eckford	Calhoun
Ecorse	Wayne
Ecorse Jct.	Wayne
Eddys	Arenac
Eden	Ingham
Edgemere	Houghton
Edgemere Jct.	Houghton
Edgerton	Kent
Edgetts	Lake
Edison	Wayne
Edjon	Luce
Edmore	Montcalm
Edna	Roscommon
Edwards	Antrim
Edwardsburg	Cass
Edwards Lake	Ogemaw
Eagleston	Muskegon
Egypt	Genesee
8-Mile Road	Wayne
Eighty Foot Grade	St. Clair

Elba	Lapeer
Elberta	Benzie
Elbon	Chippewa
Eldred	Jackson
Elkerton	Kent
Elk Rapids	Antrim
Elkton	Huron
Ellsworth	Antrim
Elm	Wayne
Elmdale	Kent
Elmer	Sanilac
Elmira	Otsego
Elmira Br. Switch	Antrim
Elm River	Houghton
Elm Street	Calhoun
Elmton	Mason
Elmwood	Berrien
Elmwood	Iron
Elmwood	Wayne
Eloise	Wayne
Elsie	Clinton
Elton	Leelanau
Elwell	Gratiot
Emanuel	Van Buren
Emens	Muskegon
Emergency	Shiawassee
Emerson	Alpena
Emery Jct.	Iosco
Emmet	Marquette
Emmett	St. Clair
Emmett Street	Calhoun
Empire	Leelanau
Empire Jct.	Benzie
Empire Mine	Marquette
Engadine	Mackinac
Engine Works	Marquette
Englishville	Kent
Ennis	Lenawee
Ensel	Ingham
Ensign	Delta
Epworth Heights	Mason

Erb	Sanilac
Erickson	Gogebic
Erico	Antrim
Erie	Monroe
Erie Mine	Marquette
Erwin	Montcalm
Erwin	Newaygo
Escanaba	Delta
Essex	Antrim
Essexville	Bay
Estey	Gladwin
Ethel	Alger
Ethelwood	Gogebic
Eureka	Wayne
Eureka Mine	Gogebic
Eureka Place	Montcalm
Eustis	Menominee
Evans	Kent
Evart	Osceola
Evelyn	Alger
Evenwood	Muskegon
Everest	Gogebic
Everett	Menominee
Evergreen	Ontonagon
Ewen	Ontonagon
Excelsior Mine	Marquette
Exeter	Monroe
Exposition Switch	Wayne
Eyke	Clare

-F-

Faben	Shiawassee
Fabius	St. Joseph
Factoryville	St. Joseph
Fairbanks	Kalkaska
Fairbanks	Otsego
Fairbanks Mine	Iron
Fairfax	St. Joseph
Fairfield	Lenawee
Fair Grounds	Kent
Fairgrove	Tuscola

Fairitys	Wexford
Fairland	Berrien
Fairview	Oscoda
Faithorn	Menominee
Faithorn Jct.	Menominee
Faleston	Houghton
Falls	Ontonagon
Falmouth	Missaukee
Fargo	St. Clair
Farleigh	Bay
Farleys	Berrien
Farm	Alger
Farm	Houghton
Farmdale	Antrim
Farmer	Iosco
Farmers	Ottawa
Farmers	Sanilac
Farmham	Menominee
Farrs	St. Clair
Farrell Spur	Delta
Farrens	Kalkaska
Farwell	Clare
Fawn River	St. Joseph
Faunus	Menominee
Fayette	Otsego
Fays	Wexford
Federman	Monroe
Felch	Dickinson
Felch Jct.	Delta
Felton	Bay
Feltz	Charlevoix
Fennville	Allegan
Fenton	Genesee
Fentonville	Genesee
Fenwick	Montcalm
Fergus	Saginaw
Ferguson	Alger
Ferguson	Chippewa
Fern	Mason
Fernald	Kent
Ferndale	Oakland

Ferris	Crawford
Ferry	Delta
Ferry	Menominee
Ferry	Washtenaw
Ferrysburg	Ottawa
Few Mine	Dickinson
Fiborn Jct.	Mackinac
Fiborn (Quarry)	Mackinac
Fibre	Chippewa
Field	Alger
Field (Crossing)	Newaygo
Fife Lake	Grand Traverse
Fifield	Saginaw
Fifteenth Street	Wayne
Filer City	Manistee
Filers Switch	Grand Traverse
Filion	Huron
Fillmore	Allegan
Findley	St. Joseph
Findley Jct.	Houghton
Finnegan	Marquette
Finns	Alger
Firmin	Marquette
Fish Creek Branch	Montcalm
Fisher	Gladwin
Fisher	Kent
Fisher	Menominee
Fisher Camp	Oceana
Fishermans Paradise	Antrim
Fishers	Wayne
Fisherville	Bay
Fish Hatchery	Alger
Fish Lake	Lapeer
Fisk	Allegan
Fisk Mine	Gogebic
Fitch	Bay
Fitch Mine	Marquette
Fitzpatrick	Iosco
Fitzpatrick	Montmorency
Fitzpatrick	Oscoda
Five Channels Dam	Iosco

Five Channels Jct.	Alcona
Five Lake	Lapeer
Fix Bros. Siding	Monroe
Flagg	Kalamazoo
Flajoles	Bay
Flanders	Alpena
Flat Lake	Oscoda
Flat Rock	Alcona
Flat Rock	Delta
Flat Rock	Wayne
Flatrock Switch	Delta
Fleming	Livingston
Fletcher	Alpena
Fletcher Jct.	Alpena
Flint	Genesee
Flint River Jct.	Genesee
Floodwood	Dickinson
Floodwood River	Ontonagon
Florence	Manistee
Florence	St. Joseph
Flowerfield	St. Joseph
Flushing	Genesee
Flynn	Marquette
FN	Wayne
Fochtman	Emmet
Fogerty Mine	Iron
Forbes Mine	Iron
Ford	Oceana
Ford	Wayne
Ford Jct.	Wayne
Fordney	Saginaw
Ford River	Delta
Ford Siding	Dickinson
Fordson	Wayne
Fordson Yard	Wayne
Fordville	Schoolcraft
Forest	Crawford
Forest Hall	Cass
Forest Hill	Gratiot
Forest Lake	Alger
Forest Lawn	Wayne

Forestville	Marquette
Fork	Antrim
Forks Switch	Monroe
Forman	Lake
Formans	Emmet
Forsyth	Marquette
Fort Custer	Calhoun
Fortesque	Roscommon
Fort Gratiot	St. Clair
Fort Howard	Ottawa
Fort Street	Wayne
Fortune Lake	Iron
Fortune Lake Mine	Iron
Fort Wayne Jct.	Hillsdale
Fort Wayne Switch	Jackson
Foss	Bay
Foster	Gogebic
Foster	Isabella
Foster City	Dickinson
Foster Mine	Marquette
Fosters	Saginaw
Fosters	Washtenaw
Fostoria	Tuscola
Fouch	Leelanau
Fouchette	Houghton
Fountain	Antrim
Fountain	Mason
Four Mile Lake	Washtenaw
Fourth Street	Kent
Fowler	Clinton
Fowlerville	Livingston
Fox	Houghton
Fox	Kalamazoo
Fox	Kent
Foy	Baraga
France	Kalkaska
France	Monroe
Francis	Montmorency
Francisco	Jackson
Franciscoville	Jackson
Francis Mine	Marquette

Francis Siding	Ontonagon
Frank	Tuscola
Frankenmuth	Saginaw
Frankentrost	Saginaw
Frankfort	Benzie
Franklin	Houghton
Franklin Jct.	Houghton
Franklin Jr. Mine	Houghton
Franklin Mine	Houghton
Franklin	Kent
Fraser	Macomb
F.R.B. Jct.	Genesee
Freda	Houghton
Freda Park	Houghton
Fredeen No. 1	Marquette
Frederic	Crawford
Freedom	Cheboygan
Freeland	Saginaw
Freeman	Bay
Freesport	Barry
Free Soil	Mason
Fremont	Newaygo
Fremont Center	Newaygo
Fremont Lake	Newaygo
French Landing	Wayne
Frenchtown	Monroe
Freys	Missaukee
Friday	Delta
Froberg	Baraga
Front Street	Kent
Frost	Clare
Frost (Jct.)	Houghton
Fruitland	Van Buren
Fruitport	Muskegon
Fruitport Jct.	Muskegon
Fruit Ridge	Lenawee
Fuller	Gogebic
Fuller	Kent
Fullerton	Wayne
Fullerton Yard	Wayne
Fulton	Keweenaw

Fumee	Dickinson
Furnace	Antrim

-G-

Gagetown	Tuscola
Gaines	Genesee
Gaines	Kent
Gale	Oceana
Gale	Ontonagon
Galesburg	Kalamazoo
Galien	Berrien
Galliver	Clare
Galloway	Grand Traverse
Galt	Montmorency
Garden	Delta
Garden City	Berrien
Gardendale	St. Clair
Gardiner	Wexford
Gardner	Menominee
Gardner Mine	Marquette
Garfield	Saginaw
Garfield	Wayne
Garnet	Mackinac
Garon	Houghton
Garth	Delta
Gasser	Wexford
Gay	Keweenaw
Gaylord	Otsego
Geddes	Washtenaw
Geels	Roscommon
Gem	Ontonagon
Genesee	Genesee
Genesee Avenue	Saginaw
Genesee Mine	Iron
Geneva	Van Buren
Geneva Mine	Gogebic
Genoa	Livingston
Gentian	Marquette
Georges Lake	Ogemaw
Georgetown	Ogemaw
Gera	Saginaw

Gerber	Benzie
Germfask	Schoolcraft
Gerrish	Missaukee
Gibbs	Alger
Gibbs	Montmorency
Gibbs City	Iron
Gibraltar	Wayne
Gibson Mine	Iron
Gibson Street	Kalamazoo
Giddings	Baraga
Gidleys	Jackson
Gilbert	Newaygo
Gilbert	Wexford
Gilberts	Manistee
Gilc(h)rist	Allegan
Gilchrist	Mackinac
Gilford	Tuscola
Gillen Yard	Wayne
Gillespie	Marquette
Gilletts	Antrim
Gillis	Cheboygan
Gladstone	Delta
Gladstone Crossing	Delta
Gladwin	Gladwin
Gladys	Chippewa
Glanville	Houghton
Glasier	Alger
Gleason	Marquette
Gleasons	Marquette
Glencoe	Bay
Glendora	Berrien
Glengarry	Wexford
Glenlord	Berrien
Glennie	Alcona
Glenwood	Cass
Glenwood	Macomb
Globe Mine	Dickinson
Glovers	Bay
Glovers	Manistee
Glovers Lake	Manistee
Gobles	Van Buren

Gobleville	Van Buren
Godfrey Ave.	Kent
Gogarnville	Alger
Gogebic	Gogebic
Gogebic Jct.	Gogebic
Golden	Bay
Golden	Dickinson
Golden	Menominee
Goo	Antrim
Goodar	Ogemaw
Goodells	St. Clair
Gooding	Kent
Goodison	Oakland
Goodman	Huron
Goodman	Marquette
Goodrich	Lake
Goodrich	Marquette
Goodrich	Oceana
Goodrichs	Manistee
Goodson	Schoolcraft
Goodyear Siding	St. Clair
Goose Lake	Marquette
Gordon	Marquette
Gorham	Osceola
Gould City	Mackinac
Gowen	Montcalm
Graafschap	Allegan
Grade	Livingston
Graffville	Montcalm
Grafton	Monroe
Graham	Saginaw
Grams (Crossing)	Alcona
Grand Beach	Berrien
Grand Blanc	Genesee
Grand Haven	Ottawa
Grand Junction	Van Buren
Grand Ledge	Eaton
Grand Marais	Alger
Grand Marais Jct.	Alger
Grand Rapids	Kent
Grand River Ave.	Wayne

Grand Trunk Jct.	St. Clair
Grand View	Cheboygan
Grandville	Kent
Granite	Marquette
Granite Bluff	Dickinson
Granot	Marquette
Grant	Cheboygan
Grant	Delta
Grant	Newaygo
Grant Center	Grand Traverse
Grant Center	St. Clair
Grass Lake	Jackson
Grassmere	Huron
Grass River	Antrim
Gratiot Avenue	Wayne
Gratiot Centre	St. Clair
Gratiot Mine	Keweenaw
Gratiot Road	Saginaw
Gratton (Spur)	Iron
Gravel Pit	Benzie
Gravel Pit	Berrien
Gravel Pit	Branch
Gravel Pit	Delta
Gravel Pit	Macomb
Gravel Pit	Menominee
Gravel Pit	St. Joseph
Gravel Pit	Schoolcraft
Gravel Pit	Tuscola
Gravel Pit Siding	Alcona
Gravel Siding	St. Clair
Graves Camp	Antrim
Grawn	Grand Traverse
Gray	Kalkaska
Grayling	Crawford
Graylock	Mackinac
Graylock	Saginaw
Grays	Berrien
Grayton	Charlevoix
Great Lakes Sand	Tuscola
Great Western	Iron
Great Western Jct.	Iron

Great Western Mine	Iron
Green	Houghton
Green	Montmorency
Green	Ontonagon
Greenbush	Alcona
Green Corners	St. Clair
Greene	Mackinac
Greene	Saginaw
Greenfield	Wayne
Green Garden	Marquette
Greenings	Monroe
Green Lake	Grand Traverse
Greenland	Ontonagon
Greenland Jct.	Ontonagon
Greenleaf	Sanilac
Green Oak	Livingston
Green River	Antrim
Greens	Clare
Greens	Saginaw
Greens Siding	Bay
Greenville	Montcalm
Greenwood	Marquette
Greenwood	Ogemaw
Greenwood Mine	Marquette
Greenwood Mine Jct.	Marquette
Gregory	Livingston
Greilickville	Leelanau
Grey	Alger
Gridley	Schoolcraft
Grindstone City	Huron
Grise	Iosco
Groesbeck	Ontonagon
Groos	Delta
Gross	Van Buren
Grosse Ile	Wayne
Grosse Ile Shops	Wayne
Grosvenor	Lenawee
Grove	Houghton
Groveland	Dickinson
Groveland Mine	Dickinson
Grover	Calhoun

Grover(ton)	Houghton
Groveton	Saginaw
Guerin	Charlevoix
Gulliver	Schoolcraft
Gulliver Lake	Schoolcraft
Gun Lake Switch	Mason
Gun Marsh	Allegan
Gustavs	Manistee
Gustin	Alcona
Gwinn	Marquette
Gwinn Mine	Marquette
Gypsum	Arenac

-H-

H & W Crossing	Bay
Haaks	Lake
Haakwood	Cheboygan
Hacker	Wexford
Hackley	Clare
Haco	Schoolcraft
Hadley	Otsego
Haff	Chippewa
Hagar	Berrien
Haggersons Spur	Delta
Haggins	Alger
Haines	Tuscola
Haire	Wexford
Haires	Jackson
Hale	Iosco
Hale Lake	Iosco
Half Way	Gladwin
Hallock	Otsego
Halls	Muskegon
Halls Siding	Huron
Hallston	Alger
Halpin	Ontonagon
Halsted	Kalkaska
Hamar (Siding)	Baraga
Hamburg	Livingston
Hamburg Jct.	Livingston
Hamby	Cheboygan

Hamilton	Allegan
Hamilton	Genesee
Hamilton	Otsego
Hamlet	Emmet
Hamlin	Dickinson
Hamlin Lake	Mason
Hammers	Charlevoix
Hammond	Kent
Hammond	Menominee
Hampshire	Iosco
Hampton Yard	Bay
Hancock	Houghton
Hand	Wayne
Handy	Alcona
Handy	Tuscola
Hanley	Alger
Hannah	Ontonagon
Hanover	Jackson
Hansen	Menominee
Hanson	Crawford
Hansons Spur	Menominee
Harbert	Berrien
Harbin	Tuscola
Harbor Beach	Huron
Harbor Springs	Emmet
Harbor Springs Jct.	Emmet
Harding	Mason
Hard Ore Mine	Marquette
Hardwood	Dickinson
Hardluck	Gladwin
Hardy	Alcona
Hardy	Oscoda
Harger	Saginaw
Haring	Wexford
Harker Street	St. Clair
Harlan	Manistee
Harlem	Ottawa
Harleys	Mason
Harold	Otsego
Harmons Mill	Wexford
Harper	Antrim

Harper Avenue	Wayne
Harper Yard	Wayne
Harrietta	Wexford
Harris	Menominee
Harrisburg	Ottawa
Harrison	Clare
Harrison	Lenawee
Harrison	Van Buren
Harrison Jct.	Clare
Harrisons	Washtenaw
Harrisville	Alcona
Harroun	Newaygo
Hart	Oceana
Hartford	Van Buren
Hartford Mine	Marquette
Hartho	Alger
Hartleys	Gogebic
Harts	Antrim
Harts	Kalkaska
Harts	Wexford
Harts Siding	Manistee
Hart Street	Bay
Hartman	Berrien
Hartman	Schoolcraft
Hartwick	Osceola
Harvard	Kent
Harvey	Marquette
Harvey Branch	Crawford
Haskins	Wexford
Haslemere	Mackinac
Haslett	Ingham
Hastings	Barry
Hatchs	Leelanau
Hatchs Crossing	Leelanau
Hatton	Clare
Hauptman	Ogemaw
Havana	Kalkaska
Hawasee	Alpena
Hawes	Alcona
Hawes Bridge	Gladwin
Hawkins	Lapeer

Hawley	Menominee
Hawthorn	Monroe
Hayes	Benzie
Hayes	Gratiot
Hayes	Osceola
Hayes Siding	Berrien
Hayes Siding	Newaygo
Haynor	Ionia
Hazel	Houghton
Hazel	Iron
Hazel Green	Shiawassee
Hazelwood	Sanilac
Headland	Osceola
Headquarters	Antrim
Hebards	Keweenaw
Hecker	Missaukee
Hecla Jct.	Bay
Heimforth	Leelanau
Helena	Antrim
Helena	Huron
Helena	Marquette
Helmers	Calhoun
Helps	Menominee
Hemans	Sanilac
Hematite Mine	Marquette
Hemlock	Iron
Hemlock	Montmorency
Hemlock	Saginaw
Hemlock Mine	Iron
Hemlock Road	Iosco
Hemmingway	Montcalm
Hemstreet	Antrim
Henderson	Dickinson
Henderson	Ionia
Henderson	Macomb
Henderson	Shiawassee
Henderson	Wexford
Hendricks	Delta
Hendricks Quarry	Mackinac
Hendricks Tank	Delta
Hendrie	Chippewa

Henrietta	Jackson
Henry	Alcona
Henry	Manistee
Henrys Crossing	Jackson
Henry Street	Bay
Henry Street	Muskegon
Herman	Baraga
Hermansville	Menominee
Herps	Allegan
Herrick	Isabella
Herrick	Missaukee
Herrick Jct.	Missaukee
Herrings	Kalkaska
Herrington	Ottawa
Herron	Alpena
Hersey	Osceola
Hess Lake	Newaygo
Hewitt Mine	Dickinson
Hewitts	Osceola
Hewitts Lake	Osceola
Hiawatha	Schoolcraft
Hiawatha Mill	Schoolcraft
Hiawatha No. 1 Mine	Iron
Hiawatha No. 2 Mine	Iron
Hickey	St. Clair
Hickory Creek	Berrien
Hicks	Oscoda
Higbee	Ionia
High Bridge	Manistee
Highland	Oakland
Highland Park	Wayne
High Top	Leelanau
Highway	Houghton
Highwood	Gladwin
Hillcrest	Kent
Hilliards	Allegan
Hilliards	Manistee
Hillman	Montmorency
Hillman Crossing	Alpena
Hillman Jct.	Alpena
Hill(s)	Oscoda

Hillsdale	Hillsdale
Hills Siding	Van Buren
Hilltop	Berrien
Hilltop	Marquette
Hilltop Mine	Iron
Himrod Mine	Marquette
Hinchman	Berrien
Hines Crossing	Muskegon
Hiram	Montcalm
Hitchcock	Antrim
Hoags	Mason
Hoags Siding	Mason
Hobart	Wexford
Hobson	Huron
Hodgemans	Roscommon
Hoey	Montmorency
Hoffman	Presque Isle
Hoffs Siding	Macomb
Hogan	Mecosta
Hogan	Washtenaw
Hogan Ore Yard	Marquette
Hoist	Marquette
Holden Road	Wayne
Holland	Ottawa
Hollister Mine	Iron
Holloway	Lenawee
Holly	Oakland
Holmes	Dickinson
Holmes	Grand Traverse
Holmes Mine	Marquette
Holt	Ingham
Holton	Muskegon
Homeier	Marquette
Homer	Calhoun
Homer Mine	Iron
Homestead	Benzie
Honor	Benzie
Hoods	Osceola
Hoop	Missaukee
Hooper	Allegan
Hoops Spur	Delta

Hope	Eaton
Hope Mine	Iron
Hopkins	Allegan
Hopkins	Kalamazoo
Hopkins Road	Lapeer
Hoppertown	Allegan
Horgan	Antrim
Horgan Jct.	Antrim
Horicon	Grand Traverse
Horner	Van Buren
Horning Spur	Macomb
Horrigan	Crawford
Horsehead Lake	Mecosta
Horton	Genesee
Horton	Jackson
Hospital Spur	Wayne
Houghton	Houghton
Houles	Menominee
Houte	Menominee
Houseman	Kalkaska
Howard	Alger
Howard	Cass
Howard City	Montcalm
Howell	Livingston
Howell Jct.	Livingston
Howells	Mason
Howells Siding	Mason
Howry(s)	Gladwin
Howrys	Saginaw
Hoxeyville	Wexford
Hoyt	Saginaw
Hubbard	Midland
Hubbell	Houghton
Hubbell	Mackinac
Hubbells Mill	Ontonagon
Hudson	Lenawee
Hudson	Ottawa
Hudsonville	Ottawa
Hughart	Kent
Hulbert	Chippewa
Hull	Benzie

Humboldt Jct.	Marquette
Humboldt Mine	Marquette
Humphrey	Manistee
Hungerford	Newaygo
Hunters Creek	Lapeer
Hunt Spur	Mackinac
Huntworth	Otsego
Huron	Huron
Huron	Wayne
Hurst	Presque Isle
Hutchinson	Tuscola
Hutula	Baraga
Hyde	Alger
Hylas	Dickinson

-I-

Ice Siding	Kalamazoo
Ice Tracks	Ogemaw
Ida	Monroe
Idlewild	Lake
Imlay	Oscoda
Imlay City	Lapeer
Imperial Mine	Baraga
Imperial Mine Jct.	Baraga
Index	Lapeer
Indiana	Ontonagon
Indiana Mine	Dickinson
Indiana Point	Emmet
Indian Creek	Kent
Indianfield	Kalamazoo
Indian Lake	Kalamazoo
Indian Landing	Antrim
Indian River	Cheboygan
Indian Town	Menominee
Industrial Home	Lenawee
Ingalls	Menominee
Ingersolls	Clinton
Inkster	Wayne
Inland	Benzie
Inland Jct.	Schoolcraft
Interior	Ontonagon

Interior Jct.	Ontonagon
Interlochen	Grand Traverse
Inverness	Cheboygan
Ionia	Ionia
Iris	Marquette
Irma	Emmet
Iron Bridge	Baraga
Iron Mountain	Dickinson
Iron Mountain Mine	Marquette
Iron River	Iron
Iron River Jct.	Iron
Iron River Jct.	Ontonagon
Irons	Lake
Iron Street Crossover	Marquette
Iron Street Jct.	Marquette
Ironton	Charlevoix
Ironton Mine	Gogebic
Iron Valley Mine	Marquette
Ironwood	Gogebic
Iroquois	Chippewa
Irving	Barry
Isadore	Leelanau
Isabella	Clinton
Isabella	Delta
Isabella	Isabella
Isabella Mine	Marquette
Ishpeming	Marquette
Ishpeming Yard	Marquette
Island Lake	Livingston
Ithaca	Gratiot
Ivanrest	Kent

-J-

Jackpot Mine	Gogebic
Jackson	Jackson
Jackson	Marquette
Jackson Crossing	Newaygo
Jackson Jct.	Jackson
Jackson Lake	Montmorency
Jackson Mine	Marquette
Jack Spur	Gogebic

Jacob City	Mackinac
James Mine	Iron
Jamestown	Cass
Jaquay	Berrien
Jasper	Lenawee
Jean	Marquette
Jeddo	St. Clair
Jefferson	Cass
Jefferson Avenue	Saginaw
Jefferson Avenue	Wayne
Jefferson Street	Muskegon
Jenison(s)	Ottawa
Jenisonville	Ottawa
Jenks	Alger
Jenney	Alger
Jennings	Missaukee
Jennings Branch Jct.	Otsego
Jerome	Hillsdale
Jeromeville	Alger
Jewell	Newaygo
JN	Allegan
Job	Antrim
Johannesburg	Otsego
Johannesburg Jct.	Otsego
Johnson	Antrim
Johnson	Huron
Johnson	Mackinac
Johnsonburg	Chippewa
Johnson Spur	Dickinson
Johnsons Siding	Marquette
Johnsons Spur	Menominee
Johnston	Otsego
Johnsville	Ottawa
Jones	Cass
Jones Spur	Houghton
Jonesville	Hillsdale
Jopling	Marquette
Joppa	Calhoun
Jordan	Isabella
Jordan River	Antrim
Judges	Crawford

Judson Mine	Iron
Jumbo	Ontonagon
Junction Switch	Benzie
Junction Yard	Wayne
Junet	Gogebic
Juniata	Tuscola
Juniper	Alger

-K-

Kalamazoo	Kalamazoo
Kalamazoo Jct.	Kalamazoo
Kaleva	Manistee
Kalkaska	Kalkaska
Kane	Oscoda
Kanitz	Muskegon
Karlin	Grand Traverse
Karr	Tuscola
Kates Lake	Marquette
KawCaChewIng	Charlevoix
Kawkawlin	Bay
Kaybee	Montmorency
Kaywood	Montcalm
Kealey	Kalamazoo
Kearsley	Genesee
Kearsarge	Houghton
Keegan	Osceola
Keeler	Baraga
Keenan	Lake
Kegomic	Emmet
Kehoe	Benzie
Kelley	Antrim
Kelley	Kalkaska
Kelleys Pit	Lenawee
Kellogg	Allegan
Kells	Menominee
Kelly Island Quarry	Presque Isle
Kellys	Kent
Kelly Siding	Shiawassee
Kelso Jct.	Iron
Kelvin	Dickinson
Keme	Chippewa

Kemps	Tuscola
Kendall	Van Buren
Kennedy	Cass
Kennedy	Mackinac
Kenneth	Mackinac
Kent City	Kent
Kenton	Houghton
Kentucky	Antrim
Kenwood	Wayne
Kerby(Mine)	Shiawassee
Kerkelas Spur	Marquette
Kerwood	Sanilac
Kerry	Grand Traverse
Kersten	Alpena
Keswick	Leelanau
Kevan	Montmorency
Kew	Menominee
Keweenaw Bay	Baraga
Keweenaw Mine	Gogebic
Keystone	Grand Traverse
Keystone Mine	Marquette
Kibbie	Van Buren
Kidd(ville)	Ionia
Kiernan Spur	Iron
Kilgore Yard	Kalamazoo
Kilns	Marquette
Kilton	Gogebic
Kilwinning	Ingham
Kimball	St. Clair
Kimball Mine	Iron
Kinde	Huron
King	Alpena
King	Benzie
King	Dickinson
King	Shiawassee
King Lake	Baraga
Kingsland	Eaton
Kingsland	Montmorency
Kingsley	Delta
Kingsley	Grand Traverse
Kingsley	St. Clair

Kings Mill	Lapeer
Kingston	Tuscola
Kings Yard	Wayne
Kinnear	Washtenaw
Kinney	Kent
Kinney	Newaygo
Kinross	Chippewa
Kinross Air Base	Chippewa
Kintner	Tuscola
Kipling	Delta
Kirby	Van Buren
Kirby	Washtenaw
Kirby Avenue	Wayne
Kirbys Spur	Menominee
Kirk	Van Buren
Kirk (Jct.)	Ottawa
Kitchi	Houghton
Klinger Lake	St. Joseph
Klingers	St. Joseph
Klingville	Houghton
Kloman	Menominee
Kloman Mine	Marquette
Klondike	Schoolcraft
Kneeland	Crawford
Knight	Kalkaska
Knights	Lenawee
Knipers	Antrim
Knorr	Hillsdale
Knorr Lake	Hillsdale
Kokomo	Missaukee
Koopman	Missaukee
Kopje	Newaygo
Koss	Menominee
Krohns Siding	Huron
Kruse Mine	Marquette
Kulmbach	Saginaw
Kunze siding	Iosco
Kuro	Baraga
Kurtz	Alcona

-L-

L & N Jct.	Lapeer
LaBranch(e)	Menominee
Lachine	Alpena
Lac La Belle	Keweenaw
Lac La Belle Jct.	Keweenaw
Lacota	Van Buren
Ladoga	Alger
Lafayette	Kent
LaGrange	Kent
Laingsburg	Shiawassee
Lake	Bay
Lake	Benzie
Lake	Clare
Lake	Muskegon
Lake	Oceana
Lake Angeline Mine	Marquette
Lake Ann	Benzie
Lake City	Missaukee
Lake Cora	Van Buren
Lake Forest	Antrim
Lake George	Clare
Lake Gerald	Houghton
Lake Gogebic	Ontonagon
Lake Harbor	Muskegon
Lake Harold	Antrim
Lake Ice House	Clare
Lake Jct.	Benzie
Lake Jct.	Houghton
Lake Jct.	Lake
Lake Jct.	Leelanau
Lakeland	Livingston
Lake Linden	Houghton
Lake Mine	Ontonagon
Lake Odessa	Ionia
Lake Orion	Oakland
Lake Part	Emmet
Lake Rest	Lenawee
Lake Roland	Houghton
Lake Sally Mine	Marquette

Lake Shore Jct.	Wayne
Lakeside	Berrien
Lakeside	Cheboygan
Lakeside	Grand Traverse
Lake Side	Muskegon
Lake Street	Berrien
Lake Street	Gogebic
Lake Superior Mine	Marquette
Laketon	Luce
Lakeview	Montcalm
Lake View	Houghton
Lake View Farm	Manistee
Lakewood	Cheboygan
Lakewood	Emmet
Lakewood	Houghton
Lakewood	Marquette
Lakewood	Muskegon
Lamar	Kent
Lamay(s)	Delta
Lambert	Delta
Lambertville	Monroe
Lamb	St. Clair
Lamont Mine	Iron
Lamson	Emmet
Lane	Ogemaw
Langworth	Osceola
Lanka	Wexford
L'Anse	Baraga
Lansing	Ingham
Lansing Avenue	Jackson
Lansingville	Isabella
Lansing Yard	Ingham
Lapan Spur	Bay
Lapeer	Lapeer
Lapeer Jct.	Lapeer
Larch	Delta
LaRocque	Presque Isle
Larsen	Osceola
Larson	Montmorency
Larsons Spur	Delta
Larsons Spur	Marquette

Larsons Spur	Menominee
LaSalle	Monroe
Lathrop	Delta
Lauris	Menominee
Laurium	Houghton
Lawndale	Saginaw
Lawrence	Van Buren
Lawson	Marquette
Lawton	Van Buren
Lawton Track Pan	Van Buren
Leapers	Menominee
Leaton	Isabella
Leaf	Lenawee
Leavells	Grand Traverse
LeBresh Spur	Delta
Lee	Allegan
Leelanau	Leelanau
Lee Peck Jct.	Iron
Lee Peck Mine	Iron
Leesburg	St. Joseph
Leetsville	Kalkaska
Lefebvres	Delta
Lefke	Marquette
LeGrand	Cheboygan
Leiphart	Kalkaska
Leland	Chippewa
Leland	Washtenaw
LeLone	Oscoda
Lemon Lake	Manistee
Lena	Marquette
Lenawee	Lenawee
Lenawee Jct.	Lenawee
Lencel	Luce
Lengsville	Bay
Lennon	Shiawassee
Lenox	Macomb
Leo	Baraga
Leonard	Oakland
Leonard Branch Jct.	Otsego
Leoni	Jackson
Leonidas	St. Joseph

Leota	Clare
Lepine	Kalkaska
Leroux	Alger
Leroy	Ingham
LeRoy	Osceola
Leslie	Ingham
Levering	Emmet
Leverington	Emmet
Levington	Clare
Lewis	Mackinac
Lewis Siding	Sanilac
Lewiston	Montmorency
Leyburns	Osceola
Lighton	Berrien
Liken	Antrim
Lilley	Newaygo
Lilley Jct.	Newaygo
Lillie Mine	Marquette
Lima Jct.	Lenawee
Limerick	Grand Traverse
Lime Siding	Eaton
Lime Spur	Arenac
Limestone	Schoolcraft
Lincoln	Alcona
Lincoln	Berrien
Lincoln	Oakland
Lincoln Fields	Mason
Lincoln Jct.	Iosco
Lincoln Lake	Kent
Lincoln Mine	Iron
Lincoln Park	Wayne
Lincoln Yard	Wayne
Linden	Genesee
Linden	Wexford
Linderman	Muskegon
Lindsley	Dickinson
Lindstedt	Ontonagon
Linkville	Huron
Linwood	Bay
Linwood	Houghton
Linwood Park	Bay

Lions Crossing	Lake
Lisbon	Kent
Liske	Presque Isle
Liston	Schoolcraft
Litchfield	Hillsdale
Little	Manistee
Little Lake	Marquette
Little Manistee	Lake
Livernois Avenue	Wayne
Livingston	Berrien
Livonia	Wayne
Lloyd Mine	Marquette
Lloyds Spur	Iron
Lockport	St. Joseph
Locks	St. Joseph
Lockwood	Kent
Lockwood	Tuscola
Logan	Kent
Logan	Otsego
Lola	Kalkaska
Lone Bridge	Roscommon
Long Lake	Iosco
Long Lake	Wexford
Long Lake Jct.	Grand Traverse
Long Lake Jct.	Wexford
Longrie	Menominee
Longs	Huron
Long Siding	Marquette
Longyear	Marquette
Loomis	Isabella
Loon Lake	Iosco
Loop Line Jct.	Dickinson
Loop Line Switch	Saginaw
Loranger	Ogemaw
Lorenzo	Kent
Loretto	Dickinson
Loretto Mine	Dickinson
Lorna	Alger
Lott	Alcona
Loud Jct.	Alcona
Louds Dam	Iosco

Louds Spur	Alger
Louds Spur	Crawford
Lovells	Crawford
Lovey	Emmet
Lowell	Bay
Lowell	Kent
Lowell	Washtenaw
Lower Big Rapids	Mecosta
Low Moor	Marquette
Lucas	Missaukee
Lucy Mine	Marquette
Ludington	Mason
Ludington Yard	Mason
Lull	Alger
Lull	Antrim
Lulu	Monroe
Lum	Lapeer
Lumberton	Newaygo
Lupton	Ogemaw
Lurmet	Wayne
Lutes	Montmorency
Luther	Lake
Lutz Siding	St. Clair
Luzerne	Oscoda
Lyle	Alpena
Lyle	Gladwin
Lymburn	Oscoda
Lyonette	Jackson
Lyons	Clinton
Lyons	Ionia
Lyons Mill	Clinton
Lyonton	Chippewa

-M-

MA	Ingham
Maas Mine	Marquette
Mable	Grand Traverse
Macatawa	Ottawa
Mackinaw City	Cheboygan
Mackinaw Mine	Marquette
Mack Road	Wayne

Macon	Monroe
Madden	Antrim
Madison	Calhoun
Madison	Lenawee
Magnetic Mine	Marquette
Mahoney	Kalkaska
Main Street	Berrien
Main Street	Macomb
Main Top	Leelanau
Maitland Mine	Marquette
Maki	Schoolcraft
Malacca	Menominee
Malcolm	Manistee
M.A.L. Crossing	Oakland
Male Spur	Presque Isle
M.A.L. Jct.	Oakland
Malta	Kent
Maltbys	Charlevoix
Maltbys	Ogemaw
Mancelona	Antrim
Mancelona Road	Antrim
Manchester	Washtenaw
Manchester Jct.	Washtenaw
Mandan	Keweenaw
Maney	Marquette
Mangum	Marquette
Mangum Mill	Marquette
Manistee	Manistee
Manistee Crossing	Manistee
Manistee Jct.	Mason
Manistee River	Otsego
Manistee Switch	Crawford
Manistique	Schoolcraft
Manistique River	Schoolcraft
Manistique Wharf	Schoolcraft
Manitou Beach	Lenawee
Manley	Osceola
Manley Siding	Gogebic
Manlius	Allegan
Manning	Saginaw
Mann Siding	Clare

Manseau	Leelanau
Mansfield	Isabella
Mansfield Mine	Iron
Manton	Wexford
Maple	Oceana
Maple Forest	Van Buren
Maple Grove	Manistee
Maple Grove	Oscoda
Maple Hill	Montcalm
Maple Ridge	Delta
Maple River Pit	Shiawassee
Maple Slope	Antrim
Maple Valley	Montcalm
Maple Wood	Berrien
Maplewood	Delta
Marble	Antrim
Marble	Ottawa
Marblehead Quarry	Schoolcraft
Marblehead Spur	Schoolcraft
Marcellus	Cass
Marcus	Marquette
Marengo	Calhoun
Marenisco	Gogebic
Marigold	Marquette
Marilla	Manistee
Marine City	St. Clair
Marion	Osceola
Marion	Otsego
Marion	Sanilac
Mark	Clare
Markell	Tuscola
Marks	Iosco
Marl	Menominee
Marl	Otsego
Marlboro(ugh)	Lake
Marlette	Sanilac
Marl Lake	Newaygo
Marne	Ottawa
Marquette	Marquette
Marquette Scales	Marquette
Marrengers	Delta

Mars	Berrien
Marsh	Alcona
Marsh	Manistee
Marsh	Oscoda
Marshall	Calhoun
Marshall Track Pan	Calhoun
Marshfield	Mecosta
Martha	Isabella
Martha	Montcalm
Martin	Allegan
Martin	Marquette
Martin	St. Clair
Martindale	Otsego
Martins Landing	Marquette
Martiny	Mecosta
Marvin	Lenawee
Mary Charlotte Mine	Marquette
Marysville	St. Clair
Mashek	Marquette
Mason	Delta
Mason	Houghton
Mason	Ingham
Masoner	Tuscola
Masonville	Delta
Mass	Ontonagon
Massie	Gogebic
Mass Mine	Ontonagon
Masson	Wayne
Masters	Alger
Mastodon	Iron
Mastodon Mine	Iron
Matchwood	Ontonagon
Mather Mine A	Marquette
Mather Mine B	Marquette
Mattawan	Van Buren
Matthews	Berrien
Maxwell	Bay
May	Allegan
Maybee	Monroe
Mayfield	Grand Traverse
Mayflower	Houghton

May Lake Jct.	Presque Isle
Mayville	Tuscola
Maywood	Iron
M.C. Jct.	Berrien
McAfee	Kalkaska
McAllister Road	Calhoun
McBain	Missaukee
McBrides	Montcalm
McCamley Street	Calhoun
McClures	Saginaw
McCollum(s)	Oscoda
McCollums	Berrien
McCool	Newaygo
McCords	Kent
McDermitts	Marquette
McDonald	Van Buren
McDonald Lake	Schoolcraft
McDonald Mine	Iron
McFarland(s)	Marquette
McGee	Kalkaska
McGills Mine	Iron
McGoverns	Iron
McGraw Jct.	Otsego
McGraws Siding	Bay
McGregor	Sanilac
McGrew Jct.	Genesee
McHale	Tuscola
McHarg	Alpena
McInnes	Schoolcraft
McIntyre	Huron
McIvor	Iosco
McKay	Clare
McKay	Mecosta
McKeever	Ontonagon
McKinley	Oscoda
McKinneys	Wayne
McLanes	Newaygo
McLaughlin	Delta
McManus	Charlevoix
McMillan	Luce
McNeils	Schoolcraft

McOmber Mine	Marquette
McPhee	Luce
McPhee	Montmorency
McPherson	Wexford
McQueen Spur	Alpena
McQueens Spur	Delta
McRae	Dickinson
McRaes Spur	Iron
McReavey	Marquette
Meads Quarry	Mackinac
Meaford	Montmorency
Mears	Oceana
Measel	Macomb
Mecosta	Mecosta
Melbourne	Saginaw
Meldrum Avenue	Wayne
Melrose	Charlevoix
Melva	Benzie
Melvin	Sanilac
Melvindale	Wayne
Memphis	St. Clair
Mendon	St. Joseph
Menominee	Menominee
Menominee Jct.	Menominee
Menonaqua Beach	Emmet
Mentha	Van Buren
Mentz	Saginaw
Meredith	Clare
Meridian	Gratiot
Meridian	Ingham
Merriam	Alger
Merrick	Bay
Merrill	Saginaw
Merrillsville	St. Clair
Merriman	Dickinson
Merritt	Mason
Merritt	Missaukee
Merritts	Cheboygan
Merritts	Newaygo
Merriweather	Ontonagon
Mershon	Saginaw

Mertz Branch Jct.	Crawford
Mesick	Wexford
Messner	Houghton
Metamora	Lapeer
Meteor Mine	Gogebic
Metheany	Wexford
Metronite Quarry	Dickinson
Metropolitan	Dickinson
Metser	Alger
Metz	Benzie
Metz	Presque Isle
Meyer	Menominee
Meyers	Monroe
Meyers Jct.	Wayne
Michelson	Roscommon
Michie	Bay
Michigamme	Marquette
Michigamme Mine	Marquette
Michigan Avenue	Ingham
Michigan Avenue	Saginaw
Michigan Avenue	Wayne
Michigan Center	Jackson
Michigan Home Spur	Lapeer
Michigan Mine	Iron
Michigan Mine	Ontonagon
Middleton	Gratiot
Middleville	Barry
Midland	Midland
Midland Gravel Co.	Mecosta
Midway	Gogebic
Midway	Houghton
Midway	Marquette
Mikado	Alcona
Mikado Mine	Gogebic
Milan	Monroe
Milan	Washtenaw
Milan Jct.	Monroe
Milford	Oakland
Military Street	St. Clair
Mill	Wayne
Millbrook	Mecosta

Mill Creek	Kent
Mill Creek Jct.	Kent
Mille Coquins	Mackinac
Millen	Oscoda
Miller	Alger
Miller	Benzie
Miller	Kalamazoo
Miller	Mecosta
Millers	Cheboygan
Millers	Montcalm
Millers	Van Buren
Millersburg	Presque Isle
Millers Mill	Ogemaw
Millers Spur	Marquette
Millersville	Wexford
Millerton	Mason
Millett(s)	Eaton
Mill Grove	Allegan
Milliken	Cheboygan
Millington	Tuscola
Millie Mine	Dickinson
Mill Mine Jct.	Houghton
Mill Point	Ottawa
Mills	Houghton
Mills	Iosco
Mill Street	Wayne
Millville	Lapeer
Milo	Barry
Milton	Macomb
Milton Jct.	Osceola
Milwaukee Jct.	Marquette
Milwaukee Jct.	Wayne
Milwaukee Mine	Marquette
Minckler Mine	Iron
Minden City	Sanilac
Mineral Branch	Marquette
Miner Lake	Allegan
Miners	Delta
Miners Rollway	Wexford
Miners Spur	Ontonagon
Missaukee (City)	Missaukee

Missaukee Jct.	Wexford
Missaukee Park	Missaukee
Mission	Baraga
Mitchell	Grand Traverse
Mitchell	Missaukee
Mitchell Mine	Marquette
Mitchell Spur	Iron
Mitchells	Osceola
Mitchells	Tuscola
Mitchells Crossing	Missaukee
Moeke	Kalkaska
Moeller	Montcalm
Moffat	Arenac
Mohawk	Keweenaw
Mohawk Mine	Keweenaw
Moiles	Mecosta
Moiles Siding	Saginaw
Moline	Allegan
Mona Lake	Muskegon
Monitor	Bay
Monitor Mine	Iron
Monroe	Monroe
Monongahela Mine	Iron
Monroeville	Newaygo
Montague	Muskegon
Montei	Tuscola
Montieth	Allegan
Montieth Jct.	Allegan
Montgomery	Hillsdale
Montreal	Gogebic
Montrose	Genesee
Moon	Charlevoix
Moon	Muskegon
Moore	Charlevoix
Moore	Roscommon
Moorepark	St. Joseph
Moores	Eaton
Moores Jct.	Arenac
Moores Siding	Clare
Mooreville	Schoolcraft
Moorland	Muskegon

Moran	Mackinac
Moran	Schoolcraft
Morenci	Lenawee
Morgan	Barry
Morgan	Marquette
Morgan	Newaygo
Morgan Park	Calhoun
Morley	Mecosta
Morrice	Shiawassee
Morris	Berrien
Morris Mine	Marquette
Morrison	Antrim
Morrisons Spur	Houghton
Morton	Wayne
Moscow	Hillsdale
Moseley	Kent
Mosher	Otsego
Mosherville	Hillsdale
Mostetlers Siding	Clare
Motley	Houghton
Mound Road Yard	Macomb
Mount Bliss	Antrim
Mount Clemens	Macomb
Mount Forest	Bay
Mount Morris	Genesee
Mount Olivet	Wayne
Mount Pleasant	Isabella
Mour	Marquette
Mud Lake	Alcona
Mud Lake Jct.	Alcona
Muir	Ionia
Mulkey Avenue	Wayne
Mullet Lake	Cheboygan
Mulliken	Eaton
Mumfords	Menominee
Mundy	Genesee
Munger	Bay
Mungerville	Shiawassee
Munising	Alger
Munising Jct.	Alger
Munith	Jackson

Munro Mine	Dickinson
Munshaw	Grand Traverse
Munson	Lenawee
Murphy	Baraga
Murphy	Isabella
Murray	Mackinac
Muskegon	Muskegon
Muskegon Heights	Muskegon
Muskegon Jct.	Kent
MX	Saginaw
Mynnings	Missaukee
Myren	Alger
Myrtle	Alger

-N-

Nadeau	Menominee
Nahma Jct.	Delta
Nallville	Wayne
Nanaimo Mine	Iron
Napier	Berrien
Naples	Kalkaska
Napoleon	Jackson
Narenta	Delta
Narrow Gauge Crossing	Newaygo
Nashs	Barry
Nashville	Barry
Nassons	Newaygo
Natalie	Luce
Nathan	Menominee
National	Marquette
National City	Iosco
National City Spur	Iosco
National Mine	Marquette
Natpo	Chippewa
Naubinway Jct.	Mackinac
Naults	Iron
Neeley	Allegan
Negaunee	Marquette
Negaunee Mine	Marquette
Nelson	Cheboygan
Nelsons Switch	Manistee

Nelsonville	Schoolcraft
Nepessing	Lapeer
Nero	Mackinac
Nessen City	Benzie
Nester	Ontonagon
Nestor Crossing	Houghton
Nestoria	Baraga
Net River	Iron
Nettles	Alger
Newark	Oakland
Newaygo	Newaygo
Newaygo Lakes	Newaygo
New Baltimore	Macomb
Newbergers	Osceola
Newberry	Luce
Newberrys	Emmet
New Boston	Wayne
Newbre	Van Buren
New Buffalo	Berrien
Newburg	Cass
New Dalton	Marquette
New Davis Mine	Gogebic
New East Branch	Otsego
Newell Branch Jct.	Cheboygan
New England Mine	Marquette
New Era	Oceana
New Furnace	Marquette
Newhall	Delta
New Haven	Macomb
New Holland	Ottawa
New Hudson	Oakland
New Kentucky	Schoolcraft
Newland	Manistee
New Minneapolis	Delta
Newport	Gogebic
Newport	Monroe
Newport Mine	Gogebic
New Richmond	Allegan
New Richmond Mine	Marquette
New South Branch Camp	Mason
New Swanzy	Marquette

Newton	Baraga
New York Hematite Mine	Marquette
New York Mine	Marquette
Nichols	Antrim
Nichols	Calhoun
Nichols	Keweenaw
Nicholsville	Schoolcraft
Nichols Yard	Calhoun
Nickerson	Berrien
Niles	Berrien
Niles Jct.	Berrien
Nine Mile	Bay
Nippesing	Lapeer
Nirvanna	Lake
Nisula	Houghton
Nizer	Otsego
Noble	Osceola
Nogi	Mackinac
Nolan	Roscommon
Nolan Yard	Wayne
Nora	Washtenaw
Norfolk	Antrim
Norrie Mine	Gogebic
Norris	Wayne
North Adams	Hillsdale
North Bay City	Bay
North Bessemer	Gogebic
North Bingham	Leelanau
North Bradley	Midland
North Branch	Alcona
North Branch	Bay
North Branch	Lapeer
North Branch Jct.	Cheboygan
North Byron	Kent
North Concord	Jackson
North Detroit	Wayne
North Elmira	Otsego
North Escanaba	Delta
North Fayette	Lenawee
Northfield	Washtenaw
North Flint	Genesee

North Grand Rapids	Kent
North Greenville	Montcalm
North Hamlin	Mason
Northampton Mine	Marquette
North Hiawatha Mine	Iron
North Holland	Ottawa
North Ironwood	Gogebic
North Jackson Mine	Marquette
North Kearsarge	Houghton
North Lake	Marquette
North Lake	Ontonagon
Northland	Marquette
North Lansing	Ingham
North Linden	Genesee
North Morenci	Lenawee
North Newport	Gogebic
Northport	Leelanau
North Raisinville	Monroe
North Saginaw	Saginaw
Norths Mill	Kent
Norths Siding	Newaygo
North Star	Gratiot
North Street	St. Clair
North Sturgis	St. Joseph
North Tamarack Mine	Houghton
North Water Street Jct.	Bay
Northwestern Mine	Marquette
Northville	Wayne
North Wye	Delta
North Yard	Kalamazoo
North Yard	Muskegon
North Yard	Wayne
North Yard	Wexford
Norton	Muskegon
Norton	Ontonagon
Norvell	Jackson
Norwalk	Manistee
Norway	Dickinson
Norway Mine	Dickinson
Norwich	Newaygo
Norwood Mine	Baraga

Nottawa	St. Joseph
Novi	Oakland
Nowicki	Presque Isle
Nugent	Otsego
Number 6 Ore Yard	Delta
Nunica	Ottawa
Nylen	Berrien

-O-

Oa-at-ka Beach	Bay
Oak	Wayne
Oak Beach	Lenawee
Oakdale	Kent
Oakdale Park	Kent
Oak Grove	Livingston
Oak Grove	Otsego
Oakhill	Berrien
Oakhill	Manistee
Oakland	Berrien
Oaklet	Lapeer
Oakley	Saginaw
Oakwood	Wayne
Oakwood Boulevard	Oakland
Oakwood Crossing	St. Joseph
Obenhoff	Houghton
O'Brien	Kent
O'Brien	Ontonagon
O'Callaghan	Dickinson
Oconto	Ottawa
OD	Jackson
Oden	Emmet
Odgers Mine	Iron
Odlam	Sanilac
Ogden	Arenac
Ogden	Lenawee
Ogden Mine	Marquette
Ogemaw	Ogemaw
Ogemaw Springs	Ogemaw
Ogontz	Delta
Ohio Mine	Baraga
Ohio Mine Spur	Baraga

Ojibway	Keweenaw
Ojibway Mine	Keweenaw
Okemos	Ingham
Ola	Gratiot
Old South Branch	Oceana
Old Richmond Mine	Marquette
Olga	Lake
Olive	Ottawa
Olive Center	Ottawa
Oliver	Huron
Olivers	Lake
Olivet	Eaton
Omega	Kalkaska
Omena	Leelanau
Omer	Arenac
Onaway	Presque Isle
O'Neill	Kalkaska
Onekama	Manistee
Onekama Jct.	Manistee
Onondaga	Ingham
Onota	Alger
Onsted	Lenawee
Ontonagon	Ontonagon
Ontonagon Jct.	Marquette
Opal	Baraga
Opeechee	Houghton
Opdyke	Muskegon
Orange	Ionia
Orchard	Presque Isle
Orchard Lake	Oakland
Ore Scale	Delta
Ore Siding	Delta
Orient	Osceola
Orion	Oakland
Orleans	Ionia
Ornum	Dickinson
Oro	Marquette
Oro	Menominee
Orono	Osceola
Ortman	Arenac
Orville	Antrim

Orville	Saginaw
Osano Mine	Iron
Osborn	Lenawee
Osborn	Menominee
Osborns	Calhoun
Osceola	Houghton
Osceola Jct.	Osceola
Osceola Mine	Houghton
Oscoda	Iosco
Oshtemo	Kalamazoo
Osier	Delta
Osin	Montcalm
Osmer	Washtenaw
Osseo	Hillsdale
Ossineke	Alpena
Otia	Newaygo
Otisco	Ionia
Otisville	Genesee
Otsego	Allegan
Otsego	Otsego
Otsego Lake	Otsego
Ottawa	Ottawa
Ottawa Beach	Ottawa
Ottawa Lake	Monroe
Ottawa Yard	Monroe
Otter	Houghton
Otterburn	Genesee
Otter Lake	Lapeer
Ovid	Clinton
Owendale	Huron
Owosso	Shiawassee
Owosso Jct.	Shiawassee
Oxford	Oakland
Ozard	Mackinac

-P-

Pabst Mine	Gogebic
Packard	Eaton
Packard	Lenawee
Packard	Van Buren
Packard Switch	Macomb

Pack Siding	Presque Isle
Packs Mills	Sanilac
Packs Siding	Sanilac
Page	Cheboygan
Page	Emmet
Page	Lenawee
Page Branch Jct.	Cheboygan
Pages	Clare
Paige	Alger
Paines	Iron
Paines	Saginaw
Painesdale	Houghton
Painesdale Jct.	Houghton
Paint River	Iron
Paint River Mine	Iron
Paisley	Alpena
Palatke	Iron
Palmer	Baraga
Palmer	Marquette
Palmer Avenue	Wayne
Palmer Mine	Marquette
Palmers	Ionia
Palms	Mackinac
Palms	Sanilac
Palms Mine	Gogebic
Palmyra	Lenawee
Palmyra Jct.	Lenawee
Panola	Iron
Pantlind City	Kent
Papin	Baraga
Paquette	Baraga
Paris	Mecosta
Park	Kent
Park	Newaygo
Park City	Newaygo
Parker	Schoolcraft
Parker Spur	Marquette
Parkington	Schoolcraft
Parkinsons	Gratiot
Park Lake	Osceola
Parks	Antrim

Park Siding	Iron
Parkville	St. Joseph
Parma	Jackson
Parmalee	Barry
Parsons	Lake
Parson Spur	Menominee
Partridge	Marquette
Pascoe Mine	Marquette
Patterson Branch Jct.	Cheboygan
Pattersons	Newaygo
Pattersons	Tuscola
Patton	Huron
Paulding	Ontonagon
Pavilion	Kalamazoo
Pavilion Jct.	Kalamazoo
Paw Paw	Van Buren
Paw Paw Lake	Berrien
Paxton	Alpena
Paxton	Genesee
Paynesville	Ontonagon
Peachville	Oceana
Peacock	Lake
Pearl(e)	Allegan
Pearl Lake	Benzie
Pearl Street	Jackson
Peat Siding	St. Clair
Peck	Sanilac
Peihl	Emmet
Pelkie	Baraga
Pellston	Emmet
Pelton	Lake
Penegor Spur	Marquette
Penfield	Calhoun
Penford	Wayne
Peninsular St.	Tuscola
Penn	Cass
Penn Jct.	Ottawa
Pennock	Clare
Pentecost	Lenawee
Pentoga	Iron
Pentwater	Oceana

Peppard	Ontonagon
Perch Creek	Baraga
Percy	Alger
Perkins	Delta
Perkins	Tuscola
Peroid	Luce
Perrin	St. Joseph
Perrinton	Gratiot
Perrons	Mackinac
Perronville	Menominee
Perry	Shiawassee
Perrys	Lake
Perues	Wexford
Peshims	Chippewa
Peters	Lake
Peterbury	Monroe
Petersburg Jct.	Monroe
Peterson	Alger
Petersons	Delta
Petersville	Benzie
Petoskey	Emmet
Petrel	Alger
Pettysville	Livingston
Pewabic Mine	Dickinson
Pewamo	Iron
Phee	Menominee
Phelps	Charlevoix
Phelps	Clare
Phillips	Houghton
Phoenix	Keweenaw
Phoenix Mine	Keweenaw
Pickand	Muskegon
Pickerel Creek	Newaygo
Pickerel Lake	Marquette
Pierson	Montcalm
Pigeon	Huron
Pigeon (River)	Ottawa
Pike Lake	Mackinac
Pilgrim	Houghton
Pilgrim Mine	Gogebic
Pilgrim Siding	St. Clair

Pinckney	Livingston
Pinconning	Bay
Pine Grove	Saginaw
Pine Grove	Van Buren
Pine Grove Ave.	St. Clair
Pinehill	Marquette
Pine Lake	Allegan
Pine Lake	Ingham
Pine Park	Grand Traverse
Pine Ridge	Antrim
Pine Ridge	Delta
Pine River	Arenac
Pine River	Chippewa
Pine Run	Genesee
Pines	Lake
Pine Street	Marquette
Pingree	Oscoda
Pioneer Mine	Marquette
Piper	Ogemaw
Pipestone	Berrien
Pitt	Shiawassee
Pittsfield	Washtenaw
Pittsfield Jct.	Washtenaw
Pittsford	Hillsdale
Plainfield Ave.	Kent
Plains	Marquette
Plainwell	Allegan
Planks Tavern	Berrien
Planter	Gogebic
Plaster Creek	Kent
Plaster Creek Jct.	Kent
Platte River	Benzie
Platte River Jct.	Benzie
Pleasant Hill	Tuscola
Pleasant Ridge	Oakland
Pleasant Street	Kent
Pleasant Street	Wayne
Pleasant View	Berrien
Plymouth	Wayne
Plymouth Jct.	Wayne
Plymouth Mine	Gogebic

Pointe Aux Barques	Huron
Point Mills	Houghton
Point Mills Jct.	Houghton
Point Nip-i-gon	Cheboygan
Pokagon	Cass
Poland	Sanilac
Polands	Lake
Polaski	Presque Isle
Pole Road Siding	Alcona
Polmantier	Tuscola
Polock Hill	Manistee
P.O.N. Jct.	Oakland
Pomeroy	Kalamazoo
Pomona	Manistee
Pompeii	Gratiot
Ponca	Iron
Ponshewaing	Emmet
Pontiac	Oakland
Pontiac Yard	Oakland
Poplar Street	St. Clair
Popple	Marquette
Pori	Houghton
Portage	Delta
Portage	Kalamazoo
Portage Coal Dock	Houghton
Portage Jct.	Crawford
Portage Street	Kalamazoo
Port Austin	Huron
Porter	Menominee
Porter Mine	Iron
Port Gypsum	Iosco
Port Hope	Huron
Port Huron	St. Clair
Portland	Ionia
Portland Mine	Baraga
Port Sherman	Muskegon
Portsmouth	Bay
Posen	Presque Isle
Potters	Osceola
Potters	Saginaw
Potterville	Eaton

Potts	Oscoda
Pound Hill	St. Clair
Powder Hill	Marquette
Powell	Marquette
Power	Marquette
Powers	Menominee
Prairie Farm	Saginaw
Prairie Farm Jct.	Saginaw
Prairie Siding	Lenawee
Pratt Lake	Kent
Pratts	Otsego
Prattville	Hillsdale
Prescott	Ogemaw
Prescy	Kalkaska
Presque Isle	Marquette
Prickett	Houghton
Princeton	Marquette
Princeton Mine #1	Marquette
Princeton Mine #2	Marquette
Prison	Jackson
Prison	Marquette
Pritchards	Alcona
Progress Dam	Newaygo
Project	Charlevoix
Provemont	Leelanau
Providence	Presque Isle
Puillions	Schoolcraft
Pulaski	Jackson
Pullman	Allegan
Purcell Mine	Iron
Purdy	Tuscola
Puritan Mine	Gogebic
Putnams	Crawford

-Q-

Quanicassee	Tuscola
Quarry	Cheboygan
Quarry	Huron
Quarry Jct.	Huron
Queen	Marquette
Queen Mine	Marquette

Quimby	Barry
Quimbys	Kalkaska
Quincy	Branch
Quincy	Houghton
Quinn	Arenac
Quinn	Houghton
Quinnesec	Dickinson
Quinnesec Jct.	Dickinson
Quinnesec Mine	Dickinson

-R-

Rabbit River	Allegan
Raby	Bay
Raco	Chippewa
Radford	Ontonagon
Radfords Spur	Menominee
Raijuels	Lake
Railo (Spur)	Alger
Rainy Lake	Presque Isle
Raish	Marquette
Raisin	Monroe
Raisin Center	Lenawee
Raisinville	Monroe
Ralph	Dickinson
Ramona	Newaygo
Ramona Park	Emmet
Ramsay	Gogebic
Rand	Isabella
Randall Beach	Oakland
Randall Spur	Cheboygan
Randville	Dickinson
Randville Mine	Dickinson
Range Jct.	Ontonagon
Ranger Spur	Alcona
Rankin	Oceana
Ransom	Calhoun
Ransom	Marquette
Rapid City	Kalkaska
Rapid River	Delta
Rapid Siding	Delta
Rapsons Siding	Huron

Rasmus	Crawford
Ravenna	Muskegon
Ravenna Mine	Iron
Rawn	Gratiot
Ray	Newaygo
Rayburn	Alpena
Rays Pit	Macomb
Rea	Monroe
Reade	Marquette
Reading	Hillsdale
Reagan	Lapeer
Reagan	Sanilac
Reavie	Mackinac
Redford	Wayne
Redford Jct.	Wayne
Red Jacket Mine	Houghton
Red Oak	Oscoda
Red Oak	St. Joseph
Redridge	Houghton
Redridge Jct.	Houghton
Redruth	Baraga
Redstone	Ionia
Redys	Bay
Reed City	Osceola
Reeds	Kent
Reedsboro	Alger
Reedsburg	Missaukee
Reeds Lake	Kent
Reeman	Newaygo
Reese	Tuscola
Reeves	Monroe
Reeves	Newaygo
Reichells Mill	Marquette
Relay Station	Menominee
Remick	Isabella
Remus	Mecosta
Remwick	Clare
Rennies	Leelanau
Reno	Lake
Renton	Calhoun
Reo Jct.	Ingham

Republic	Marquette
Republic Jct.	Marquette
Republic Mine	Marquette
Resort	Crawford
Rexford	Chippewa
Rexton	Mackinac
Reynolds	Jackson
Reynolds	Montcalm
Rhodes	Gladwin
Ribble Road	Huron
Ricedale	Houghton
Richard	Iron
Richardi	Antrim
Richardson	Schoolcraft
Richland	Kalamazoo
Richland Jct.	Kalamazoo
Richmond	Allegan
Richmond	Macomb
Richs	Osceola
Richville	Tuscola
Ricker	Kalkaska
Riddle Jct.	Ontonagon
Riddles Spur	Schoolcraft
Ridge	Alger
Ridgeway	Lenawee
Ridgeway (Jct.)	Macomb
Rifle Range	Chippewa
Riga	Lenawee
Ripley	Houghton
Riskes Siding	Clare
Riverbank	Osceola
River Branch Jct.	Manistee
Riverdale	Gratiot
River Raisin	Washtenaw
River Rouge	Wayne
Riverside	Berrien
Riverside Mine	Marquette
River Siding	Dickinson
Riverton	Mason
Riverton Mine	Iron
Riverview	Berrien

Riverview	Kalkaska
Rives Jct.	Jackson
Rix	Kalamazoo
RK	St. Joseph
Roaring Brook	Emmet
Robbins	Charlevoix
Robbins Spur	Marquette
Roberts	Alger
Roberts Landing	St. Clair
Roberts Siding	Delta
Robinson	Baraga
Robinson	Clare
Robinson	Iosco
Robinson	Ottawa
Robinson	Tuscola
Robinsons	Huron
Robys Jct.	Newaygo
Robys Spur	Saginaw
Rochester	Oakland
Rochester Jct.	Oakland
Rock	Delta
Rock Elm	Charlevoix
Rockford	Kent
Rockland	Ontonagon
Rockport	Alpena
Rock River	Alger
Rockton	Alger
Rockwell	Berrien
Rockwood	Wayne
Rodney	Mecosta
Roe Lake	Alcona
Rogers	Ontonagon
Rogers	Otsego
Rogers City	Presque Isle
Rogers City Jct.	Presque Isle
Rogers Mine	Iron
Rogersville	Genesee
Rolfe	Osceola
Rollin	Lenawee
Rolling Mill Mine	Marquette
Romeo	Macomb

Romulus	Wayne
Rondo	Cheboygan
Rondo	Menominee
Rooney	Bay
Rooney	Menominee
Roosevelt Hills	Van Buren
Roots	Jackson
Roscoe	Alger
Roscommon	Roscommon
Roscommon Gravel Pit	Crawford
Roseburg	Sanilac
Rosebush	Isabella
Rose Center	Oakland
Rose City	Ogemaw
Rose Island	Huron
Rose Lake	Osceola
Rosevear	Huron
Ross	Kent
Ross	Marquette
Ross Crossing	Tuscola
Ross Siding	Gogebic
Rosemound	Ottawa
Rothbury	Oceana
Rougemere	Wayne
Rouge Yard	Wayne
Round Lake	Emmet
Round Lake	Wexford
Round Lake Jct.	Missaukee
Rousseau	Ontonagon
Rowena	Ogemaw
Rowley	Kalkaska
Royal Mine	Gogebic
Royal Oak	Oakland
Royalton	Berrien
Ruby	St. Clair
Ruby Mine	Gogebic
Rudds	Oakland
Rudyard	Chippewa
Rugg	Kalkaska
Ruggles	Lake
Rugsten	Mackinac

Rumbo	Wexford
Rumely	Alger
Rumley Yard	Calhoun
Ruprechts	Dickinson
Rushton	Livingston
Russell	Alcona
Russell	Delta
Russell	Dickinson
Russell Siding	Lenawee
Russell Street	Wayne
Rust	Mecosta
Rust	Montmorency
Ruth	Huron
Ruthards	Leelanau
Rutland	Emmet
Ryerson	Newaygo

-S-

Sabin	Grand Traverse
Saddlebag Siding	Kent
Saganing	Arenac
Sage	Luce
Sages Lake	Ogemaw
Saginaw	Saginaw
Saginaw City	Saginaw
Saginaw City Jct.	Saginaw
Saginaw Crossing	Kent
Saginaw E.S.	Saginaw
Saginaw Jct.	Saginaw
Saginaw Jct.	St. Clair
Saginaw Mine	Marquette
S.B. Jct.	Saginaw
Sagola	Dickinson
Saile	Manistee
Saint Anthonys	Monroe
Saint Charles	Saginaw
Saint Clair	St. Clair
Saint Clare Springs	St. Clair
Saint Collins	Ontonagon
Saint Helen	Roscommon
Saint Ignace	Mackinac

Saint Jacques	Delta
Saint Johns	Bay
Saint Johns	Clinton
Saint Joseph	Berrien
Saint Joseph Jct.	Berrien
Saint Lawrence	Marquette
Saint Louis	Gratiot
Saint Marys Jct.	Houghton
Saint Marys Transfer	Chippewa
Saint Paul Avenue	Wayne
Salem	Washtenaw
Saline	Washtenaw
Salisbury Mine	Marquette
Sallings	Otsego
Salmon Trout	Houghton
Salt River	Isabella
Salt Wells	Wayne
Salva	Delta
Salzburg	Bay
Samaria	Monroe
Samson	Alger
San	Shiawassee
Sanborn	St. Clair
Sand Beach	Huron
Sand Creek	Lenawee
Sandhurst	Ontonagon
Sand Lake	Kent
Sand Lake	Lenawee
Sand Lake	Van Buren
Sand Pit	Cheboygan
Sand Pit	Muskegon
Sand Ridge	Saginaw
Sand River	Alger
Sand River	Marquette
Sands	Kalkaska
Sands	Marquette
Sands Siding	Manistee
Sandstone	Jackson
Sandstown	Missaukee
Sandusky	Sanilac
Sandy	Huron

Sandy Beach	Cass
Sanford	Midland
Sangsters	Ionia
Sanson	Tuscola
Saranac	Ionia
Sauble	Lake
Sauble	Mason
Sault Sainte Marie	Chippewa
Saunders	Iron
Saunders	Kalkaska
Saunders	Wexford
Sawyer	Berrien
Sawyer Lake	Dickinson
Saxon	Kent
Schaeffer	Wayne
Schaffer	Delta
Schemms	Bay
Schneider	Marquette
Schomberg	Leelanau
Schoolcraft	Kalamazoo
Schriver	Ontonagon
Scio	Washtenaw
Scipio	Hillsdale
Scofield	Monroe
Scotdale	Berrien
Scott Lake	Iron
Scotts	Kalamazoo
Scotts	Schoolcraft
Scotts Camp	Schoolcraft
Scotts Point	Mackinac
Scotts Quarry	Chippewa
Scottville	Mason
Scranton	Sanilac
Scully Siding	Huron
Seager	Ontonagon
Seamans	Wexford
Sears	Osceola
Sebewaing	Huron
Second Avenue	Kent
Secords	Wayne
Section 10	Antrim

Section 10	Missaukee
Seed	Charlevoix
Seeley	Tuscola
Seewhy	Chippewa
Segwan	Kent
Selina	Alpena
Selma	Marquette
Selma	Wexford
Seneca	Lenawee
Seney	Schoolcraft
Senter	Houghton
Seola	Monroe
Setif	Delta
Sevastapol	Eaton
Seven Mile Hill	Iosco
17th Street	Wayne
Severns	Van Buren
Seville	Gratiot
Seymour	Kent
Shafer Mine	Iron
Shaftsburg	Shiawassee
Shanahan	St. Clair
Shanghai Pit	Washtenaw
Shanty Plains	Montcalm
Sharon	Kalkaska
Sharpville	Tuscola
Shaw	Muskegon
Shearer	Arenac
Sheboyganing	Bay
Sheepdale	Lake
Sheffield	Kent
Shelby	Allegan
Shelby	Macomb
Shelby	Oceana
Shelbyville	Allegan
Sheldon	Ottawa
Sheldon	Wayne
Shelldrake	Kalamazoo
Shenango Mine	Marquette
Shepards	Antrim
Shepards	Eaton

Shepardsville	Clinton
Shepherd	Isabella
Sheridan	Barry
Sheridan	Montcalm
Sheridan Avenue	Saginaw
Sherman	Allegan
Sherman	Wexford
Shermans Mill	Benzie
Sherwood	Branch
Sherwood Mine	Iron
Shields	Saginaw
Shiloh	Ionia
Shingleton	Alger
Shirley	Baraga
Shoecraft	Genesee
Shops	Houghton
Shore Acres	Cass
Shore Line Jct.	Houghton
Shore Line Quarry	Monroe
Short Cut	Wayne
Shoup	Oakland
Shultz	Barry
Shultz	Otsego
Sibley	Wayne
Siding No. 1	Delta
Siding No. 2	Iron
Siding No. 2	Menominee
Siding No. 3	Iron
Siding No. 4	Menominee
Siding No. 5	Dickinson
Siding 145	Marquette
Siding 339	Gogebic
Siding 378	Schoolcraft
Siding M-7	Houghton
Siding R-358	Delta
Sidnaw	Houghton
Sidney	Montcalm
Siemens	Gogebic
Sigan	Marquette
Sigma	Kalkaska
Sillberg	Gogebic

Silver Beach	Cheboygan
Silver Creek	Kalamazoo
Silver Creek	Tuscola
Silverwood	Tuscola
Simar	Ontonagon
Simmonds	Newaygo
Simons	Antrim
Simpson	Muskegon
Sisson	Lenawee
Sisson	Newaygo
Six Lake	Montcalm
Six Mile Mine	Shiawassee
16th Street	St. Clair
6th Street	Wayne
Skandia	Marquette
Skeel	Iosco
Skellingers	Lake
Slagh	Oceana
Slaghts Track	Montcalm
Slapneck	Alger
Slaters Pit	Oakland
Slayton	Ogemaw
Slights	Grand Traverse
Slingerland	Iosco
Slocum	Muskegon
Slocum Jct.	Wayne
Slocums Grove	Muskegon
Sly	Emmet
Smith	St. Clair
Smith Jct.	Ogemaw
Smith Mill	Cheboygan
Smith Mine	Marquette
Smith Mine Jct.	Marquette
Smiths	Gladwin
Smiths	Saginaw
Smiths	Tuscola
Smiths	Charlevoix
Smiths Creek	St. Clair
Smiths Creek	Schoolcraft
Smiths Crossing	Midland
Smiths Siding	Cheboygan

Smyrna	Ionia
Snover	Sanilac
Snow	Berrien
Snowflake	Antrim
Snowshoe	Keweenaw
Snyder	Jackson
Snyder	Oscoda
Sobieski	Presque Isle
Sodus	Berrien
Soldiers Home	Kent
Solon	Leelanau
Solvay	Kent
Somerleyton	Berrien
Somerset	Hillsdale
Somerset Center	Hillsdale
Sonoma	Calhoun
Soo Jct.	Luce
Sorenson	Manistee
Soules	Kalkaska
South Adrian	Lenawee
South Allens	Osceola
South Arm	Charlevoix
South Bay City	Bay
South Boardman	Kalkaska
South Branch	Ogemaw
South Branch Camp	Oceana
South Buffalo Mine	Marquette
South End	Antrim
South Flint	Genesee
South Frankfort	Benzie
South Grand Blanc	Oakland
South Grand Rapids	Kent
South Haven	Van Buren
South Kearsarge	Houghton
South Lake Linden	Houghton
South Lansing	Ingham
South Lyon	Oakland
South Main Jct.	Marquette
South Manistique	Schoolcraft
South Norway	Dickinson
Southport	Monroe

South Range	Houghton
South Rockford	Kent
South Rogers City	Presque Isle
South Saginaw	Saginaw
South St. Clair	St. Clair
South Shore Jct.	Chippewa
South Street	Ingham
South Traverse City	Grand Traverse
South Wye	Cheboygan
South Wye	Chippewa
South Yard	Kalamazoo
South Yard	Wayne
Souveigny	Arenac
Spalding	Menominee
Sparr	Otsego
Sparta	Kent
Spears	Marquette
Spencer	Kalkaska
Spies Mine	Iron
Spies-Thompson	Ontonagon
Spinning	Macomb
Spires	Muskegon
Spoonville	Ottawa
Spratt	Alpena
Spring Arbor	Jackson
Spring Brook	Emmet
Spring Brook	Kalamazoo
Spring City	Grand Traverse
Springdale	Manistee
Springer	Schoolcraft
Springfield	Kalkaska
Springfield	Oakland
Spring Lake	Ottawa
Springport	Jackson
Spring Water	Charlevoix
Springwells	Wayne
Spruce	Baraga
Spruce	Dickinson
Spruceville	Schoolcraft
Spur 1	Presque Isle
Spur 3	Antrim

Spur 8	Schoolcraft
Spur 13	Schoolcraft
Spur 15	Schoolcraft
Spur 21	Menominee
Spur 24	Schoolcraft
Spur 25	Schoolcraft
Spur 28	Schoolcraft
Spur 42	Chippewa
Spur 75	Luce
Spur 80	Schoolcraft
Spur 81	Marquette
Spur 81	Schoolcraft
Spur 88	Schoolcraft
Spur 91	Schoolcraft
Spur 97	Schoolcraft
Spur 139-T	Alger
Spur 201	Baraga
Spur 203	Baraga
Spur 205	Baraga
Spur 208	Baraga
Spur 216	Baraga
Spur 234	Iron
Spur 237	Houghton
Spur 247	Iron
Spur 250	Marquette
Spur 255	Iron
Spur 257	Iron
Spur 259	Iron
Spur 265	Iron
Spur 267	Ontonagon
Spur 274	Ontonagon
Spur 275	Ontonagon
Spur 280	Gogebic
Spur 283	Houghton
Spur 284	Houghton
Spur 287	Gogebic
Spur 293	Houghton
Spur 301	Gogebic
Spur 309	Menominee
Spur 314	Ontonagon
Spur 315	Menominee

Spur 318	Ontonagon
Spur 409	Mackinac
Spur 416	Mackinac
Spur 428	Mackinac
Spur 447	Chippewa
Spur 458	Chippewa
Spur 459	Chippewa
Spur 477	Chippewa
Spur D-5	Baraga
Spur D-14	Baraga
Spur D-15	Baraga
Spur D-38	Houghton
Spur D-39	Houghton
Spur H-3	Houghton
Spur R-370	Alger
Spurr	Baraga
Spurr Mine	Baraga
Stack	Marquette
Stackpole	Houghton
Staffords	Antrim
Stager	Iron
Stambaugh	Iron
Stambaugh Mine	Iron
Stan	Lenawee
Standish	Arenac
Stanley Pit	Lapeer
Stanton	Montcalm
Stanton Jct.	Ionia
Stantons Spur	Houghton
Stanwood	Houghton
Stanwood	Mecosta
Star Lake	Lake
Star Siding	Alger
Stark	Wayne
Starr Wye	Schoolcraft
Star West Mine	Marquette
Statefair	Wayne
State Hospital	Grand Traverse
State Line	Gogebic
State Prison	Ionia
State Road	Allegan

State Road	Bay
State Road	Benzie
State Road	Eaton
State Road	Manistee
State Road	Saginaw
State Road	Schoolcraft
States Switch	Lake
Station Nine	Schoolcraft
Station 51	Delta
Statts Spur	Mackinac
Stearns	Lake
Stebbins(ville)	Ionia
Stegmiller Mine	Marquette
Steiner	Monroe
Stella	Gratiot
Stemms	Berrien
Stephen	Saginaw
Stephens	Lapeer
Stephens Siding	Gladwin
Stephenson	Menominee
Stephenson Mine	Marquette
Sterling	Arenac
Sterling	Macomb
Stetson	Oceana
Steuben	Schoolcraft
Stevens	Berrien
Stevens	Emmet
Stevens	Lenawee
Stevens	Montmorency
Stevensburg	Chippewa
Stevenson	Ontonagon
Stevensville	Berrien
Stewarts	Kent
Stewarts	Tuscola
Stickley	Gogebic
Stillman	Alger
Stillson	Sanilac
Stimson	Kalkaska
Stimson	Marquette
Stimson Jct.	Mecosta
Stinsons	Alpena

Stirling	Isabella
Stirling	Mecosta
Stockbridge	Ingham
Stock Yards	Wayne
Stoddards	Montmorency
Stone	Tuscola
Stoneville	Marquette
Stonington	Houghton
Stony Creek	Monroe
Stone Island	Wayne
Stony Point	Jackson
Stormer	Benzie
Stowes	Lake
Strasburg	Monroe
Stratford	Missaukee
Stratton	Ontonagon
Streeter	Kalamazoo
Street Railway	Marquette
Stronach	Manistee
Strong	Ionia
Strongs	Chippewa
Strongs	Monroe
Strongs Siding	Monroe
Strongs Siding	Wayne
Sturgeon	Baraga
Sturgeon	Dickinson
Sturgeon Branch	Cheboygan
Sturgeon Point	Alcona
Sturgeon River	Delta
Sturgis	St. Joseph
Sugar Loaf	Marquette
Sullivan	Muskegon
Sumac	Dickinson
Summerville	Montcalm
Summit	Alger
Summit	Baraga
Summit	Berrien
Summit	Charlevoix
Summit	Clare
Summit	Dickinson
Summit	Livingston

Summit	Ogemaw
Summit	Wexford
Summit City	Grand Traverse
Summitville	Lake
Sunday Lake Mine	Gogebic
Sunfield	Eaton
Sunn Spur	Iron
Sunny Brook	Emmet
Sunnyside	Kent
Sunnyside	St. Clair
Sunnyside	Wayne
Sunrise Landing	Alger
Superior	Charlevoix
Superior	Chippewa
Superior	Marquette
Superior Jct.	Chippewa
Sutliffs	Osceola
Sutton	Lenawee
Suttons Bay	Leelanau
Swains Crossing	Newaygo
Swan Creek	Monroe
Swan Creek	Saginaw
Swanson	Menominee
Swanzy	Marquette
Swartz Creek	Genesee
Swedetown	Houghton
Sweet	Muskegon
Sweet Siding	St. Clair
Sweetwater Tank	Lake
Swift	Mackinac
Sylvan	Washtenaw
Sylvania	Gogebic
Sylvan Lake	Oakland

-T-

Taft	Iosco
Talbot	Menominee
Talcott	Charlevoix
Tallman	Mason
Tamarac(k)	Gogebic
Tamarack	Houghton

Tamarack Mine	Houghton
Tanning	Alger
Tappan	St. Clair
Tarry	Huron
Tawas Beach	Iosco
Tawas Beach Jct.	Iosco
Tawas City	Iosco
Taylor	Isabella
Taylor (Jct.)	Baraga
Taylor Mine	Baraga
Taylors	Marquette
Taymouth	Saginaw
Tecumseh	Lenawee
Tecumseh Jct.	Lenawee
Tecumseh Pit	Lenawee
Tekonsha	Calhoun
Temperance	Monroe
Temple	Clare
Ten Mile Spur	Delta
Tenth Street	St. Clair
Terminal Jct.	Kent
Terre Coupee	Berrien
Terry	Bay
Tesch	Delta
Thayer	Gogebic
Thelma	Antrim
Third Street	Muskegon
Third Street	Wayne
Thomas	Oakland
Thomas	Van Buren
Thomas Road	Wayne
Thomas Street	St. Clair
Thomaston	Gogebic
Thompson	Kalkaska
Thompsonville	Benzie
Thorn Apple	Barry
Thornton	St. Clair
Thread	Genesee
Three Lakes	Baraga
Three Oaks	Berrien
Three Rivers	St. Joseph

Three Rivers Jct.	St. Joseph
Thumb Lake	Charlevoix
Thumb Lake Jct.	Charlevoix
Tibbets	Baraga
Tierney	Roscommon
Tietsorts	Cass
Tilden Mine	Gogebic
Tilden Mine	Marquette
Tindall	Antrim
Tioga	Alger
Tioga	Baraga
Tipton	Lenawee
Titan Mine	Baraga
Tittabawassee Jct.	Saginaw
Tobico	Bay
Tobin Mine	Iron
Tobin Siding	Gogebic
Todds	Monroe
Toivola	Houghton
Tolands	Kent
Toledo Crossing	Muskegon
Toledo Jct.	Monroe
Toleens (Spur)	Iron
Toma Siding	Baraga
Tomlin	Mason
Tong	Oscoda
Topaz	Ontonagon
Topinabee	Cheboygan
Toquin	Van Buren
Torch Lake Jct.	Houghton
Torrey	Genesee
Totten	Lake
Tower	Cheboygan
Tower 1	Kalamazoo
Town House	Jackson
Town Line	Bay
Town Line	Berrien
Town Line	Montcalm
Town Line	Wayne
Traders Jct.	Dickinson
Traders Jct.	Dickinson

Train Falls	Alger
Transit Jct.	Wayne
Transport	Isabella
Traunik	Alger
Traverse	Keweenaw
Traverse City	Grand Traverse
Traverse Resort	Leelanau
Traverse Roads	Newaygo
Travis	Kalamazoo
Trenary	Alger
Trent	Muskegon
Trenton	Wayne
Trenton Jct.	Wayne
Triangle Spur	Iron
Trimountain	Houghton
Trombley	Delta
Trombley	Otsego
Trout Creek	Ontonagon
Trout Lake	Chippewa
Trowbridge	Cheboygan
Trowbridge	Ingham
Troy	Berrien
Truax	Alpena
Trufant	Montcalm
Truitts	Cass
Trumbull Avenue	Wayne
Trumbulls	Jackson
Trumbulls Siding	Newaygo
Tucker	Iosco
Tucker Farm	Iosco
Tula	Gogebic
Tully Mine	Iron
Tunis	Baraga
Tunk	Grand Traverse
Tunnel Jct.	St. Clair
Tunnel Yard	St. Clair
Turkey	Wayne
Turnbull	Alpena
Turner	Arenac
Turner	Dickinson
Turner Jct.	Dickinson

Turner Street	Ingham
Turtle	Gogebic
Turtle	Iosco
Turtle Lake	Benzie
Tuscola	Tuscola
Tustin	Osceola
Tuxbury	Manistee
Twecoma	Gogebic
Twelfth Street	St. Clair
12th Street	Wayne
12 Mile Siding	Mason
20th Street	Wayne
23rd Street	Bay
24th Street	Wayne
26th Street	Bay
Twining	Arenac
Twin Lake	Muskegon
Twin Lake Branch	Grand Traverse
Twin Lake Jct.	Oscoda
Twin Lakes	Houghton
Twin Moutain	Grand Traverse
Tylers	Crawford
Tylers	Marquette
Tyre	Sanilac
Tyrone	Kent
Tyrus	Otsego

-U-

Ubly	Huron
Uhl	Newaygo
Umatilla	Wexford
Umstead	Arenac
Underwood	Alger
Underwood	Ingham
Ungers	Lake
Union City	Branch
Union Mine	Iron
Union Park	Marquette
Union Pier	Berrien
Unionville	Tuscola
Upjohn	Kalamazoo

Upper Big Rapids	Mecosta
Upper Mills	Houghton
Upper Paris	Mecosta
Upton Works	St. Clair
Urania	Washtenaw
Urbanrest	Oakland
Utica	Macomb
Utica Bend Switch	Macomb
Utica Plank	Macomb

-V-

V	Tuscola
Vail	Alger
Valda	Wexford
Valentine Lake	Montmorency
Valley	Alger
Valley Center	Sanilac
Valley Switch	Antrim
Van	Emmet
Van Buren	Kalkaska
Vandalia	Cass
Vandalia Track Pan	Cass
Van Demans	Benzie
Vanderbilt	Otsego
Van Horn	Jackson
Van Iderstine	Marquette
Van Meer	Alger
Van Patten	Tuscola
Van Platen	Charlevoix
Vans Harbor	Delta
Van Winkle	Delta
Vassar	Tuscola
Vaughn(s)	Alcona
Vaughn Mine	Gogebic
VE	St. Joseph
Veenfliets	Saginaw
Vega	Menominee
Veneer Jct.	Missaukee
Veneklassen	Ottawa
Vergennes	Kent
Vermilac	Baraga

Vermontville	Eaton
Verne	Saginaw
Verne Mine Jct.	Saginaw
Vernon	Shiawassee
Verona	Calhoun
Verona	Gogebic
Verona Mine	Dickinson
Vesper	Menominee
Vestaburg	Montcalm
Vick	Marquette
Vickeryville	Montcalm
Vicksburg	Kalamazoo
Victoria Avenue	Wayne
Victoria Mine	Iron
Vida	Alger
Vienna	Monroe
Vienna Jct.	Monroe
Vienna Jct.	Montmorency
Vincent	Presque Isle
Vine	Berrien
Vine	Kalamazoo
Vineland	Berrien
Vinewood Avenue	Wayne
Virgil	Montcalm
Virgil Mine	Iron
Vista	Dickinson
Vivian Mine	Dickinson
Volinia	Cass
Volunteer Mine	Marquette
Voss	Muskegon
Vriesland	Ottawa
Vrooman	Berrien
Vulcan	Dickinson
Vulcan Mine	Dickinson

-W-

Wabik	Marquette
Wabememe	Emmet
Wadhams	St. Clair
Wadsworth	Huron
Wagers	Montcalm

Waggoner	Charlevoix
Wagner	Missaukee
Wagner Lake	Missaukee
Wahjamega	Tuscola
Wah Wah Soo	Otsego
Wainola	Ontonagon
Wakefield	Gogebic
Wakefield Mine	Gogebic
Wakelee	Cass
Waldo	Berrien
Waldron	Hillsdale
Wales	St. Clair
Walhalla	Mason
Walker	emmet
Walker	Kalamazoo
Walker	Ottawa
Walkers	Sanilac
Walkerville	Oceana
Wallace	Huron
Wallace	Menominee
Walled Lake	Oakland
Wallin	Benzie
Wallis	Eaton
Wall Lake	Barry
Walloon Lake	Charlevoix
Walloon Lake Jct.	Charlevoix
Walls	Wexford
Walsh	Schoolcraft
Walton	Grand Traverse
Walton Jct.	Grand Traverse
Waltz	Wayne
Wampson	Tuscola
Wann	Dickinson
Wapano	Lenawee
Ward	Dickinson
Ward	Saginaw
Warden	Ionia
Wards	Antrim
Wards	Manistee
Wards	Schoolcraft
Wardville	Missaukee

Warner	Monroe
Warner Mine	Iron
Warner Mine Jct.	Iron
Warren	Macomb
Warren Yards	Wayne
Wasas	Ontonagon
Wasepi	St. Joseph
Washington	Macomb
Washington Avenue	Ingham
Washington Avenue	Saginaw
Washington Mine	Marquette
Washington Street	Monroe
Waterford	Oakland
Waterford	Wayne
Waterloo Street	Wayne
Water Tank	Gogebic
Water Tank	Oceana
Water Tank	Otsego
Watertown	Sanilac
Waters	Otsego
Watersmeet	Gogebic
Water Street Jct.	Bay
Watervliet	Berrien
Water Works Spur	Bay
Watkins	Jackson
Watrous	Huron
Watrousville	Tuscola
Watson	Marquette
Watson	Montmorency
Watson Mine	Marquette
Watsonville	Emmet
Watton	Baraga
Waucedah	Dickinson
Wauseca Mine	Iron
Waveland	Cheboygan
Waverly	Ottawa
Way	Antrim
Wayagamung	Emmet
Wayland	Allegan
Wayne	Wayne
Wayne Jct.	Wayne

WB	Lenawee
Weale	Huron
Wealthy	Manistee
Wealthy Street	Kent
Webb	Antrim
Webber	Ionia
Webberville	Ingham
Webster	Antrim
Webster Mine	Baraga
Weeks	Monroe
Weidman	Isabella
Weimer	Mason
Welch	Mackinac
Welch	Ogemaw
Welden	Benzie
Weldon	Benzie
Weldon Bridge	Benzie
Weldon Centre	Benzie
Weldon Creek	Mason
Weller	Chippewa
Wellington	Gogebic
Wells	Allegan
Wells	Antrim
Wells	Arenac
Wells	Delta
Wells	Tuscola
Wellsburg	Chippewa
Wells Branch	Antrim
Wellsford	Tuscola
Wells Spur	Dickinson
Wellston	Manistee
Wellsville	Lenawee
Wenatchee	Berrien
Wenona	Bay
Wenona Beach	Bay
Wentworth	Kent
Wenzells	Chippewa
Wequetonsing	Emmet
West AuTrain	Alger
West Branch	Marquette
West Branch	Ogemaw

West Chapin Mine	Dickinson
West Chester	Ottawa
West Detroit	Wayne
West End Avenue	Wayne
West End Bridge	Houghton
West End Mine	Marquette
Western Avenue	Muskegon
West Flint	Genesee
West Gladstone	Delta
West Grand Ledge	Eaton
West Grand Rapids	Kent
West Greenbush	Alcona
West Harrisville	Alcona
West Hill	Jackson
West Ishpeming	Marquette
Westminster	Grand Traverse
West Niles	Berrien
West Olive	Ottawa
Weston	Lenawee
Westover	St. Clair
West Percy	Alger
West Point	Delta
West Pontiac	Oakland
West Republic Mine	Marquette
West Tappan	St. Clair
West Troy	Newaygo
West Troy Jct.	Newaygo
West Vulcan Mine	Dickinson
West Watson	Allegan
West Wequetonsing	Emmet
Westwood	Kalkaska
West Yard	Mackinac
West Yard	Marquette
Wetmore	Alger
Wetmore Mine	Baraga
Wetzell	Antrim
Wexford	Wexford
Weyant	Emmet
Whatcheer Mine	Bay
Wheatfield	Calhoun
Wheeler	Gratiot

Wheeler Spur	Arenac
Wheelerton	Jackson
Wheeling	Emmet
Wheeling Mine	Marquette
Whipple	Grand Traverse
White	Delta
White	Houghton
White Camp	Charlevoix
White City	Alger
White Cloud	Newaygo
White Dale	Schoolcraft
White Feather	Bay
Whitefish	Alger
Whitefish Tank	Alger
White Fish River	Delta
Whitehall	Muskegon
White Lake Jct.	Muskegon
White Oak	Van Buren
White Pigeon	St. Joseph
White Pigeon Jct.	St. Joseph
White Pine	Ontonagon
White River Club	Newaygo
White Rock	Iosco
Whites	Gratiot
Whites (Crossing)	Calhoun
White Siding	Antrim
Whites Jct.	Charlevoix
White Star Track	Washtenaw
Whitewood	Wayne
Whitman	Marquette
Whitmore Lake	Livingston
Whitmore Lake	Washtenaw
Whitney	Menominee
Whitneys	Kent
Whitneyville	Kent
Whittaker	Washtenaw
Whittemore	Iosco
Wiard	Washtenaw
Wickwire Mine	Iron
Widdicomb	Missaukee
Wiggins	Oscoda

Wilbur Road	Sanilac
Wilcox	Alger
Wilcox	Newaygo
Wilders	Calhoun
Wildeys	Van Buren
Wileys	Mason
Wilkins	Kalkaska
Wilkinson	Berrien
Williams	Barry
Williams	Kalamazoo
Williams	Wexford
Williams Crossing	Alger
Williamburg	Grand Traverse
Williams Jct.	Roscommon
Williams Street	Kent
Williamston	Ingham
Willis	Benzie
Willis	Washtenaw
Willets	Monroe
Willow	Wayne
Willow Run	Washtenaw
Wilman	Mackinac
Wilmot	Tuscola
Wilson	Menominee
Wilson	Montmorency
Wilson	Sanilac
Wilsons	Jackson
Wilsons Siding	Lapeer
Winchester	Mecosta
Winchester	Monroe
Winde	Delta
Windermere	Berrien
Windiate	Oakland
Windling	Antrim
Windling	Antrim
Winegars	Gladwin
Wingleton	Lake
Wings Jct.	Osceola
Winona	Houghton
Winona Mine	Gogebic
Winsor	Huron

Winter Street	Kent
Winthrop	Marquette
Winthrop Jct.	Marquette
Winthrop Mine	Marquette
Wisconsin Mine	Gogebic
Wise	Isabella
Witbeck	Marquette
Witch Lake	Marquette
Wixom	Oakland
Wolcott	Antrim
Wolf Lake	Lake
Wolverine	Cheboygan
Wolverine	Cheboygan
Wolverine	Houghton
Wolverine	Marquette
Wolverine Mine	Houghton
Wolverine Mine #1	Bay
Wolverine Mine #2	Bay
Wolverine Road	Cheboygan
Wolverine Switch	Cheboygan
Wood	Branch
Wood	Lenawee
Woodbury	Eaton
Woodhull	Shiawassee
Wood Lake	Montcalm
Woodland	Barry
Woodlawn	Delta
Woodman	Tuscola
Woodmere	Wayne
Woodrow	Ogemaw
Woods Corners	Ionia
Woodside	Bay
Woodside	Houghton
Woods Mill	Montcalm
Wood Spur	Ontonagon
Woodstock	Lenawee
Woodville	Bay
Woodville	Jackson
Woodville	Newaygo
Woodward	Lenawee
Woodward Avenue	Wayne

Woodway	Tuscola
Wooster	Newaygo
Worcester (Hill)	Newaygo
Worden	Washtenaw
Worth	Arenac
Worthing	Iron
Wright	Gratiot
Wrights	Alger
Wrights	Ogemaw
Wrights Lake	Otsego
Wyandotte	Wayne
Wylies	Grand Traverse
Wyman	Montcalm
Wyoming	Kent
Wyoming	Keweenaw

-Y-

Yale	St. Clair
Yale Mine	Gogebic
Yalmer	Marquette
Yandell	Houghton
Yates	Oakland
Yatton	Mackinac
YD	Wayne
York	Shiawassee
Yorks	Sanilac
Yorkville	Kalamazoo
Young	Marquette
Youngs Mine	Iron
Youngstown Mine	Iron
Ypsilanti	Washtenaw
Ypsilanti Jct.	Washtenaw
Yuill	Otsego
Yuma	Wexford

-Z-

Zams Spur	Ottawa
Zeeland	Ottawa
Zerbel	Alger
Zilwaukee	Saginaw
Zimmerman Mine	Iron
Zion	St. Clair

PART TWO:

Railroad Lines and Stations, Lower Peninsula, Michigan

DIRECTORY OF RAILROAD LINES

AA	Ann Arbor
AA-A	Toledo-Owosso
AA-B	Owosso-Cadillac
AA-C	Cadillac-Frankfort
AA-F	junction-Boat Landing
AA-O	Old main line, near Ann Arbor-near Whitmore Lake
AA-S	Leland-South Lyon
AA-2	Old main line, Ithaca-St. Louis-Alma
A&BR	Arcadia & Betsey River
	Arcadia-Copemish
ASNW	AuSable & Northwestern
ASNW-A	AuSable-Comins
ASNW-AO	Russell-McKinley
ASNW-B	Hardy-Beevers
ASNW-1	Russell-Luzerne
ASNW-2	Twin Lake Jct.-Lewiston
ASNW-3	Comins-Hills
ASNW-4 +	Comins-LeLone
AT	Algonac Transit
	Marine City-Algonac
BC	Boyne City
BC-A	Boyne City-Alpena
BC-2 +	Thumb Lake + other east branches
BC-3 +	South branches
BC-5 +	Miscellaneous branches
BF	Cleveland, Cincinnati, Chicago & St. Louis (Big Four)
	Elkhart-Benton Harbor

CCS	Canada Southern
	Slocum Jct.-Fayette, Ohio
CK&S	Chicago, Kalamazoo & Saginaw
CK&S	Kalamazoo-Woodbury
CK&S-S	Kalamazoo-Pavilion Jct.
CN	Cincinnati Northern
	Jackson-Alvordton, Ohio
C&NE	Cadillac & North Eastern
	Cadillac-Lake City
D&C	Detroit & Charlevoix
	Frederic-East Jordan
D&M	Detroit & Mackinac
D&M-A +	National City-Alger
D&M-B +	National City-Rose City
D&M-E	Erie & Michigan Ry. & Nav.
D&M-G	AuGres-Omer
D&M-H	Hillman Branch
D&M-K	Black Lake Branch
D&M-M +	Mud Lake Branch
D&M-N	Alpena-Cheboygan
D&M-L	LeGrand Branch
D&M-O	Old main line (later Lincoln Branch)
D&M-Q	Rockport Branch
D&M-R	Rogers City Branch
D&M-S	Foss-Alpena
D&M-T	Tawas Beach Branch
D&M-V	Jackson Lake Branch
D&M-W	Wolverine Branch
DCS	Detroit, Caro & Sandusky
	Bay City-Tappan
DT	Detroit Terminal
DTI	Detroit, Toledo & Ironton
DTI-A	Malinta, Ohio-Tecumseh

DTI-D	D & I Jct.-Dearborn
DTI-M	West End Avenue-Metamora, Ohio
DTI-T	Petersburg Jct.-Toledo
DTI-T2	Dundee-Petersburg, Jct.
DTI-Z	Raisinville-Dundee
DTM	Detroit, Toledo & Milwaukee
	Dundee-Allegan
DTSL	Detroit & Toledo Shore Line
	Toledo-River Rouge
EJ&S +	East Jordan & Southern
	East Jordan-Bellaire, plus branches
E&SE +	Empire & South Eastern
	Empire Jct.-Empire, plus branch
FSUD	Fort Street Union Depot
(DURS	includes Detroit Union Railway Station)
GR&I	Grand Rapids & Indiana
GR&I-K +	Missaukee Jct.-Michelson, plus branches
GR&I-H	Harbor Springs Branch
GR&I-M	Muskegon Branch
GR&I-N	Grand Rapids-Mackinaw City
GR&I-S	Fort Wayne-Grand Rapids
GR&I-T	Walton Jct.-Traverse City
GR&I-2	Osceola Jct.-west
GR&I-3	Milton Jct.-Carey
GR&I-4	Stimson Jct.-west
GR&I-5 to 10	Other branches
GR&I-YG	Madison Square Branch
GTW	Grand Trunk Western
GTW-A	Richmond-Pontiac-Jackson
GTW-B	Cass City-Bad Axe
GTW-C	Chicago-Port Huron
GTW-D +	Detroit-Grand Haven
GTW-H	West Detroit-Port Huron
GTW-K	Pavilion-Kalamazoo

GTW-M	Ashley-Muskegon
GTW-P	Pontiac-Caseville
GTW-S +	Durand-Bay City
GTW-YF	Old main line at Flint
GTW-YK	Kalamazoo yard
GTW-YM	Muskegon Ry. & Nav. Co.
GTW-YP	Pontiac Belt Line
KLSC	Kalamazoo, Lake Shore & Chicago
	Kalamazoo-South Haven, plus branch
L&N	Ludington & Northern
	Ludington-Epworth, plus branch
LS	Lake Shore & Michigan Southern
LS-A	Toledo-Elkhart via Old Road
LS-D	Toledo-Detroit
LS-F	Grosvenor-Fayette
LS-G	White Pigeon-Grand Rapids
LS-J	Lenawee Jct.-Jackson
LS-L	Jonesville-Lansing
LS-M	Lenawee Jct.-Monroe
LS-S	Sturgis-Goshen
LS-W	Jackson-Fort Wayne
LS-Y	Hillsdale-Ypsilanti
LS-2	Erie & Kalamazoo original line
M&O	Mason & Oceana
	Buttersville-Maple
M&GR	Manistee & Grand Rapids
M&GR	Manistee-Marion
M&GR-1 to	
M&GR-6	Other branches
M&NE	Manistee & Northeastern
M&NE-A	Manistee-Traverse City
M&NE-E	Platte River Jct.-Empire Jct.
M&NE-N	Hatchs-Northport
M&NE-O	Onekama Jct.-Onekama
M&NE-P	Solon-Provemont

M&NE-R	Kaleva-Grayling
M&NE-YM +	Manistee yard
M&NE-1 to 5	Other branches
MC	Michigan Central
MC-A	Air Line (Jackson-Niles)
MC-B	Detroit-Bay City
MC-BC	Vassar-Caro
MC-BL	Lapeer & Northern
MC-BS	Denmark Jct.-Saginaw
MC-C	Jackson-Niles
MC-DD	Delray-Dearborn Jct.
MC-DM	St. Clair-Ridgeway
MC-DZ	YD-Town Line
MC-E	Detroit-Jackson
MC-G	Jackson-Grand Rapids
MC-H	Kalamazoo-South Haven
MC-J +	South Bend-St. Joseph & Benton Harbor
MC-K	Battle Creek-Sturgis
MC-L	Bay City-Midland
MC-L +	Branches off Midland Branch
MC-M	Bay City-Mackinaw City
MC-MB +	Sallings-Johannesburg
MC-ME	Edwards Lake Branch
MC-MH +	Haakwood Branch
MC-MP +	Pigeon River Branch
MC-MR	Camp Grayling Branch
MC-MT +	Grayling-Lewiston
MC-M +	Branches off Mackinaw Branch
MC-N	Niles-South Bend
MC-P +	Gladwin Branch
MC-S	Jackson-Bay City
MC-T	Detroit-Toledo
MC-TG	Grosse Isle Branch
MC-W	Niles-Chicago
MC-YB +	Bay City yard lines
MC-YD +	Detroit yard lines
MC-YL +	Lansing yard lines
MEC	Mecosta
	Byers-Horseshoe Lake

PHD   Port Huron & Detroit
             Port Huron-Marine City

PM   Pere Marquette
PM-A   Allegan-Muskegon-Pentwater
PM-AH   Mears-Hart
PM-AM   Macatawa Branch
PM-AO   Old main line, Holland-Muskegon
PM-B +   Saginaw-Bay City
PM-C   Grand Rapids-Chicago
PM-D   Detroit-Grand Rapids
PM-DW   West Detroit Branch
PM-F   Flint-Fostoria
PM-FB   Flint Belt
PM-G   Edmore-Freeport
PM-H   Lawton-South Haven
PM-I   Grand Ledge-Howard City
PM-J   Ionia-Big Rapids
PM-JB   Barryton Branch
PM-JC   Chippewa Lake Branch
PM-JW   Weidman Branch
PM-K   Rapid City-Kalkaska
PM-K +   Branches off Kalkaska Branch
PM-L   Saginaw-Ludington
PM-LG   Coleman-Beaverton
PM-LH   Clare-Harrison
PM-LH +   Branches off Harrison Branch
PM-LL   Harrison-Leota
PM-LM   Coleman-Mt. Pleasant
PM-L +   Other Branches off Ludington Branch
PM-M   Walhalla-Manistee
PM-N   Port Huron-BadAxe-Grindstone City
PM-NA   Port Huron-Almont
PM-NH   Palms-Port Hope
PM-NS   Poland-Sandusky
PM-NZ   Yale-Zion
PM-P   Grand Rapids-Bay View
PM-PE   Williamsburg-Elk Rapids
PM-P +   Other branches off Petoskey Branch
PM-Q   Saginaw-Port Huron
PM-R   Berry-Big Rapids

PM-S	Saginaw-Bad Axe
PM-T +	Saginaw-Toledo
PM-U	Benton Harbor-Buchanan
PM-V +	Saginaw-Howard City
PM-W	New Buffalo-LaCrosse, Ind.
PM-YB	Bay City yard
PM-YM	Muskegon yard
PM-YS +	Saginaw yard lines
PRR	Pennsylvania (see also Grand Rapids & Indiana listing)
PRR	Carleton-Detroit
PRR +	Other Detroit yard lines
WAB	Wabash
WAB	Delray-Montpelier, Ohio
WAB +	Other Detroit yard lines

Note. New York Central System lines are listed by constituent owners; see listings for BF, CCS, CK&S, CN, D&C, DTM, LS, and MC.

ALCONA COUNTY

Alcona	12	27N	9E	D&M-S 98.4
Bamfield	11	25N	5E	ASNW-A 26.9
Batton	(now Lott?)			
Beever(s)	9	27N	6E	ASNW-B 50.0
Black River	14	28N	9E	D&M-S 102.7 —
				D&M-O 108.4
Bryant	35	25N	6E	ASNW-A 18.8
Byers	24	27N	5E	ASNW-B 45.7
#Cedarmere		25N	9E	D&M-S 83?
Chevriers	17	25N	5E	ASNW-A 24.2
Code	16	27N	5E	ASNW-B 41.5
Crooked Lake Jct.	(now Hardy)			
Curran	22	27N	5E	ASNW-B 43.6
#Dault Spur				D&M-S
#Davidson				D&M
Five Channels Jct.	(see same, Iosco Co.)			
Flat Rock	3	25N	5E	ASNW-A 29.1
Glennie	15	25N	6E	ASNW-A 23.1
#Grams (Crossing)		26N	5E	ASNW-A 32
Gravel Pit Siding	31	25N	9E	D&M-O 81.8
Greenbush	3	25N	9E	D&M-S 86.3
Gustin	25	26N	8E	D&M-O 89.9
Handy	18	25N	9E	D&M-O 84.9
Hardy	19	27N	5E	ASNW-A 39.2 —
				ASNW-B 39.2
Harrisville	12	26N	9E	D&M-S 91.8
Hawes	24	27N	8E	D&M-O 97.2 —
				D&M-M 0
Henry	12	27N	8E	D&M-O 99.8
Kurtz	18	25N	7E	ASNW-?
Lincoln	36	27N	8E	D&M-O 93.9
Lott	27	25N	6E	ASNW-A 20.9
Loud Jct.	32	27N	7E	D&M-M 11.3
Marsh	(now Code)			

Mikado	1	25N	8E	D&M-O 87.4
Mud Lake	32	27N	7E	D&M-M 10.5
Mud Lake Jct.	(now Hawes)			
North Branch	(now Russell)			
#Pole Road Siding				D&M-S
Pritchards	31	27N	8E	D&M-M 6.0
#Ranger Spur				D&M-S
Roe Lake	36	28N	8E	D&M-O 101.9
Russell	17	26N	5E	ASNW-A 33.5 — ASNW-AO 33.5
Sturgeon Point	25	27N	9E	D&M-S 95.5
Vaughn(s)	(now Glennie)			
West Greenbush	(now Mikado)			
West Harrisville	(now Lincoln)			

ALLEGAN COUNTY

Abronia	32	2N	12W	LS-G 56.0
Allegan	28	2N	13W	DTM 132.9 — LS-G 61.8 — PM-A(old) 1.0 + 0.8; PM-A(new) 0
Black River	(now Lee)			
#Bowens				GR&I-S 201
Boyd	21	4N	15W	PM-C 29.9
Bradley	19	3N	11W	GR&I-S 210.0
Bravo	32	2N	15W	PM-C 46.0
Brick Yard	8	3N	14W	PM-A 11.7
Clyde	(now Pearl)			
Dorr	16	4N	12W	LS-G 76.7
Doster	13	1N	11W	DTM 114.1
Dunning(ville)	27	3N	14W	PM-A 8.4
East Saugatuck	4	3N	15W	PM-C 32.9
Fennville	5	2N	15W	PM-C 40.4
Filmore	23	4N	15W	PM-A 17.1
Fisk	27	2N	12W	DTM 125.5

Gilc(h)rist	21	3N	15W	PM-A 9.8
#Graafschap				PM-C 28?
Gun Marsh	(now Pine)			
Hamilton	6	3N	14W	PM-A 13.3
Herps	4	4N	12W	LS-G 79.6
Hilliards	4	3N	12W	LS-G 73.0
Hooper	36	2N	11W	DTM 118.2
Hopkins	19	3N	12W	LS-G 69.1
Hoppertown	(now Pullman)			
JN	29	1N	11W	GR&I-S 196.6— LS-G 48.1
Kellogg	29	2N	12W	DTM 128.1
Lee	20	1N	15W	PM-C 50.4
Manlius	19	3N	15W	PM-C 37.2
Martin	29	2N	11W	GR&I-S 203.1
May	3	4N	15W	PM-A 18.6
Mill Grove	12	2N	14W	PM-A 3.9
Miner Lake	2	2N	13W	LS-G 65.5
Moline	12	4N	12W	GR&I-S 217.6
Montieth	32	2N	11W	DTM 121.7— GR&I-S 202.1
Montieth Jct.	32	2N	11W	DTM 121.8
Neely	1	1N	11W	DTM 117.3
New Richmond	17	3N	15W	PM-C 36.2
Otsego	23	1N	12W	LS-G(old) 52.0; LS-G(new) 52.7
Pearl(e)	20	2N	15W	PM-C 43.6
Pine Lake	(now Neely)			
Plainwell	29	1N	11W	GR&I-S 196.7; LS-G 48.0
Pullman	8	1N	15W	PM-C 48.1
Rabbit River	(now Hamilton)			
Richmond	8	3N	15W	PM-C 35.4
Shelby	(now Shelbyville)			
Shelbyville	5	2N	11W	GR&I-S 207.2
Sherman	(now Bravo)			
State Road	(now East Saugatuck)			
Wayland	6	3N	11W	GR&I-S 213.0
Wells	17	2N	15W	PM-C 42.4
West Watson	(now Abronia)			

ALPENA COUNTY

Alpena	22	31N	8E	D&M-S 124.0
Alpena	23	31N	8E	BC-A 91.7; D&M-S(old) 124.4 + 0.7
Alpena Jct.	15	31N	8E	D&M-N 124.8 – D&M-S 124.8 – D&M-Q 0
Beebe Spur	21	30N	8E	D&M-S 117.8
Bolton	9	32N	7E	D&M-N 135.5
#Canfield		30N	5E	BC-A 69
Cedar Spur	17	30N	5E	BC-A 68.1
Cathro	23	32N	7E	D&M-N 133.2
#Cranberry Spur				D&M-S
Emerson	23	31N	6E	D&M-H 12.5
#Flanders				D&M-H
Fletcher	17	30N	5E	BC-A 69.0
Fletcher (Jct.)	5	31N	8E	D&M-N 127.7
Herron	1	30N	6E	BC-A 79.3
Hillman Crossing	8	31N	7E	BC-A 85.5 – D&M-H 5.3
Hillman Jct.	28	31N	8E	D&M-S 123.3 – D&M-H 0.7
#Hiwasee				D&M-Q
Kerston	27	31N	7E	D&M-H 7.6
King	25	31N	6E	D&M-H 11.1
Lachine	17	31N	6E	D&M-H 15.8
#Lyle				D&M-Q
McHarg	31	31N	7E	BC-A 81.4
#McQueen Spur				D&M-H
Ossineke	11	29N	8E	D&M-S 112.5
#Paisley				BC-A
Paxton	30	31N	7E	D&M-H 10.1
#Rayburn		30N	5E	BC-A 71
Rockport	6	32N	9E	D&M-Q 13.6
Selina	18	31N	6E	D&M-H 17.6
Spratt	7	30N	6E	BC-A 74.4

Stinsons	10	30N	6E	BC-A 76.8
#Truax				D&M-Q
#Turnbull				D&M-Q

ANTRIM COUNTY

Aabee	(now Comfort?)			
Alba	25	30N	6W	D&C 25.5; GR&I-N 391.6
Alden	28	29N	8W	PM-P 171.7
Antrim	19	29N	6W	GR&I-N 383.8
#Bacon				PM
#Barnards		30N	6W	GR&I-N 390
Bellaire	30	30N	7W	EJ&S 18.0 — PM-P 183.6
#Blanchards New Spur		30N	6W	D&C 28
Blosser	28	29N	7W	PM-P8A 2.7
Blue Lake Jct.	25	29N	5W	D&C 15.2
#Brennan		30N	6W	D&C 27 1/2
#Brickerville				BC-3B 4.0?
#Buckley & Douglas Spur				D&C 17
Cameron	26	31N	8W	PM-P 190.8
#Camp 10				BC-A
#Camp 11				BC-A
Cascade	(now Alba)			
Central Lake	23	31N	8W	PM-P 191.6
Chestonia	30	31N	6W	EJ&S 7.8
#Churchill				EJ&S
Comfort	18	29N	7W	PM-P 178.9 — PM-P8 0
#Danford				GR&I-N
#Dennis				GR&I-?
Dingmans	8	31N	7W	EJ&S-2 6.4
Dix	2	31N	8W	PM-P 194.3 — PM-P9 0
#Dow				BC-3 5.2? — BC-3C 0

#East End				BC-3C 2.5?
#Eaton				BC
#Edwards				GR&I-N
Elk Rapids	21	29N	9W	PM-PE 8.8
Ellsworth	14	32N	8W	PM-P 198.3
Elmira Branch Switch	2	29N	5W	D&C 19.6
#Erico				PM
Essex	28	32N	8W	PM-P9 2.7
Farmdale	11	30N	7W	EJ&S 13.2
Fishermans Paradise	31	30N	7W	PM-P 181.8
Fork	29	29N	7W	PM-P8A 1.5
Fountain	27	31N	7W	EJ&S-2 3.5
Furnace	(now Antrim)			
Gilletts	19	29N	7W	PM-P8A 0.3
#Goo				BC
#Grass River				PM
Graves Camp	32	31N	6W	D&C 34.1
Green River	28	30N	6W	D&C 30.8
Harper	23	32N	8W	PM-P 196.8
#Harts				PM
#Headquarters				BC-3 7.0?— PM-3D 0
#Helena		29N	8W	PM-P 172.2?
#Hemstreet				PM
Hitchcock	2	30N	7W	EJ&S 11.6— EJ&S-2 0
Horgan				GR&I
Horgan Jct.				GR&I
Indian Landing	(now Fishermans Paradise)			
#Job				PM
#Johnson				PM-P
Jordan River	29	31N	6W	D&C 35.8
Kelley	28	30N	5W	D&C 22.3
#Kentucky				BC-3D 1.1?
#Knipers				PM-P
Lake Forest	(current name for Comfort)			
Lake Harold	34	30N	5W	D&C 21.0
#Liken				PM
#Lull		29N	8W	PM-P 176

#Madden				GR&I
Mancelona	20	29N	6W	GR&I-N 384.9
Mancelona Road	13	29N	5W	D&C 16.5
#Maple Slope				BC-3 4.0?
Marble	17	31N	6W	D&C 37.2 −
				EJ&S 6.4
#Morrison		30N	5W	D&C 20.8?
Mt. Bliss	1	31N	7W	EJ&S 4.0
#Nichols				PM
Norfolk	31	29N	7W	PM-P8 2.9
#Orville				BC-A 11
#Parks				PM
Pine Ridge	31	31N	6W	EJ&S 9.2
#Richardi				PM
Section 10	10	30N	7W	EJ&S 12.6
Shepards	28	30N	6W	D&C 28.9
Simons	4	31N	5W	GR&I-N 395.3
Snowflake	2	30N	8W	PM-P 188.7
#South End				BC-3 8.67?
#Spur 3				BC-A 10
#Staffords		30N	7W	EJ&S 14
Thelma	17	30N	5W	GR&I-N 393.9
Tindall	19	29N	7W	PM-P8 0.7
Valley Switch	8	30N	6W	D&C 32.2 −
				EJ&S-3 spur
				1.9 + 1.1
Wards		(now Marble)		
#Way				PM
Webb	30	29N	7W	PM-P8 1.9
Webster	20	31N	7W	D&C 36.1
Wells	30	29N	7W	PM-P8A 0.8
Wells Branch	19	29N	7W	PM-P8 1.3 −
				PM-P8A 0
Wetzell	10	29N	6W	GR&I-N 387.4
#White Siding				BC-3 6.0?
#Windling				BC
Wolcott	22	30N	7W	EJ&S 14.9

ARENAC COUNTY

Alger	21	20N	3E	D&M-A 23.0 –
				MC-M 40.7
#Arenac Spur				D&M-S
AuGres	13	19N	6E	D&M-G 8.1
Babcocks Wye	7	19N	3E	MC-PN 15.2
Clydes	(now Dunham?)			
Culvers	17	20N	3E	MC-M 41.5
Davidson	5?	19N	3E	MC-PN
				15.2 + 1.8
Deep River	33	19N	4E	MC-M 30.2
Dunham	19	19N	4E	MC-M 32.9
#Eddys		18N	4E	MC-M
Gypsum	8	20N	6E	D&M-S 42.3
#Lime Spur				D&M-S
Moffat	12	20N	3E	D&M-A 18.7
Moores Jct.	33	19N	3E	MC-PN 9.4
Ogden	21	19N	3E	MC-PN 10.9
Omer	15	19N	5E	D&M-G 0 –
				D&M-S 34.2
#Ortman		19N	4E	MC-M 34
Pine River	8	18N	5E	D&M-S 29.4
Quinn	13	19N	3E	MC-M 35.2
Saganing	30	18N	5E	D&M-S 25.7
Saganing	(now Worth on MC-M)			
Shearer	5	20N	4E	D&M-A 16.1
Souveigny	15	19N	6E	D&M-G 6.4
Standish	11	18N	4E	MC-M 27.7
Sterling	20	19N	4E	MC-M 32.4
Turner	17	20N	6E	D&M-S 41.5
Twining	30	20N	6E	D&M-S 39.3
Umstead	16	19N	6E	D&M-G 4.4
Wells	(now Alger)			
Wheeler Spur	16	19N	6E	D&M-G 4.7
Worth	35	18N	4E	MC-M 23.6

BARRY COUNTY

#Ackers Point		2N	9W	CK&S 21
Cloverdale	20	2N	9W	CK&S 20.5
Coats Grove	6	3N	7W	CK&S 36.1
Cressey	34	1N	10W	CK&S 11.1
Crooked Lake	7	2N	9W	CK&S 16.5
Delton	6	1N	9W	CK&S 17.3
Doster	(see same, Allegan Co.)			
Freeport	1	4N	9W	PM-G 116.8
Hastings	17	3N	8W	CK&S 30.4; MC-G 62.0
Irving	31	4N	9W	MC-G 69.5
Middleville	23	4N	10W	MC-G 73.2
Milo	23	1N	10W	CK&S 13.6
Morgan	29	3N	7W	MC-G 54.9
#Nashs		2N	9W	CK&S 23
Nashville	36	3N	7W	MC-G 49.8
Parmalee	10	4N	10W	MC-G 76.2 (also sp. Parmelee)
Quimby	26	3N	8W	MC-G 57.7
Sheridan	(now Morgan)			
Shultz	11	2N	9W	CK&S 24.2 (also sp. Schultz)
Thorn Apple	30	3N	8W	MC-G 55.5
#Wall Lake				CK&S
#Williams Crossing				CK&S
Woodbury	(see same, Eaton Co.)			
Woodland	22	4N	7W	CK&S 40.4

BAY COUNTY

Arn	27	13N	6E	PM-B 98.2
#Arnold				PM-YBH
Arrow	20	14N	4E	PM-L 8.1

Auburn	24	14N	3E	MC-L 11.0
Bangor	20	14N	4E	MC-L 8.3
Bangor Street	9	14N	5E	PM-YBH 0.9
Banks	16	14N	5E	GTW-S 55.0
Bay City	20	14N	5E	GTW-S 53.0
Bay City	21	14N	5E	GTW-S 51.7 + 1.2; DCS 0; PM-B 17.0 − PM-BP 12.5
Bay City East Side	21	14N	5E	MC-B 108.9 − MC-M 0 − (DCS 0)
Bay City West Side	21	14N	5E	MC-M 0.7 − MC-S 114.6
#Bay County Spur				D&M-S
Bay Jct.	22	14N	4E	MC-L 6.8 − MC-L2 0
B. C. & B. C. Jct.	17	14N	5E	MC-L 1.6 − MC-M 1.6
#Beardsleys				MC-P 2.6
Beaver Mine	2	13N	4E	MC-LS 5.6
Beebe	7	13N	5E	MC-S 109.4
Bentley	20	18N	3E	MC-PN 4.4
#Betts				PM-B
Bridge Jct.	(now Foss)			
Brooks	31	14N	5E	GTW-S 50.4; MC-S 111.6
Brundage Spur	23	16N	4E	D&M-S 15.0
Center Street	26	14N	5E	DCS 1.9 − MC-B 107.2 − PM-B 13.2
Cheboyganing	16	13N	5E	PM-B 7.8
Colden	18	14N	3E	MC-L 15.9
Colfax	33	14N	4E	MC-L2 2.1
Columbus Avenue	28	14N	5E	PM-BP 11.9
Coryell	19	14N	4E	MC-L 9.5
Cranage	(now Farleigh)			
#Davenport				PM-B
Essexville	14	14N	5E	MC-YBL 0.3 − PM-B 14.8
Farleigh	28	14N	6E	DCS 6.9

Felton	12	14N	4E	PM-YBH 6.6
Fisherville	22	14N	3E	MC-L 13.0
#Fitch				PM-B 7
Flajoles	20	14N	3E	MC-L 15.0
Foss	15	14N	5E	D&M-S 1.9 –
				MC-YBN 1.8 –
				PM-B 15.0 –
				PM-YBH
				0 + 1.1
#Freeman				MC-PN 4.0
#Glencoe				MC-PO 10.5
Glovers	5	18N	3E	MC-PN 7.3
Golden	(see Colden)			
Greens Siding	5	13N	5E	GTW-S 49.6
H. & W. Crossing	8	14N	5E	MC-M 2.0 –
				PM-YBH 2.2
Hampton Yard	34	14N	5E	PM-B 13.5
Hart Street	17	14N	5E	GTW-S 54.1 –
				MC-M 1.1
Hecla Jct.	4	13N	4E	MC-Ls 3.6
#Houseback				PM-B
Henry Street	8	14N	5E	PM-YBH 1.8
Interurban				
Crossing	16	13N	5E	GTW-S 47.8
Kawkawlin	1	14N	4E	MC-M 4.7
#Krabbe				PM-B
Lake	30	17N	5E	MC-P2 2.3
#Lakeside				D&M-S
Lapan Spur	12	17N	4E	D&M-S 22.5
#Lawrence Spur				D&M-S
Lengsville	26	16N	4E	D&M-S 13.6;
				MC-M 12.3
Linwood	35	16N	4E	D&M-S 12.0;
				MC-M 10.7
Linwood Park	12	15N	4E	D&M-S 10.2
#Lowell				MC-P?
Maxwell	(now State Road)			
McGraws Siding	4	13N	5E	PM-B 9.5
#Merrick				MC-P3 4
Michie	11	16N	4E	D&M-S 16.5
Millers Crossing	12	14N	4E	PM-YBH 4.8

Monitor	21	14N	4E	MC-L 7.1
Mt. Forest	9	17N	3E	MC-P 7.9 – MC-PN 0
Munger	16	13N	6E	MC-B 101.0
Nine Mile (new)	13	17N	3E	MC-P 5.4
Nine Mile (old)	15	17N	3E	MC-P 6.6 – MC-P5 0
North Bay City	10	14N	5E	D&M-S 3.0 – GTW-S 56.4 – MC-YBH 2.4 – PM-YBH 0
#North Branch				MC-P?
North Water St. Jct.	21	14N	5E	MC-YBN 0.4 – PM-B 16.5
Oa-at-ka Beach	33	15N	5E	GTW-S 58.7
Oakwood	1	15N	4E	D&M-S 10.8
Pinconning	23	17N	4E	D&M-S 19.9; MC-M 18.9 – MC-P 0
#Portsmouth				PM-BP 11
Raby	23	14N	6E	DCS 3.8
#Redy's				MC-PN 4.8
Rooney	23	14N	3E	MC-L 12.0
St. Johns	13	17N	3E	MC-P 5.0 – MC-P3 0
Salzburg	32	14N	5E	GTW-S 51.4; MC-S 112.6
#Schemms				MC-B 96
Seven Mile Road	9	14N	4E	PM-YBH 8.8
Sheboyganing	(see Cheboyganing)			
#Smithville				PM-YBH
South Bay City	4	13N	5E	PM-B 10.0
State Road	11	16N	4E	MC-M 15.1
Terry	(now Linwood)			
Tobico	24	15N	5E	D&M-S 6.7
#Tobico Ice House Spur				D&M-S
#Town Line				MC-P5 2.4
23rd Street	33	13N	5E	PM-B 11.1 – PM-BP 11.1

26th Street	33	13N	5E	MC-YBL 5.8 — PM-B 10.9
Water Street Jct.	35	14N	5E	MC-B 106.1 — MC-YBL 3.0
Water Works Spur	30	15N	5E	D&M-S 5.7
Wenona	8	14N	5E	MC-M 2.7
Wenona Beach	3	14N	5E	GTW-S 58.3
Whatcheer Mine	30	13N	6E	PM-B2 3.4
White Feather	2	17N	4E	MC-M 21.6
Wolverine Mine #2	17	14N	4E	PM-YBH 7.7 + 1.5
Wolverine Mine #3	7	14N	4E	PM-YBH 9.9
Woodside	21	14N	5E	MC-M 0.2 — MC-YBS 0 — PM-B 16.7
Woodville	17	17N	4E	MC-P 3.3

BENZIE COUNTY

#Achas				M&NE-E 14
Allyn	6	26N	13W	M&NE-E 4.1
#Alpha				PM-P5 3.8
Bay Point	20	26N	15W	AA-C 286.3
Bendon	23	26N	13W	PM-P 130.5
Benzonia	35	26N	15W	AA-C 281.5
#Betsey				PM
Beulah	26	26N	15W	AA-C 282.8
Blake	33	16N	13W	PM-P6 1.2
Boat Landing	27	26N	16W	AA-F 291.8
#Bridges				PM
#Bye				PM-P5 2.6
Carters	29	26N	13W	PM-P6 4.2
Case	22	26N	14W	PM-P6 7.0
Cases	(Now Benzonia? on AA-C)			
Clary	34	26N	13W	PM-P 128.2 — PM-P6 0
#Cranes				AA-C
#Colfax				PM-P5 2.1

Cruse	15	26N	14W	M&NE-E 8.6
Crystal City	(now Beulah)			
Crystal Lake	(now Bay Point)			
Elberta	27	26N	16W	AA-F 290.7
Empire Jct.	21	27N	14W	E&SE 0 –
				M&NE-E 16.7
Frankfort	28	26N	16W	AA-C 292.4
Gerber	17	25N	13W	PM-P 124.2 –
				PM-P5 0
Gravel Pit	21	26N	15W	AA-C 285.8
Hayes	13	26N	14W	M&NE-E 6.8
Homestead	33	26N	14W	AA-C 277.9
Honor	8	26N	14W	M&NE-E 10.6;
				PM-P6 9.1
Hull	28	26N	13W	PM-P6 1.5
Inland	(now Bendon)			
Junction Switch	35	25N	16W	AA-C 290.3 –
				AA-F 290.3
Kehoe	(now Turtle Lake)			
#King				PM-P5 1.7
Lake	27	25N	15W	AA-C 283.3
Lake Ann	23	27N	13W	M&NE-A 51.7
Lake Jct.	(see same, Leelanau Co.)			
Melva	(current name for Platte River Jct.)			
#Metz				AA-C
#Miller				M&NE
Nessen City	33	25N	13W	M&NE-A 32.9
Pearl Lake	6	27N	13W	E&SE-2 3.0
#Petersville	15	27N	14W	E&SE 2
Platte River	35	27N	13W	PM-P6 7.5
Platte River Jct.	35	27N	13W	M&NE-A 49.3 –
				M&NE-E 0
Shermans Mill	(now Platte River Jct.)			
South Frankfort	(now Boat Landing)			
State Road	(now Cruse)			
Stormer	29	27N	14W	M&NE-E 15.4
Thompsonville	36	25N	14W	AA-C 270.4 –
				PM-P120.9
Turtle Lake	29	26N	13W	PM-P6 2.7
Van Demans	27	26N	15W	AA-C 284.0
Wallin	16	25N	13W	PM-P 125.2

Welden	4	25N	14W	AA-C 276.6
#Weldon	29?	25N	14W	M&NE-1 8.0?
Weldon Bridge	25	25N	14W	AA-C 271.3
#Weldon Centre	15?	25N	14W	AA-C 273.4?
#West End				PM-P5 4.6
Willis	36	25N	14W	AA-C 270.9

BERRIEN COUNTY

Alfred	16	8S	21W	PM-C 116.3 − PM-W 34.0
Avery(s)	1	8S	20W	MC-W 210.2
Avery Track Pan	6	8S	19W	MC-W 209.9
#Bainton				PM-U 25
Bakertown	3	8S	18W	MC-W 200.5
#Bankers				PM-U 1
Barnetts Siding	5	8S	19W	MC-W 209.1
Baroda	14	6S	19W	MC-J 28.3
Benton Harbor	24	4S	19W	BF 0; PM-C 86.0 − PM-U 0; MC-J 38.3 + 1.5
Berrien Centre	16	6S	17W	BF 15.0
Berrien Springs	13	6S	18W	PM-U 16.1
Bertrand	14	8S	17W	MC-N 4.5
#Blakes				KLSC-P 4½
Bridgman	19	6S	19W	PM-C 100.1
Browns	(now Oakhill)			
Buchanan	35	7S	18W	MC-W 198.5; PM-U 26.0
#Carl				PM-U
Chamberlins	2	8S	20W	MC-W 211.2
Chickaming	16	7S	20W	PM-C 107.8
Coloma	20	3S	17W	PM-C 76.2 − PM-CP 0
Corymbo	(now Grand Beach)			
Dayton	7	8S	18W	MC-W 203.0
Derby	26	5S	19W	MC-J 32.3

#Dunbars			PM-U
Eau Claire	4	6S 17W	BF 12.7
#Elmwood			KLSC-P 3 1/2
Fairland	34	6S 17W	BF 19.0
#Farleys			PM-U
Galien	3	8S 19W	MC-W 206.0;
			MC-J 17.8
#Garden City			PM-C
Glendora	11	5S 19W	MC-J 23.3
Glenlord	15	5S 19W	PM-C 92.8
Grand Beach	19	8S 21W	MC-W 222.1
#Gravel Pit			PM-U 22
#Grays			PM-U
Hagar	33	3S 18W	PM-C 82.0
Harbert	15	7S 20W	PM-C 106.8
Hartman	30	5S 17W	BF 10.1
#Hayes Siding			BF
Hickory Creek	35	4S 19W	MC-J 36.5
Hilltop	(now Summit)		
Hinchman	5	6S 18W	PM-U 10.9
Jaquay	14	7S 18W	PM-U 19.6
Lakeside	20	8S 21W	PM-C 109.2
Lake Street	26	7S 17W	MC-C 191.5
#Lighton	35	6S 18W	PM-U
Lincoln	10	5S 19W	PM-C 92.4
Livingston	8	6S 19W	PM-C 97.3
Main Street	28	7S 17W	MC-N 0.8
Maple Wood	16	3S 17W	PM-CP 1.4
Mars	2	6S 19W	MC-J 29.8
Matthews	23	7S 19W	MC-J 20.3
M.C. Jct.	(now Niles Jct.)		
#McCollums			PM-U
Morris	(now Livingston)		
Napier	29	4S 18W	BF 2.8
Napier	31	4S 18W	PM-U 3.2
New Buffalo	9	8S 21W	MC-W 219.0 —
			PM-C(old)
			111.1 + 4.3 —
			PM-W 35.5
New Buffalo	10	8S 21W	PM-C(new)
			115.1

Nickerson	31	4S	18W	PM-U 3.6
Niles	26	7S	17W	MC-C 192.0 −
				MC-N 0 −
				MC-A 104.0 −
				MC-W 192.0;
				BF 23.8
Niles Jct.	2	8S	17W	MC-N 1.9 − BF
				26.1
Nylen				PM-C 92
Oakhill	36	6S	20W	PM-C 103.3
#Oakland				PM-U 19
#Paw Paw Lake	15	3S	17W	PM-CP 2.7;
				KLSC-P 5
Pipestone	(now Hartman)			
#Planks Tavern				PM-C 87
Pleasant View	16	3S	17W	PM-CP 1.6
Riverside	27	3S	18W	PM-C 80.1
#Riverside				PM-U
#Riverview				PM-U 24
#Rockwell				PM-?
Royalton	20	5S	18W	PM-U 7.8
St. Joseph	23	4S	19W	MC-J 39.4;
				PM-C 87.9
St. Joseph Jct.	25	4S	19W	MC-J 38.2
Sawyer	2	7S	20W	PM-C 104.7
Scotdale	18	5S	18W	PM-U 5.7
Snow	26	6S	19W	MC-J 26.0
Sodus	11	5S	18W	BF 7.1
Somerleyton	(now Scotdale)			
Stemms	9	6S	18W	PM-U 12.3
Stevens	(now Stevensville)			
Stevensville	28	5S	19W	PM-C 94.9
Summit	34	4S	19W	PM-C 90.5
Terre Coupee	(now Dayton)			
Three Oaks	2	8S	20W	MC-W 211.8
Town Line	(now Union Pier)			
Troy	(now Sawyer)			
Union Pier	25	7S	21W	PM-C 111.1
Vine	10	5S	19W	PM-C 92.0
Vineland	2	5S	19W	MC-J 35.3
Vrooman	26	3S	18W	PM-C 79.1

#Waldo				PM-C 84
Watervliet	23	3S	17W	PM-C 73.8
#Wenatchee				PM-U
#West Niles				MC-W
Wilkinson	(now Lakeside)			
#Windermere				KLSC-P 4

BRANCH COUNTY

Batavia	27	6S	7W	LS-A 389.8
Bronson	11	7S	8W	LS-A 395.4
Coldwater	21	6S	6W	LS-A 384.6
Gravel Pit	6	5S	8W	MC-K 21.6
Quincy	15	6S	5W	LS-A 378.2
Ray	(station located in Indiana)			
Sherwood	28	5S	8W	MC-A 49.0
Union City	4	5S	7W	MC-A 42.2
Wood	17	7S	8W	LS-A 398.4

CALHOUN COUNTY

A	2	3S	4W	LS-L 21.9 −
				MC-C 96.0
Adams	25	2S	8W	MC-K 5.6
Airport	9	2S	8W	GTW-C 172.0
Albion	2	3S	4W	LS-L 22.3;
				MC-C 95.8
Athens	28	4S	8W	MC-K 18.6
Battle Creek	1	2S	8W	MC-C 120.6 −
				MC-K 0
Battle Creek	7	2S	7W	GTW-C(new)
				176.6

Battle Creek	12	2S	8W	DTM 90.9; GTW-C(old) 175.8; MC-K(old) 1.3
Beadle Lake	29	2S	7W	DTM 87.0
Bedford	29	1S	8W	MC-C 126.2
Brick Yard Siding	(now Adams)			
Browns Siding	21	4S	8W	MC-K 17.0
Burlington	25	4S	7W	MC-A 38.0
Ceresco	30	2S	7W	MC-C 112.8
Ceresco	25	2S	7W	DTM 82.6
Clarendon	14	4S	5W	MC-A 27.4
Condit	21	3S	4W	LS-L 17.3
East Leroy	34	3S	8W	MC-K 12.8
Eckford	23	3S	5W	DTM 70.2
Elm Street	7	2S	7W	GTW-C 176.7 − MC-K 0.8
Emmett Street	5	2S	7W	GTW-C 178.6
Fort Custer	32	1S	8W	MC-C 124.9 + 1.0
Fort Custer Crossover	32	1S	8W	MC-C 124.9
Grover	12	4S	4W	DTM 60.8
Helmers	9	2S	8W	GTW-C(old line) 171.5
Hinman Yard	8	2S	7W	MC-C 118.9
Homer	8	4S	4W	DTM 65.1-MC-A 24.3; LS-L 13.9
Joppa	23	3S	8W	MC-K 11.3
#Madison	13	1S	7W	GTW-C 135
Main Yard	7	2S	7W	MC-C 120.3
Marengo	25	2S	5W	MC-C 101.1
Marshall	25	2S	6W	DTM 77.1; MC-C 107.5
Marshall Track Pan	36	2S	6W	MC-C 106.5
McAllister Road	5	1S	7W	GTW-C 181.2
McCamley Street	1	2S	8W	DTM 91.2-GTW-C 175.6

Morgan Park	19	2S	8W	DTM 88.7 – MC-K 3.3
Nichols	7	2S	7W	GTW-C 176.9 – MC-C 119.7
Nichols Yard	5	2S	7W	GTW-C 177.3
Osborns	29	4S	6W	MC-A 36.0
Penfield	22	1S	7W	GTW-C 182.8
Ransom	13	1S	7W	GTW-C 184
Renton	20	2S	8W	GTW-C 169.2
Rumley Yard	2	2S	8W	MC-C 122.0
Sonoma	2	3S	8W	MC-K 8.1
Tekonsha	27	4S	6W	MC-A 34.0
Verona	5	2S	7W	GTW-C 179.0
Wheatfield	23	2S	7W	MC-C 114.4
Whites (Crossing)	(now Wheatfield)			
Wilders	8	3S	5W	DTM 73.3

CASS COUNTY

Air Line Junction	11	7S	16W	MC-A 92.9
Barron Lake	21	7S	16W	MC-A 99.9
#Beebe				BF
Cassopolis	36	6S	15W	GTW-C 122.9; MC-A 90.5
Corey	36	6S	13W	MC-A 77.4
Cross Bank	21	5S	13W	GTW-C 134.3
Dailey	6	7S	15W	MC-A 94.7
Diamond Lake	(now Forrest Hall)			
Dowagiac	1	6S	16W	MC-C 179.6
#Dyer		6S	13W	MC-A
East End	7	7S	16W	MC-C 188.0 – MC-A 97.6 + 3.6
Edwardsburg	8	8S	15W	GTW-C 114.0
For(r)est Hall	36	6S	15W	MC-A 89.4
Glenwood	3	5S	15W	MC-C 173.3

Howard	(now Dailey)			
Jamestown	(now Penn)			
Jefferson	22	7S	15W	GTW-C 118.7
Jones	34	6S	13W	MC-A 79.4
Kennedy	20	7S	16W	MC-A 100.7
Marcellus	22	5S	13W	GTW-C 135.8
Newburg	33	6S	13W	MC-A 81.2
Penn	16	6S	14W	GTW-C 127.3
Pokagon	28	6S	16W	MC-C 185.4
Sandy Beach	29	6S	14W	MC-A 87.9
Shore Acres	30	6S	14W	MC-A 88.7
Tietsorts	(now Glenwood)			
Truitts	10	8S	16W	BF 31.0
Vandalia	26	6S	14W	MC-A 85.3
#Vandalia Track Pan				MC-A
Volinia	(now Wakelee)			
Wakelee	36	5S	14W	GTW-C 131.5

CHARLEVOIX COUNTY

Ballous Siding	(now Phelps)			
Bayshore	12	34N	7W	PM-P 218.2
Bear Lake Jct.	(now Walloon Lake Jct.)			
Belvedere	35	34N	8W	PM-P 209.4
Boyne	(now Boyne City)			
Boyne City	35	33N	6W	BC-A 0
Boyne Falls	21	32N	5W	BC-A 6.1 + 1.1 − GR&I-N 409.0
Branch Lake	33	32N	4W	BC-2A 5.0 − BC-2B 0 − BC-2C 0
#Brown				BC-3 2.0? − BC-3B
Burgess	9	34N	7W	PM-P 214.9
#Camp 1				BC-2 8½
#Camp 2				BC-2A 3.5

#Camp 3				BC-2A 6.0
#Camp 4				BC-2B 0.5
#Camp 5				BC-2C 0.6
#Camp 6				BC-2B 3.3
#Camp 8				BC-2D 2.6
#Camp 8				BC-2E 1.5
Campbell	4	33N	5W	GR&I-N 417.3
Charlevoix	35	34N	8W	PM-P 209.8
#Charltons				GR&I-N 415
Cherrie	35	34N	8W	PM-P 207.1 — PM-P10 0
Clarion	(now Campbell)			
#Crampton				PM
#Curfew				PM
Cushman	8	32N	5W	BC-A 4.4 — BC-2 0
#Deer Lake				BC-3A?
#Doyles		32N	5W	BC-A 4
#Durham				PM
East Jordan	23	32N	7W	D&C 43.2; EJ&S 0.6
Easton	10	32N	5W	BC-2 1.4 — GR&I-N 410.3
#Feltz				PM
#Grayton				GR&I
#Guerin				BC-2 5
#Hammers				HR&I-N 413
Ironton	17	33N	7W	PM-P10 4.1
KawCaChewIng	2	34N	7W	PM-P 216.9
#Maltbys				GR&I
McManus	21	33N	5W	GR&I-N 414.9
#Melrose				GR&I
#Moon				GR&I
Moore	21	32N	5W	BC-A 6.1
Phelps	25	33N	8W	PM-P 202.6
Project	21	32N	5W	BC-A 6.9
#Robbins				GR&I-N
Rock Elm	(now South Arm)			
#Seed				PM
#Smiths				PM
South Arm	22	32N	7W	D&C 43.6

#Spring Water	35	32N	5W	GR&I-N
#Summit		32N	4W	BC-2 7
#Superior				PM-P 216
Talcott	(now Walloon Lake (old))			
#Thumb Lake	2?	32N	4W	BC-2 10
Thumb Lake Jct.	(now Cushman)			
Van Platen	9	32N	4W	BC-2 6.4 —
				BC-2A 0 —
				BC-2D 0
Waggoner	13	32N	5W	BC-2 4.0 —
				BC-2F 0
Walloon Lake (new)	9	33N	5W	GR&I-N 416.2 —
				GR&I-5 0
Walloon Lake (old)	9	33N	5W	GR&I-5 1.1
Walloon Lake Jct.	(now Walloon Lake (new))			
White Camp	(now Whites Jct.)			
Whites Jct.	(now Moore)			

CHEBOYGAN COUNTY

Afton	36	35N	2W	MC-MH 11.3
Aloha	8	36N	1W	D&M-N 188.4
Birchwood	3	36N	2W	MC-M 158.6
Bushville	16	36N	2W	MC-M 156.8
Cheboygan	31	38N	1W	MC-M 166.3 —
				D&M-N 196.5
Cheboygan Dock	29	38N	1W	D&M-N 197.7
Churchill	5	34N	1E	D&M-L 2.3
#Cleveland				D&M
Diver	(now Hamby)			
Freedom	35	39N	3W	MC-M 176.5
#Gillis				D&M
Grand View	6	35N	2W	MC-M 151.8
Grant	22	37N	1W	D&M-N 184.9
Haakwood	36	34N	3W	MC-M 140.5 —
				MC-MH 0
Hamby	1	34N	3W	MC-M 145.3
Indian River	24	35N	3W	MC-M 148.4

Inverness	18	37N	1W	D&M-N 193.1
Lakeside	15	38N	2W	MC-M 170.5
Lakewood	(now Birchwood)			
LeGrand	21	35N	1W	D&M-L 8.1
Long Point	9	36N	2W	MC-M 157.2
Mackinaw City	18	39N	3W	GR&I-N 459.7 – MC-M 182.3
#Merritts	12?	34N	3W	MC-M 143
Millers	27	35N	1W	D&M-L 5.9
#Milliken				D&M-W
Mullett Lake	35	37N	2W	MC-M 160.4
Nelson	6	38N	2W	MC-M 174.5
North Branch Jct.	29	34N	2W	MC-MH 2.0 – MC-MH 3
Newell Branch Jct.	12	34N	2W	MC-MH 10.0 – MC-MH 2
Page	35	33N	1W	MC-MP 13.1
Page Branch Jct.	35	33N	1W	MC-MP 13.0
Patterson Branch Jct.	35	39N	3W	MC-M 175.9 – MC-M2 0
Point Nip-i-gon	5	38N	2W	MC-M 173.0
Quarry	36	35N	2W	MC-MH 12.1
Randall Spur	32	37N	1W	D&M-N 190.7
Rondo	25	34N	3W	MC-M 141.5
#Sand Pit				D&M-W
Silver Beach	34	37N	2W	MC-M 159.3
#Smith Mill		33N	2W	MC-MP 1
Smiths Siding	7	33N	2W	MC-M 137.8
South Wye	31	34N	2W	MC-MH 0.7
#Sturgeon Branch				MC-MP 5.2
Topinabee	30	36N	2W	MC-M 153.9
Tower	3	34N	1E	D&M-N 174.3 – D&M-L 0 – D&M-W 0
Trowbridge	29	33N	2W	MC-M 135.0 – MC-MP 0
Waveland	18	35N	1E	D&M-N 178.8
Wolverine	7	33N	2W	MC-M 138.3
#Wolverine Road	26	33N	1W	D&M-W2
Wolverine Switch	31	34N	1E	D&M-W 6.4 – D&M-W2

CLARE COUNTY

Arnold Lake	2	19N	4W	PM-LH 22.0
Atwoods Siding	31	18N	4W	PM-LH 7.8
#Cairns				AA-B
Campbell	(now Temple)			
Clare	34	17N	4W	AA-B 178.8 —
				PM-L 50.4
Clarence	25	19N	6W	AA-B 197.6
Clintons	10	17N	5W	AA-B 186.8
Crooked Lake	(now Lake)			
Dodge	19	19N	3W	PM-LH2 9.8
Eyke	16	20N	3W	PM-LH 28.0
Farwell	25	17N	5W	AA-B 183.7;
				PM-L 55.0
Frost	29	20N	3W	PM-LH 26.0
Galliver	31	18N	4W	PM-LH 8.0
#Greens				PM-?
#Hackley				PM-LH 23
Harrison	21	19N	4W	PM-LH 16.8 —
				PM-LL 0
Harrison Jct.	29	17N	4W	PM-L 52.7 —
				PM-LH 2.3
Hatton	29	18N	4W	PM-LH 9.1 —
				PM-LH2 0
Lake	23	17N	6W	PM-L 62.5 —
				PM-LJX 0
Lake George	8	18N	5W	AA-B 194.2
Lake Ice House	16	17N	6W	PM-L 64.5
Leota	10	20N	5W	PM-LL 8.8
Levington	29	20N	3W	PM-LH 25.1
Mann Siding	9	18N	4W	PM-LH 12.3
#Mark				PM-LH
#McKay				PM-LH
Meredith	13	20N	3W	PM-LH 31.7
Moores Siding	18	17N	4W	PM-LH 4.2
Mostetlers Siding	25	19N	4W	PM-LH2 8.4
#Pages				PM-LH
Pennock	17	19N	6W	AA-B 203.4

Phelps	28	18N	5W	AA-B 190.0
#Remwick	?30	17N	5W	PM-L 60
#Riskes Siding		20N	3W	PM-LH 28
#Robinson	16	17N	6W	PM-L 65.2
Summit	4	17N	5W	AA-B 189.0
Temple	21	19N	6W	AA-B 200.7

CLINTON COUNTY

Bath	17	5N	1W	MC-S 45.0
Chandler	25	5N	2W	MC-S 42.3
Dallas	11	7N	3W	GTW-D 106.7
Daniels	(now Ingersolls)			
Delta	34	5N	3W	PM-D 94.1
Eagle	21	5N	4W	PM-I 4.3
Elsie	12	8N	1W	AA-B 120.3
Fowler	11	7N	3W	GTW-D 107.4
#Ingersolls	32	5N	3W	PM-D 96
Isabella	(now Fowler)			
#Lyons	11	7N	3W	GTW-D
Lyons Mill	(now Lyons)			
Ovid	12	7N	1W	GTW-D 88.8
St. Johns	9	7N	2W	GTW-D 98.1
Shepardsville	9	7N	1W	GTW-D 91.5

CRAWFORD COUNTY

Alexander	21	27N	3W	MC-MT 5.1
AuSable River	23	28N	4W	D&C 1.7
#Bills		28N	1W	MC-MT 22
Bucks	8	27N	2W	MC-MT 10.8
Cheney	11	25N	3W	MC-M 83.7
Clear Lake Jct.	17	28N	1W	MC-MT 19.0–
				MC-MT2 0
Crawford	(now Grayling)			

#Dale Branch				D&C 3
Deward	7	28N	4W	D&C 11.5 + 0.4
#Ferris				D&C
Forest	(now Frederic)			
Frederic	35	28N	4W	D&C 0 – MC-M 101.0
Grayling	7	26N	3W	MC-M 92.4 – M&NE-R 78.7
Hanson	23	27N	4W	MC-M 97.0
Harvey Branch	22	28N	4W	D&C 2.5
Horrigan	32	26N	3W	MC-M 87.5
Judges	35	28N	2W	MC-MT 14.6
Kneeland	14	27N	3W	MC-MT 7.6
#Louds Spur		25N	3W	MC-M 81
Lovells	19	28N	1W	MC-MT 17.6
Manistee Switch	32	26N	3W	MC-M 87.7
Mertz Branch Jct.	22	27N	3W	MC-MT 5.7 – MC-MT4 0
Portage Jct.	2	26N	1W	MC-MR 2.6 – M&NE-R 76.1
Putnams	(current name for Clear Lake Jct.)			
Rasmus	22	26N	1W	MC-MR 5.9
Roscommon Gravel Pit	27	25N	2W	MC-M5 3.8
#Resort	5	26N	1W	M&NE-R 74
Smith Siding	10	28N	4W	D&C 3.9
Tyler(s)	29	27N	3W	MC-MT 4.4 – MC-MT3 0

EATON COUNTY

Ainger	(now Olivet)			
#Alperos				GTW-C
Bellevue	28	1N	6W	GTW-C 189.2
Brockway	(now Charlesworth)			
Charlesworth	29	1N	3W	LS-L 37.7
Charlotte	12	2N	5W	GTW-C 202.4 – MC-G 35.0

Charlotte	18	2N	4W	MC-G 34.9
Chester	33	3N	5W	MC-G 40.2
Clay	5	4N	4W	PM-D 103.0
Dimondale	15	3N	3W	LS-L 51.9
Eaton Rapids	3	1N	3W	MC-G 24.2
Eaton Rapids	33	2N	3W	LS-L 42.4
Grand Ledge	1	4N	4W	PM-D 99.3
Hope	24	4N	3W	GTW-C 217.6
Kingsland	3	2N	3W	LS-L 42.4
Lime Siding	32	1N	6W	GTW-C 188.2
Millett(s)	26	4N	3W	GTW-C 216.2
Moores	(now Shepards)			
Mulliken	3	4N	5W	PM-D 107.1
Olivet	18	1N	5W	GTW-C 194.3
Packard	(see same, Ingham Co.)			
Potterville	23	3N	4W	GTW-C 208.7
Sevastapol	18	3N	3W	GTW-C 210.4
Shepards	4	1N	5W	GTW-C 196.6
State Road	23	1N	6W	GTW-C 191.8
Sunfield	2	4N	6W	PM-D 112.2
Vermontville	28	3N	6W	MC-G 46.2
#Wallis				GTW-C 200
West Grand Ledge	2	4N	4W	PM-D 100.1 – PM-I 0.8
Woodbury	6	4N	6W	PM-D 116.2 – CK&S 44.2

EMMET COUNTY

Alanson	10	35N	4W	GR&I-N 434.9
Bay View	32	35N	5W	GR&I-N 425.7 – PM-P 226.2
#Beahan				GR&I
#Bells Landing				PM-P 220
#Benham				GR&I
#Bogardus				GR&I-7
Brutus	22	36N	4W	GR&I-N 438.5
Carpenter	8	34N	6W	PM-P 219.2

Carp Lake	10	38N	4W	GR&I-N 452.7
Conway	24	35N	5W	GR&I-N 430.0
#Curtis				GR&I
#East Wequetonsing				GR&I-H 4
#Fochtman				GR&I
Formans	7	34N	5W	GR&I-N 423.0
#Hamlet				GR&I
Harbor Springs	13	35N	6W	GR&I-H 5.6
Harbor Springs Jct.	(now Kegomic)			
Indiana Point	17	35N	4W	GR&I-N 432.9
#Irma				GR&I
Kegomic	28	35N	5W	GR&I-N 427.0 −
				GR&I-H 0
#Lake Park				GR&I
Lakewood	10	37N	4W	GR&I-N 446.8
Lamson	10	34N	6W	PM-P 221.7
Levering	34	38N	4W	GR&I-N 448.6
Leverington	(now Levering)			
#Lovey				GR&I
Mackinaw City	(see same, Cheboygan Co.			
Menonaqua Beach	21	35N	5W	GR&I-H 2.1
#Newberrys				GR&I-?
Oden	17	35N	4W	GR&I-N 432.2
Page	21	35N	5W	GR&I-H 2.1
#Peihl				PM-P
Pellston	34	37N	4W	GR&I-N 442.6 −
				GR&I-7 0 −
				GR&I-12 0
Petoskey	5	34N	5W	GR&I-N 424.8
Petoskey	6	34N	5W	PM-P 225.2
Ponshewaing	16	35N	4W	GR&I-N 433.3
Ramona Park	17	35N	5W	GR&I-H 3.2
Roaring Brook	17	35N	5W	GR&I-H 3.6
Round Lake	26	35N	5W	GR&I-N 428.1
#Rutland				GR&I-?
#Sly				PM
#Spring Brook				PM-P
#Stevens				GR&I-N 426
Sunny Brook	13	35N	5W	GR&I-N 430.9
Van	15	37N	4W	GR&I-N 445.6
#Wabememe		34N	5W	GR&I-N 421

#Walker				GR&I
#Watsonville				GR&I
Wayagamung	26	35N	5W	GR&I-N 428.7
Wequetonsing	18	35N	5W	GR&I-H 4.4
#West Wequetonsing				GR&I-H 5
#Weyant				GR&I-?
#Wheeling				GR&I

GENESEE COUNTY

Atwood Jct.	4	6N	7E	PM-FB 37.7— PM-T 38.4
Belsay	10	7N	7E	GTW-C 275.2
Belsay Yard	9	7N	7E	GTW-C 274.2
Branch Siding	11	9N	8E	PM-F 17.5
Brent Creek	9	8N	5E	GTW-S 17.1
Clay Track	21	8N	5E	GTW-S 14.1
Clio	15	9N	6E	PM-T 21.3
County Line	(see same, Saginaw Co.)			
Crapo	8	6N	5E	GTW-C 258.2
Crapo Farm	3	6N	5E	GTW-C 259.8
Crapo Street	7	7N	7E	GTW-YF 270.7
Davison	10	7N	8E	GTW-C 279.2
#Dawson		7N	6E	GTW
Duffield	8	6N	5E	GTW-C 257.2
East Flint	7	7N	8E	GTW-C 276.7
#Egypt				GTW-D
Fenton	36	5N	6E	GTW-D 50.7
Fentonville	(now Fenton)			
Flint	13	7N	6E	PM-T 33.3
Flint	18	7N	7E	GTW-C 270.1;(old site now North Flint)
Flint River Jct.	(now Horton)			
Flushing	27	8N	5E	GTW-S 12.9
F. R. B. Jct.	(now Flint River Jct.)			
Gaines	31	6N	5E	GTW-D 62.6

Genesee	11	8N	7E	PM-F 8.2
Grand Blanc	16	6N	7E	PM-T 40.6
Hamilton	(now Swartz Creek)			
Horton	19	8N	7E	PM-F 4.7 − PM-T 28.6
Kearsley	9	7N	7E	GTW-YF 272.5 − PM-FB 32.9
Lennon	(see same, Shiawassee Co.)			
Linden	20	5N	6E	GTW-D 55.3
McGrew Jct.	30	8N	7E	PM-FB 29.5 − PM-T 29.5
Montrose	20	9N	5E	GTW-S 21.2
Mt. Morris	7	8N	7E	PM-T 26.1
Mundy	31	7N	6E	GTW-C 262.7 − GTW-YF 262.7
North Flint	7	7N	7E	GTW-YF 270.2 (old station for Flint)
North Linden	(now Linden)			
Otisville	21	9N	8E	PM-F 14.4
Otterburn	32	7N	6E	GTW-YF 264.1
Paxton	21	5N	6E	GTW-D 53.6
Pine Run	23	9N	6E	PM-T 22.1 (moved and renamed Clio)
Rogersville	6	8N	8E	PM-F 10.6
Shoecraft	12	9N	7E	PM-F 9.4
Swartz Creek	2	6N	5E	GTW-C 261.5
Thread	19	7N	7E	PM-T 35.1
Torrey	26	7N	6E	GTW-C 267.2
West Flint	32	7N	6E	GTW-C 263.8

GLADWIN COUNTY

Beaverton	12	17N	2W	PM-LG 11.1
Bliss Branch	9	18N	1W	MC-P 25.1
Bricks	9	19N	2E	MC-PN 21.1

Estey	14	17N	2E	MC-P7 3.1
#Fisher				PM-LG?
Gladwin	6	18N	1W	MC-P 27.4
Half Way	(now Lyle)			
Hardluck	1	19N	2E	MC-PN 17.9
Hawes Bridge	(now Highwood)			
Highwood	36	18N	1E	MC-P 17.8
Howry(s)	15	18N	1W	MC-P 23.3
Lyle	34	17N	2W	PM-LG 5.9
Rhodes	1	17N	2E	MC-P 11.1 –
				MC-P7 0
Smith(s)	33	18N	2E	MC-P 14.8
Stephens Siding	8	18N	1W	MC-P 26.0
Winegars	13	18N	1W	MC-P 21.3

GRAND TRAVERSE COUNTY

Acme	3	27N	10W	PM-P 153.2
Angell	8	28N	9W	PM-PE 4.5
Bates	6	27N	9W	PM-P 156.8
Beitners	9	26N	11W	PM-P 141.1
Beitners	(now Keystone)			
#Blair				GR&I
Boardman	10	27N	11W	PM-P 147.2
Boardman Jct.	(now Boardman)			
Cedar Run	6	27N	12W	M&NE-A 55.3
Cobb Jct.	21	26N	10W	GR&I-T 13.1
#Dennis				PM-P
East Bay	9	27N	10W	PM-P 151.5
Fife Lake	12	25N	9W	GR&I-N 357.8
Filers Switch	6	26N	12W	M&NE-A 47.3
#Galloway				PM
Grant Center	33	26N	12W	M&NE-A 41.0
Grawn	7	26N	11W	PM-P 138.0
Green Lake	(now Grant Center)			
Holmes	30	25N	9W	GR&I-T 2.8
Horicon	(now Karlin)			

Interlochen	16	26N	12W	M&NE-A 44.6 –
				PM-P 134.2
Karlin	8	25N	12W	M&NE-A 39.2
Kerry	11	27N	11W	GR&I-T 25.6 –
				PM-P 147.8
Keystone	3	26N	11W	GR&I-T 19.6
Kingsley	4	25N	10W	GR&I-T 9.3
#Lakeside	33	26N	12W	M&NE
#Leavells		25N	10W	GR&I-T
#Limerick				PM-P
Long Lake Jct.	8	26N	12W	M&NE-A 45.7 –
				M&NE-5X
Mable	35	28N	9W	PM-P 160.9
Mayfield	28	26N	10W	GR&I-T 12.6
Mitchell	7	27N	10W	PM-P 150.2
#Munshaw				GR&I
Pine Park	21	26N	12W	M&NE-A 43.6
Sabin	27	27N	11W	PM-P 143.4
Slights	12	26N	11W	GR&I-T 17.2
South Traverse City	10	27N	11W	PM-P 146.1
Spring City	(now Mayfield)			
State Hospital	9	27N	11W	PM-P 147.0 + 1.4
Summit City	22	25N	10W	GR&I-T 6.2
Traverse City	2	27N	11W	GR&I-T 26.0;
				M&NE-A 69.8
Traverse City	3	27N	11W	PM-P 147.2 + 0.6
				(old station)
Traverse City	11	27N	11W	PM-P 147.7 (new
				station)
Tunk	36	28N	9W	PM-P 162.0
Twin Lake Branch	18	25N	12W	M&NE-A 37.6
#Twin Mountain	18	25N	12W	M&NE-A 38
Walton	(name for Walton Jct. on			
	M&NE-R)			
Walton Jct.	33	25N	9W	GR&I-N 352.8 –
				GR&I-T 0 –
				M&NE-R 38.8
Westminster	17	25N	10W	GR&I-T 8.0
#Whipple				GR&I-T
Williamsburg	4	27N	9W	PM-P 158.7 –
				PM-PE 0
Wylies	(now Pine Park)			

GRATIOT COUNTY

Alma	3	11N	3W	AA-b 145.4 — PM-V 40.2
Alma	34	12N	3W	AA-2 12.3 — PM-VO 40.2
Ashley	7	9N	1W	AA-B 128.3 — GTW-M 0
Bannister	27	9N	1W	AA-B 123.8
#Beet				PM-V
Boyers	34	12N	4W	PM-V 46.5
Breckenridge	19	12N	1W	PM-V 29.8
#Brown				PM-V
Detroiter Mobile	25	12N	3W	PM-V 37.2
Doyle	(now Eaton)			
Eaton	24	12N	1W	PM-V 24.3
Elwell	36	12N	4W	PM-V 44.5
Forest Hill	16	12N	3W	AA-B 149.8
Hayes	21	9N	1W	AA-B 125.8
Ithaca	1	10N	3W	AA-B 138.3; PM-VT 6.7
Ithaca	31	11N	2W	AA-2 0.9
Meridian	(now Doyle)			
Middleton	7	9N	3W	GTW-M 12.0
North Star	15	10N	2W	AA-B 133.7
Ola	9	9N	2W	GTW-M 4.5
Parkinsons	9	12N	3W	AA-B 150.8
Perrinton	8	9N	3W	GTW-M 10.5
Pompeii	7	9N	2W	GTW-M 6.4
Rawn	6	10N	2W	AA-B 137.8
Riverdale	31	12N	4W	PM-V 49.3
St. Louis	30	12N	2W	AA-2 8.4 + 1.4; PM-V 36.3 — PM-VO 36.3
#Seville		12N	4W	PM-V
#Stella				AA-B
Wheeler	21	12N	1W	PM-V 27.8

Whites	26	10N	2W	AA-B 131.2
Wright	3	11N	3W	AA-B 144.7—
				(PM-VT 0.4)

HILLSDALE COUNTY

Allen	3	6S	4W	LS-A 371.1
Bakers	29	5S	1W	DTM 42.2
Bankers	6	7S	3W	LS-W 31.1—
				LS-Y 65.3
#Baw Beese				LS-A
Camden	(now Montgomery)			
Clear Lake	(now Montgomery)			
East Mosherville	(now Scipio)			
Fort Wayne Jct.	9	6S	3W	LS-A 366.0—
				LS-W 25.3
Hillsdale	27	6S	3W	LS-A 362.1—
				LS-Y 61.1
Jerome	19	5S	1W	DTM 43.9; LS-Y
				48.9
Jonesville	4	6S	3W	LS-W 24.5
Jonesville	5	6S	3W	LS-A 366.6—
				LS-L 0
Knorr	36	5S	1W	DTM 38.3
Knorr Lake	(now Knorr)			
Litchfield	10	5S	4W	LS-L 6.6
Montgomery	17	8S	4W	LS-W 41.5
Moscow	11	5S	2W	DTM 46.8
Mosherville	11	5S	3W	LS-W 18.9
North Adams	3	6S	2W	LS-Y 53.6
Osseo	4	7S	2W	LS-A 354.3
Pittsford	13	7S	2W	LS-A 353.5
Prattville	16	8S	1W	CN 35.7
Reading	26	7S	4W	LS-W 35.8
Scipio	(now Mosherville)			
Somerset	12	5S	1W	LS-Y 43.4
Somerset Centre	10	5S	1W	LS-Y 45.3
Waldron	34	8S	1W	CN 39.5

Along the Tracks

HURON COUNTY

Adams Corners	(now Ruth)			
#Andersons Siding				GTW-P
Atherton	22	17N	15E	PM-NH 22.3
Atwater	27	15N	12E	GTW-B 11.1
Bach	25	15N	9E	MC-BC 28.1
Bad Axe	19	16N	13E	GTW-B 18.8;
				PM-N 70.1
Bart	1	16N	9E	PM-S 44.9 –
				PM-SB 0
Bay Port	36	17N	9E	PM-SB 1.4
Bay Port Jct.	(now Bart)			
Berne	35	17N	10E	GTW-P 93.1
Berne	(On PM-S now Berne Jct.)			
Berne Jct.	(now Pigeon)			
Caseville	35	18N	10E	GTW-P 99.4
#Clarks	30	17N	13E	PM-N 75
Creevy Siding	18	17N	13E	PM-N 77.6
Dwight	(now Kinde?)			
Eagle Bay	23	19N	13E	PM-N 90.9
Elkton	10	16N	11E	PM-S 54.6
Filion	19	17N	13E	PM-N 76.4
Goodman	(now Grassmere)			
Grassmere	18	16N	12E	PM-S 57.5
Grindstone City	25	19N	13E	PM-N 92.2
Halls Siding	19	15N	10E	MC-BC 30.7
Harbor Beach	1	16N	15E	PM-NH 18.3
Helena	34	16N	15E	PM-NH 12.5
Hobson	26	17N	15E	PM-NH 20.7
Huron	19	16N	13E	GTW-B 18.7 –
				PM-N 69.6
Johnson	18	18N	13E	PM-N 82.6
Kinde	31	18N	13E	PM-N 79.6
#Krohns Siding				PM-N 62
Linkville	35	16N	10E	GTW-P 86.9
Longs	15	16N	12E	PM-S 60.6
McIntyre	10	15N	12E	GTW-B 13.0
Oliver	(now Elkton)			

Owendale	11	15N	10E	GTW-P 84.8— MC-BC 33.9
Patton	20	15N	10E	MC-BC 31.6
Pigeon	11	16N	10E	GTW-P 91.8— PM-S 50.0
Pointe Aux Barques	21	19N	13E	PM-N 89.2
Port Austin	30	19N	13E	PM-N 86.7
Port Hope	4	17N	15E	PM-NH 25.7
Quarry	6	16N	10E	PM-S 46.1
Quarry Jct	5	16N	10E	PM-S 47.2
Rapsons Siding	31	17N	13E	PM-N 73.6
#Ribble Road				PM-S
Robinsons	(now Goodman)			
Rose Island	33	16N	9E	PM-S 39.5
Rosevear	7	16N	11E	PM-S 52.4
Ruth	20	15N	15E	PM-NH 7.7
Sand Beach	(now Harbor Beach)			
#Sandy				PM
#Scully Siding		16N	13E	PM-N
Sebewaing	10	15N	9E	PM-S 36.9
#Tarry		16N	9E	PM-S 42
Ubly	27	15N	13E	PM-N 62.9
Wadsworth	8	15N	13E	PM-N 66.4
Wallace	5	16N	10E	PM-S 46.5
#Watrous				GTW-P 84
Weale	15	16N	9E	PM-S 42.7
Winsor	(now Linkville)			

INGHAM COUNTY

Cedar Street	22	4N	2W	GTW-C 221.4— MC-S 35.9
Chapins	(now Eden)			
Chicago Jct.	(now Trowbridge)			
College Farm	24	4N	2W	PM-D 83.4
Dana	6	4N	2E	PM-D 72.3
Delhi	(now Holt)			

Eden	33	2N	1W	MC-S 20.6
Ensel	4	4N	2W	PM-D 89.9
Haslett	10	4N	1W	GTW-C 229.0
Holt	14	3N	2W	MC-S 30.3
Kilwinning	16	2N	1W	MC-S 23.1
Lansing	15	4N	2W	MC-S 36.9 −
				PM-D 87.4
Lansing	16	4N	2W	LS-L 60.1
Lansing	21	4N	2W	GTW-C 220.9
Lansing Yard	34	4N	2W	MC-S 34.0
Leroy	(now Webberville)			
Leslie	21	1N	1W	MC-S 15.5
MA	15	4N	2W	PM-D 87.3 −
				MC-S 36.8
Mason	5	2N	1W	MC-S 25.0
Meridian	36	3N	1W	PM-D 77.5
#Meridian				GTW-C 226½
Michigan Avenue	(PM-D name for MA)			
North Lansing	10	4N	2W	MC-S 37.9 −
				PM-D 88.3
Okemos	28	4N	1W	PM-D 81.2
Onondaga	29	1N	2W	MC-G 17.5
Packard	6	4N	2W	LS-L 54.9
Pine Lake	(now Haslett)			
Reo Jct	21	4N	2W	LS-L 58.7 −
				GTW-C 221.2
#South Lansing				LS-L 59
South Street	(see Reo Jct.)			
Stockbridge	26	1N	2E	GTW-A 87.6
Trowbridge	24	4N	2W	GTW-C 223.5 −
				PM-D 84.8
Turner Street	9	4N	2W	LS-L 61.3 −
				MC-YLM 0 −
				PM-D 88.8
Underwood	4	1N	1W	MC-S 19.0
Washington				
Avenue	21	4N	2W	GTW-C 220.8
Webberville	11	3N	2E	PM-D 67.7
Williamston	1	3N	1E	PM-D 73.4

IONIA COUNTY

Belding	11	8N	8W	PM-G 88.2
Chadwick	7	8N	7W	PM-I 37.5
Clarksville	10	5N	8W	PM-D 126.4
Collins	6	6N	5W	PM-I 17.4
Danby	2	5N	5W	PM-I 8.8
Elmdale	(see same, Kent Co.)			
Haynor	12	7N	7W	PM-I 30.4 – PM-J 30.4
Henderson	36	8N	6W	PM-J 32.7
Higbee	35	8N	7W	PM-J 32.1
Ionia	19	7N	6W	GTW-D 124.2; PM-I 26.1
Kidd(ville)	1	8N	8W	PM-G 86.5 – PM-I 39.6
Lake Odessa	33	5N	7W	PM-D 120.1
Lyons	24	7N	6W	PM-I 20.8
Muir	17	7N	5W	GTW-D 117.7
Orange	(now Stebbins)			
Orleans	21	8N	7W	PM-I 34.9
#Otisco				PM-G
Palmers	(now Orleans)			
Pewamo	13	7N	5W	GTW-D 112.8
Portland	28	6N	5W	PM-I 12.1
#Redstone				PM-I
Sangsters	27	8N	7W	PM-I 33.7
Saranac	1	6N	8W	GTW-D 132.5
Shiloh	1	8N	7W	PM-J 36.8
Smyrna	28	8N	8W	PM-G 92.2
Stanton Jct.	(now Haynor)			
Stebbins(ville)	7	6N	5W	PM-I 16.4
Strong	(now Stanton Jct.)			
Warden	23	7N	7W	PM-I 27.6
Webber	30	7N	5W	PM-I 19.6
Woods Corners	24	8N	7W	PM-J 34.6

IOSCO COUNTY

Alabaster	26	21N	7E	D&M-E 4.0
Alabaster Jct.	2	21N	7E	D&M-S 57.0 –
				D&M-E 0
Arn	(now McIvor)			
AuSable	3	23N	9E	ASNW-A 0
AuSable River Jct.	4	23N	9E	ASNW-A 0.9 –
				D&M-S 73.6
Beadle	(now Bisonette)			
Bisonette	14	24N	7E	ASNW-A 11.9
Bristol	14	22N	8E	D&M-S 64.7
Cedarmere	(see same, Alcona Co.)			
Cooke Dam	10	24N	7E	ASNW-A 13.5
Coopers Corners	13	22N	6E	D&M-B 5.0
#Cowley(s Spur)				D&M-S
Doane	18	24N	8E	ASNW-A 10.0
East Tawas	20	22N	8E	D&M-S 61.0
(old sta.)				
Emery Jct.	8	21N	6E	D&M-A 0.3 –
				D&M-B 0.3
#Farmer				D&M-S
#Fitzpatrick				ASNW-A 15
Five Channels Dam	23	24N	6E	ASNW-A2 5.2
Five Channels Jct.	6	24N	7E	ASNW-A 17.5 –
				ASNW-A2 0
Grise	10	21N	7E	D&M-E 0.9
Hale	14	23N	5E	D&M-B 11.5
Hale Lake	(now Hale)			
#Hampshire				D&M-B
Hemlock Road	30	22N	6E	D&M-B 3.8
Kunze Siding	6	22N	9E	D&M-S 67.4
Lincoln Jct.	9	24N	9E	D&M-S 79.3 –
				D&M-O 79.3
Long Lake	31	24N	5E	D&M-B 16.5
Loon Lake	9	23N	5E	D&M-B 13.1
Louds Dam	21	24N	6E	ASNW-A2 7.4
Marks	5	21N	7E	D&M-S 54.2
McIvor	10	21N	6E	D&M-S 50.5

Mills	6	21N	5E	D&M-A 7.2
National City	9	21N	6E	D&M-S 48.6 –
				D&M-A 0
National City Spur	11	21N	6E	D&M-S 47.3
Oscoda	4	23N	9E	D&M-S 74.2
Port Gypsum	2	21N	7E	D&M-E 0.6 + 0.7
Robinson	23	21N	7E	D&M-E 3.7
#Seven Mile Hill	26	24N	8E	ASNW-A 7
Skeel	33	24N	9E	D&M-S 75.4
Slingerland	22	21N	7E	D&M-E 2.9
Taft	11	22N	5E	D&M-B 6.7
Tawas Beach	27	22N	8E	D&M-T 62.6
Tawas Beach Jct.	21	22N	8E	D&M-S 61.6 –
				D&M-T 61.6
Tawas City	30	22N	8E	D&M-S 60.3 (old
				station 59.6)
Tucker (Farm)	32	24N	9E	ASNW-A 2.5
Turtle	19	21N	6E	D&M-S 45.5
White Rock	12	21N	6E	D&M-S 51.9
Whittemore	2	21N	5E	D&M-A 4.1

ISABELLA COUNTY

Blanchard	18	13N	6W	PM-J 67.8
Brodie	35	14N	4W	AA-B 159.9
Buchtel	(now Loomis)			
Bundy	3	14N	6W	PM-JW 8.1
Burdick	6	13N	3W	AA-B 158.4
Burnham	15	16N	4W	AA-B 176.1
Calkinsville	(now Rosebush)			
Cowdens	34	16N	4W	AA-B 172.5
Delwin	16	15N	3W	PM-LM 6.5
#Denver		15N	3W	PM-LM
Dingmans	27	15N	4W	AA-B 168.3
Doherty	27	16N	4W	AA-B 174.0
Drew	26	15N	6W	PM-JW 11.2
Foster	17	14N	6W	PM-JW 5.6
Herrick	6	16N	3W	PM-L 46.9

Isabella	2	14N	4W	PM-LM 11.7
Jordan	25	15N	4W	PM-LM 10.3
Lansingville	(now Herrick)			
Leaton	19	15N	3W	PM-LM 9.0
Loomis	9	16N	3W	PM-L 44.7
Mansfield	(now Foster)			
Martha	3	14N	4W	AA-B 166.3
Mt. Pleasant	15	14N	4W	AA-B 163.8; PM-LM 14.7
Murphy	29	13N	6W	PM-J 64.9
Rand	20	13N	6W	PM-J 66.0
Remick	33	13N	6W	PM-J 63.7
Rosebush	15	15N	4W	AA-B 170.5
Salt River	(now Shepherd)			
Shepherd	18	13N	3W	AA-B 156.2
Stirling	7	14N	6W	PM-JW 4.2
Taylors	26	14N	4W	AA-B 160.8
Transport	15	14N	4W	AA-B 164.2
Weidman	13	15N	6W	PM-JW 13.3
Wise	2	15N	3W	PM-LM 3.6

JACKSON COUNTY

A	34	2S	1W	MC-G 1.5
Ackerson Lake	30	3S	1E	CN 5.7
Arland	3	1S	2W	MC-G 14.4
Aspinwall	10	3S	1W	MC-A 1.8
Baldwin Mills	(now Horton)			
Barry	(now Sandstone)			
Bath Mills	5	3S	3W	MC-C 92.2
Brooklyn	19	4S	2E	LS-Y 35.7
Clark Lake	18	4S	1E	CN 9.7
Coalville	19	2S	3W	LS-L 26.3
Concord	27	3S	3W	MC-A 14.7
Concord	(on MC-C now North Concord)			
Devereux	7	2S	3W	LS-L 28.7
East Avenue	2	3S	1W	MC-E 75.1— LS-W 0.4

East Yard	6	3S	1E	MC-E 73.1
Eaton Rapids Jct.	(now Rives Jct.)			
Eldred	20	3S	1E	LS-J 36.4
Fort Wayne Switch	(now OD)			
Francisco	25	2S	2E	MC-E 61.1
Friciscoville	(now Francisco)			
Gidleys	(now Parma)			
Grass Lake	32	2S	2E	MC-E 65.2
Haires	20	3S	1W	LS-W 5.1 — MC-A 4.8
Hanover	21	4S	2W	DTM 51.2 — LS-W 14.0
Henrietta	23	1S	1E	GTW-A 95.4
Henrys Crossing	32	1S	1W	MC-G 7.8
Horton	2	4S	2W	LS-W 10.4
Jackson	2	3S	1W	GTW-A 105.9; LS-J 42.4; MC-C & MC-E 75.5
Jackson Jct.	1	3S	1W	MC-A 0 — MC-E 74.4
Lansing Avenue	22	2S	1W	MC-G 2.7
Leoni	1	3S	1E	MC-E 68.2
Lyonette	24	3S	1W	CN 4.3
Michigan Center	9	3S	1E	MC-E 70.5
Munith	13	1S	1E	GTW-A 92.9
Napoleon	31	3S	2E	LS-J 32.0
North Concord	10	3S	3W	MC-C 89.2
Norvell	3	4S	2E	LS-J 28.7
OD	2	3S	1W	CN 1.2 — LS-J 41.3 — LS-W 1.2 — MC-A 0.8
Parma	36	2S	3W	MC-C 86.3
Pearl Street	34	2S	1W	MC-C 75.5 — MC-G 0.2
Prison	13	2S	1W	GTW-A 102.2
Pulaski	6	4S	3W	Mc-A(old line) 19.1
Pulaski	(non DTM now Wheelerton)			
Reynolds	25	3S	3W	MC-A 12.7
Rives Jct.	18	1S	1W	MC-G 10.4 — MC-S 10.4

Roots	4	2S	1E	GTW-A 98.1
Sandstone	35	2S	2W	MC-C 81.7
Snyder	22	3S	2W	MC-A 8.2
Spring Arbor	28	3S	2W	MC-A 10.3
Springport	17	1S	3W	LS-L 32.7
Stony Point	31	4S	2W	LS-W 16.2
#Town House				CN
Trumbulls	36	2S	2W	MC-C 80.8
Van Horn	4	2S	1W	MC-G 6.2
Watkins	13	4S	2E	LS-Y 29.7
West Hill	32	2S	1W	MC-C 78.4
Wheelerton	15	4S	3W	DTM 55.8
Wilsons	(now Haires?)			
Wilsons	30	3S	1W	LS-W 6.6
Woodville	31	2S	1W	MC-C 79.1

KALAMAZOO COUNTY

Alamo	22	1S	12W	MC-H 9.1
Argenta	3	1S	11W	LS-G 45.5
Augusta	34	1S	9W	MC-C 130.2; DTM 99.8
Augusta Coal Chutes	4	2S	9W	MC-C 131.4
Austin	(now Austin Lake)			
Austin Lake	24	3S	11W	GR&I-S 178.0
#Baker	25	3S	11W	GR&I-S
Balch	35	1S	12W	MC-H 5.9
Beckwiths Siding	6	3S	10W	GTW-K 6.3
#Bly		3S	12W	KLSC
BO	15	2S	11W	CK&S 0.2 – GTW-YK 3.3 – LS-G 36.8 – MC-C 143.1
Botsford	14	2S	11W	MC-C 142.0
Brady	(now Vicksburg)			
Brighton	34	3S	12W	KLSC 6.6

Brownell	6	2S	11W	MC-H 4.0
Camp St. Louis	20	1S	9W	DTM 102.5
Carrolls	19	1S	10W	CK&S 5.9
Climax	3	3S	9W	GTW-C 165.0
Comfort Siding	34	2S	11W	LS-G 33.8
Comstock	17	2S	10W	MC-C 139.6
Cooper	15	1S	11W	GR&I-S 191.3;
				LS-G 42.3
County Spur	15	1S	11W	GR&I-S 191.8
Dock	10	2S	11W	GR&I-S 187.1
Doubling Track	2	2S	12W	MC-H 5.5
#Eassom		3S	12W	KLSC 10
East Avenue	(now Botsford)
East Cooper	26	1S	11W	CK&S 4.2
Flagg	(now Richland Jct.)
Fox	15	2S	11W	GR&I-S 185.8
Galesburg	13	2S	10W	MC-C 134.6
Gibson Street	15	2S	11W	GR&I-S 185.0 —
				GTW-K 11.0 —
				LS-G 36.2
	(not so named on GTW-K and LS-G)
Hopkins	(now Balch)
#Ice Siding		4S	11W	GTW-C 152
Indianfield	13	3S	11W	GR&I-S 180.4
Kalamazoo	15	2S	11W	CK&S 0 —
				CK&S-S 0;
				GR&I-S 185.4;
				GTW-K 11.3;
				MC-C 143.4 —
				MC-H 0; LS-G 36.3
Kalamazoo	16	2S	11W	KLSC 0
Kalamazoo Jct.	(now Tower 1 on MC-C; now Richland Jct. on DTM)
Kealey	8	3S	10W	GTW-K 4.3
Kilgore Yard	31	2S	10W	GTW-K 6.5
Miller	28	2S	12W	MC-C 150.7
North Yard	15	2S	11W	LS-G 36.9
Oshtemo	35	2S	12W	KLSC 5.2

Ostemo	(spelling for Oshtemo when on MC-C)			
Pavilion	34	3S	10W	GTW-C 157.2— GTW-K 0
Pavilion Jct.	25	2S	11W	CK&S-S 1.3— GTW-K 9.5— GTW-YK 1.3
Pomeroy	21	3S	10W	GTW-K 2.5
Portage	21	3S	11W	LS-G 29.8
Portage Street	22	2S	11W	LS-G 35.8
Richland	14	1S	10W	DTM 106.1
Richland Jct.	8	1S	10W	CK&S 8.9— DTM 108.8
Rix	5	3S	12W	KLSC 7.8
Schoolcraft	19	4S	11W	GTW-C 146.8— LS-G(new) 23.0; LS-G(old) 23.4
Scotts	24	3S	10W	GTW-C 160.1
#Shelldrake				GR&I-S
Silver Creek	(now Argenta)			
South Yard	34	2S	11W	LS-G 34.1
Spring Brook	(now Carrolls)			
#Streeter				CK&S 3
Tower 1	15	2S	11W	GR&I-S 185.7— MC-C 143.2
Travis	4	1S	11W	GR&I-S 193.5
Upjohn	13	3S	11W	GR&I-S 179.0
Vicksburg	18	4S	10W	GR&I-S 173.0— GTW-C 152.5
Vine	23	2S	11W	GR&I-S 184.6
Walker	8	3S	12W	KLSC 8.6
Williams	30	1S	12W	MC-H 11.3
Yorkville	19	1S	9W	DTM 103.4

KALKASKA COUNTY

#Aarwood				GR&I
Angling	11	26N	6W	M&NE-R 62.8

Barker Creek	31	28N	8W	PM-P 163.8
#Barnes				PM
Blue Lake	22	28N	5W	D&C-2 9.6
#Butcher		25N	6W	PM-K 30.8
#Chapman				PM
Clearwater	15	28N	8W	PM-K 1.8
#Clement				PM
Crofton	2	26N	8W	GR&I-N 366.6
#Culver				M&NE-R
Deiberts	11	25N	8W	M&NE-R 48.5
#Dempsey		25N	6W	PM-K 30
#Eastman		26N	7W	PM-K 18
#Fairbanks				PM
#Farrens		26N	8W	GR&I-N 363
#France		28N	8W	PM-P 165
#Gray				PM-K
Halsted	35	26N	6W	PM-K 29.0
#Hamiltons				GR&I
#Harts		26N	8W	GR&I-N 361
Havana		(now Westwood)		
#Herrings		27N	7W	GR&I-N 373
Houseman	32	26N	8W	GR&I-N 360.9
Kalkaska	17	27N	7W	GR&I-N 371.5; PM-K 11.1
#Kelley				PM-K
#Knight				PM-K
Leetsville	27	28N	7W	GR&I-N 376.1
Leiphardt	31	28N	7W	PM-K 6.9
#Lepine				PM-K
#Lola				GR&I
Mahan	7	27N	7W	PM-K 9.1 – PM-K2 0
#McAfee				GR&I
McGee	32	26N	7W	M&NE-R 52.2
#Moeke				PM-K
Naples	21	25N	6W	PM-K 27.0
#Omega				GR&I
O'Neill	19	26N	6W	M&NE-R 58.0
#Prescy				PM-K
#Quimbys		27N	8W	GR&I-N 367

Rapid City	9	28N	8W	PM-P 168.6—
				PM-K 0
#Rice				PM
Ricker	13	28N	8W	PM-K 3.4
Riverview	2	26N	5W	M&NE-R 70.6
Rowley	36	26N	8W	M&NE-R 50.1
Rugg	30	28N	7W	PM-K 5.5
Sands	6	25N	6W	PM-K 22.3
Saunders	3	26N	7W	PM-K 15.6
Sharon	6	25N	6W	PM-K 23.2
Sigma	9	26N	6W	M&NE-R 61.0
#Soules		27N	8W	PM-K2 4.8
South Boardman	21	26N	8W	GR&I-N 363.4
Spencer	14	26N	7W	PM-K 18.4
Springfield	18	25N	8W	M&NE-R 43.6
#Squaw Lake				D&C
Stimson	15	26N	8W	GR&I-N 364.8
#Thompson		27N	8W	GR&I-N 368
Van Buren	(now Rapid City)			
Westwood	1	28N	7W	GR&I-N 381.1
Wilkins	11	28N	7W	GR&I-N 379.6

KENT COUNTY

Ada	34	6N	10W	GTW-D 148.0
Alpine	24	8N	12W	PM-P 8.6
Alto	4	5N	9W	PM-D 133.9
Avenue Jct.	(now Sunnyside)			
Ball Creek	(now Kent City)			
Bartlett Street	25	7N	12W	MC-G 94.1—
				GR&I-S
				233.6—
				GR&I-YG 3.1
Belmont	16	8N	11W	GR&I-N 243.7
Bowen	28	6N	11W	MC-G 87.9
Brannin	32	6N	9W	PM-D 135.2

Bridge Street	25	7N	12W	GR&I-N 235.1 (West Grand Rapids on PM-P)
Bristol	10	7N	12W	GR&I-M 4.4
Burch's Mill	1	9N	11W	GR&I-N 253.0
#Bushs				GR&I-N 246
Byron				(now Byron Center)
Byron Center	21	5N	12W	LS-G 82.6
Caledonia	29	5N	10W	MC-G 79.8
Camp Lake	12	9N	12W	GTW-M 63.3
Carlisle	12	5N	12W	GR&I-S 224.3
#Cascade				PM-D 141
Casnovia				(see same, Muskegon Co.)
Cedar Springs	25	10N	11W	GR&I-N 255.2
Cedar Springs	31	10N	10W	GTW-M 56.4
Childsdale				(now South Rockford)
Child's Mill				(now Childsdale)
Comstock Park	36	8N	12W	GR&I-N 239.4; PM-P 5.5
Dewey	26	6N	11W	GTW-D 152.6
#Dickson		10N	9W	PM-I
Dutton	11	5N	11W	MC-G 84.0
Eagle Mills	34	7N	12W	LS-G 92.5
#East Grand Rapids				PM-D
#East Paris	14	6N	11W	PM-D 144
Edgerton	13	9N	11W	GR&I-N 250.8
Elkerton	12	5N	9W	PM-G 111.6
Elmdale	1	5N	9W	PM-D 130.4 – PM-G 110.5
Englishville	1	8N	12W	PM-P 11.6
Evans	2	10N	10W	GTW-M 50.9
Fair Grounds	18	6N	11W	MC-G 90.0
#Fernald				PM-G
Fisher	36	6N	12W	GR&I-S 227.5
Fourth Street	24	7N	12W	PM-P 1.5
Fox	19	6N	10W	PM-D 142.5
Franklin Street	36	7N	12W	MC-G 93.5
Freeport				(see same, Barry Co.)
Front Street	25	7N	12W	PM-P 0.3
Fuller	13	7N	12W	GR&I-N 236.9 – GTW-D

				158.9 – PM-P 3.0
Gaines	(now Hammond)			
Godfrey Avenue	36	7N	12W	GR&I-YG 2.2 – PM-C 0.8
Gooding	18	9N	12W	GTW-M 69.7
Grand Rapids	19	7N	12W	GTW-D(new) 157.5
Grand Rapids	24	7N	12W	GTW-D(old) 158.2 + 1.5
Grand Rapids	25	7N	12W	GR&I-N & GR&I-S 234.0 – MC-G(new) 94.4 – PM-C 0; LS-G 94.5; MC-G(old) 94.1
Grandville	18	6N	12W	PM-C 6.0
Grandville	21	6N	12W	LS-G
Hammond	(now Dutton)			
Harvard	6	10N	9W	GTW-M 49.1
Hillcrest	36	6N	9W	PM-G 109.2
Hughart	1	6N	12W	GR&I-S 232.1 – MC-G 92.6
Indian Creek	6	7N	12W	GTW-D 163.1
Ivanrest	9	6N	12W	PM-C 4.9
Kellys	9	6N	12W	LS-G 89.8
Kent City	33	10N	12W	PM-P 20.0
Kinney	8	7N	12W	GR&I-M 7.4
Lafayette	19	7N	11W	GTW-D 157.0
LaGrange	(now Moseley)			
Lamar	3	6N	12W	LS-G 91.1 – PM-C 3.5
Lincoln Lake	2	9N	9W	GTW-M 45.7
Lisbon	(now Gooding)			
Lockwood	18	10N	10W	GR&I-N 257.8
Logan	24	5N	9W	PM-G 113.3
#Lorenzo				GTW-M
Lowell	2	6N	9W	PM-G 104.1
Lowell	11	6N	9W	GTW-D 139.4

Malta	11	6N	9W	GTW-D 139.0—
				PM-G 104.9
McCords	35	6N	10W	PM-D 137.3
Mill Creek	(now Comstock Park)
Mill Creek Jct.	(now Comstock Park)
Moseley	35	8N	9W	PM-G 96.6
Muskegon Jct.	13	7N	12W	GR&I-N 236.6—
				GR&I-M 2.6
North Byron	4	5N	12W	LS-G 85.2
#North Grand Rapids				PM-P
Norths Mill	(now Mill Creek)
Oakdale	5	7N	11W	PM-D 149.2—
				PM-DR 0
Oakdale Park	(now Oakdale)
O'Brien	25	8N	12W	PM-P 6.9
#Pantlind City				GR&I-N 245
Park	1	7N	12W	PM-P 4.9
Plainfield Avenue	18	7N	11W	GTW-D 157.6
Plaster Creek(new)	2	6N	12W	PM-C 1.8
Plaster Creek(old)	3	6N	12W	PM-C 3.0
Plaster Creek Jct.	13	6N	12W	GR&I-S 231.2—
				GR&I-YG 0
Pleasant Street	36	7N	12W	GR&I-S 233.2—
				MC-G 93.7—
				PM-D 151.5
#Pratt Lake	25	6N	9W	PM-G
Reeds	5	9N	11W	GTW-M 61.4
Reeds Lake	34	7N	11W	PM-DR 2.5
Rockford	36	9N	11W	GR&I-N 247.9
Ross	26	5N	12W	GR&I-S 221.0
Saddleback Siding	(now Dewey)
Saginaw Crossing	14	9N	12W	GTW-M 65.3—
				PM-P 15.2
				(Saxon on GTW-M)
Sand Lake	5	10N	10W	GR&I-N 260.3
Saxon	14	9N	12W	GTW-M 65.3—
				PM-P 15.2
				(Saginaw Cross. on PM-P)

Second Avenue	(GR&I-S and MC-G name for Pleasant Street)			
Segwan	(now Lowell on GTW-D)			
Seymour	8	7N	11W	PM-D 148.1
Sheffield	4	9N	10W	GTW-M 52.6
Soldiers Home	6	8N	11W	PM-P 5.1
Solvay	25	6N	12W	GR&I-S 229.0
South Grand Rapids	1	6N	12W	GR&I-S 231.6; MC-G 92.2
South Rockford	2	8N	11W	GR&I-N 246.3
Sparta	14	9N	12W	GTW-M 65.5
Sparta	23	9N	12W	PM-P 14.9
Stewarts	23	5N	12W	GR&I-S 222.7
Sunnyside	36	7N	12W	PM-C 0.7 – PM-DZ 0.4 – PM-P 0
Terminal Jct.	24	7N	12W	GTW-D 158.2
#Tolands				GR&I-S 220
Tyrone	(now Ball Creek)			
#Vergennes				PM-G
Wealthy Street	25	7N	12W	PM-C 0.4 – PM-D 151.6
Wentworth	16	6N	12W	LS-G 88.7
West Grand Rapids	25	7N	12W	PM-D 1.2 (Bridge St. on GR&I-N)
Whitneys	(now Belmont?)			
#Whitneyville				PM-D
Williams Street	25	7N	12W	GR&I-S 233.7 – PM-C 0.3
Winter Street	25	7N	12W	GR&I-N 234.7 – PM-P 0.8
Wyoming	2	6N	12W	PM-C 2.5

LAKE COUNTY

#Alyn				GR&I-2 7.0
Baldwin	3	17N	13W	PM-L 107.3 – PM-P 73.6; old PM-L 106.9

#Bennett				PM
Branch	(see same, Mason Co.)			
Canfields	(now Peacock)			
#Canfields "Y"				M&GR-3 45
Carey(ville)	15	19N	12W	GR&I-3 14.5; M&GR 39.7
Chase	9	17N	11W	PM-L 95.9
#Conley		19N	13W	PM-P
#Danaher				GR&I-3
Deer Lake	11	18N	11W	GR&I-3 5.1
Edgetts	11	19N	11W	M&GR 47.0
Forman	1	17N	13W	PM-L
Goodrich	(now Sheepdale)			
#Haaks				M&GR-4 45
Idlewild	5	17N	12W	PM-L 102.4
Irons	7	20N	13W	PM-P 91.7
Keenan	8	19N	11W	M&GR 43.9
Lake Jct.	10	18N	11W	GR&I-3 5.3 − GR&I-3A 0
Lions Crossing	(now Goodrich)			
Little Manistee	30	20N	13W	PM-P 88.6
Luther	13	19N	12W	GR&I-3 11.7; M&GR 41.8
Marlboro(ugh)	15	17N	13W	PM-P 71.1
Nirvanna	2	17N	12W	PM-L 99.8
#Olga		20N	11W	GR&I-2
Olivers	12	17N	11W	PM-L 93.0
#Parsons		17N	13W	PM-P 72
Peacock	17	19N	13W	M&GR 31.2 − PM-P 84.9
Pelton	(now Raijuels)			
#Perrys		19N	11W	M&GR 47
Peters	8	19N	13W	PM-P 85.6
#Pines				M&GR 34
#Polands				GR&I-3
#Raijuels		18N	12W	GR&I-3A 7.0
#Reno				PM-L
Roby's Jct.	(now Marlboro)			
#Ruggles				?
Sauble	16	19N	14W	M&GR 25.3
Sheepdale	(now Sauble?)			

#Skellingers				GR&I-3
Star Lake	25	17N	14W	PM-LSX 4.8
#States Switch	21	19N	12W	M&GR 38 —
				M&GR-4
Stearns	27	18N	14W	PM-L 112.7
#Stowes				GR&I-3
Summitville	6	17N	11W	PM-L 98.0
Sweetwater Tank	28	18N	14W	PM-L 114.6
Totten	32	19N	11W	GR&I-3 8.8
Ungers	(now Idlewild)			
Wingleton (old)	6	17N	13W	PM-L 109.5 —
				PM-LSX 0
Wingleton (new)	36	18N	14W	PM-L 110.8
Wolf Lake	27	19N	13W	PM-P 81.8

LAPEER COUNTY

Almont	24	6N	12E	PM-NA 34.0
Attica	15	7N	11E	GTW-C 297.3
Carpenter	14	8N	9E	MC-B 65.5
Clifford	4	10N	11E	GTW-P 54.7 —
				PM-Q 39.9
Columbiaville	33	9N	9E	MC-B 69.0
Dryden	12	6N	11E	GTW-P 27.3
Elba	7	7N	7E	GTW-C 283.3
#Fish Lake				MC-BL
Five Lakes	1	8N	10E	MC-BL 8.0
#Hawkins				GTW-P
Hopkins Road	25	6N	12E	PM-NA 31.6
Hunters Creek	33	7N	10E	MC-B 55.3
Imlay City	17	7N	12E	GTW-C 302.0;
				GTW-P 32.9
Index	22	10N	12E	PM-Q 49.6
Kings Mills	3	8N	11E	GTW-P 42.7
L&N Jct.	5	7N	10E	MC-B 60.7 —
				MC-BL 0.3
Lapeer	5	7N	10E	GTW-C 290.0;
				MC-B 60.4

Lapeer Jct.	5	7N	10E	GTW-C 290.0; MC-B 59.8
Lum	23	8N	11E	GTW-P 39.3
Metamora	16	6N	10E	MC-B 52.0
Michigan Home Spur	6	7N	10E	GTW-C 288.0
Millville	24	8N	9E	MC-B 63.7
Nepessing	(now Oaklet; also sp. Nipissing)			
North Branch	4	9N	11E	GTW-P 48.6
Oaklet	11	7N	9E	GTW-C 286.8
Otter Lake	7	9N	9E	MC-B 73.6 — PM-F 19.1
Reagan	(see same, Sanillac Co.)			
Silverwood	(see same, Tuscola Co.)			
#Stanley Pit				GTW-C 300
#Stephens		8N	10E	MC-BL 6.0
#Wilsons Siding				GTW-P

LEELANAU COUNTRY

#Bahles Switch		28N	12W	M&NE-A 61
Bingham	32	29N	11W	M&NE-N 9.4
Bodus	20	29N	12W	M&NE-P 7.4
Carp Lake	(now Fouch)			
Cedar	(now Cedar City)			
Cedar City	5	28N	12W	M&NE-P 3.2
#Clovers				M&NE-A
#East Empire	28	28N	14W	E&SE 9
#Elton				M&NE-P 11
Empire	24	28N	15W	E&SE 11
Fouch	11	28N	12W	M&NE-A 62.5
Greilickville	(now Rennies)			
Hatchs	18	28N	11W	M&NE-A 64.6 — M&NE-N 5.5
Hatchs Crossing	(now Hatchs)			
Heimforth	6	28N	11W	M&NE-N 7.5
#High Top				E&SE
Isadore	32	29N	12W	M&NE-P 5.3

Keswick	20	29N	11W	M&NE-N 11.5
Lake Jct.	35	28N	14W	E&SE 4.6
Leelanau	9	29N	11W	M&NE-N 13.1
#Main Top		28N	14W	E&SE 7
#Manseau		30N	11W	M&NE-N 20
#North Bingham		29N	11W	M&NE-N
Northport	34	32N	11W	M&NE-N 29.0
Omena	26	31N	11W	M&NE-N 23.7
Provemont	26	30N	12W	M&NE-P 14.5
Rennies	33	28N	11W	M&NE-A 68.6
Ruthardts	36	28N	12W	M&NE-A 56.2
Schomberg	16	29N	12W	M&NE-P 8.7
Solon	21	28N	12W	M&NE-A 59.7 –
				M&NE-P O
Suttons Bay	28	30N	11W	M&NE-N 16.7
Traverse Resort	28	28N	11W	M&NE-A 67.6

LENAWEE COUNTY

#Abbott	4	6S	1E	CN 20
Addison	31	5S	1E	DTM 36.8
Addison Jct.	32	5S	1E	CN 18.8 – DTM
				35.9
Adrian	1	7S	3E	WAB 58.8
Adrian	2	7S	3E	DTI-A 46.6;
				LS-A 328.8;
				LS-2 7.1
Balch	(now Britton on WAB)			
Baldwins Crossing	34	7S	4E	LS-F 9.7
Bimo	26	8S	2E	DTI-A 32.0 –
				LS-F 22.0
Birdsall	24	7S	3E	DTI-A 50.0
Blissfield	30	7S	5E	LS-A 318.6
Blissfield Jct.	(now Grosvenor)			
Britton	3	6S	5E	DTM 9.4 – WAB
				46.7
Cadmus	11	7S	2E	LS-A 336.0
Cambridge	(now Onsted)			

Cement City	4	5S	1E	LS-Y 40.7
Cement City	5	5S	1E	CN 13.5
Chases	28	6S	4E	LS-J 3.3
Clay	5	7S	1E	CN 25.9
Clayton	18	7S	2E	LS-A 339.8
Clinton	5	5S	4E	LS-J 13.5
Corbus	14	7S	5E	CCS 53.5 — LS-M 22.2
#Cowham				CN
Deerfield	12	7S	5E	LS-M 20.5; CCS 51.8
Devils Lake	27	5S	1E	DTM 33.8
Dover	(now Cadmus)			
Ennis	(now Seneca)			
Fairfield	(now Jasper on LS-F; now Sand Creek on DTI-A)			
#Fruit Ridge	2	8S	2E	DTI-A; WAB
Grosvenor	25	7S	4E	CCS 59.0 — LS-A 321.2 — LS-F 7.6
Harrison	26	7S	4E	LS-F 8.1
Holloway	26	6S	4E	WAB 52.4
Hudson	18	7S	1E	CN 29.9; LS-A 346.3
Industrial Home	26	7S	3E	DTI-A 48.0
Jasper	11	8S	3E	LS-F 15.3
#Kelleys Pit				CN 14
Knights	(now Riga)			
Lake Rest	26	5S	1E	DTM 33.1
Leaf	2	8S	2E	DTI-A 36.0 — WAB 68.4
Lenawee	(now Leaf on DTI-A)			
Lenawee Jct.	9	7S	4E	LS-A 324.7 — LS-J 0 — LS-M 29.3
Lima Jct.	(now Leaf on WAB)			
Madison	23	7S	3E	DTI-A 42.2; WAB 61.7
Manitou Beach	4	6S	1E	CN 20.8
Marvin	(now Packard)			
Morenci	32	8S	2E	LS-F 25.7

Munson	5	8S	1E	WAB 79.5
North Fayette	(now Munson)			
North Morenci	19	8S	2E	WAB 73.2
Oak Beach	(now Manitou Beach)			
Ogden	5	8S	4E	LS-F 12.1
Onsted	28	5S	2E	DTM 28.3
Osborn	34	5S	4E	DTM 16.1 – LS-J 8.5 (Tecumseh on DTI-A)
Packard	14	8S	2E	DTI-A 35.1
Page	12	7S	3E	DTI-A 44.3 – WAB 59.8
Palmyra	15	7S	4E	LS-A 322.9
Palmyra Jct.	23	7S	4E	LS-A 322.1 – LS-2 0
Pentecost	30	5S	3E	DTM 24.9
#Prairie Siding				DTI-A 53
Raisin Center	33	6S	4E	LS-J 2.1 – WAB 54.8
Ridgeway	5	6S	5E	DTM 11.3
Riga	3	8S	5E	DTI-M 52.7; LS-A 316.4
Rollin	33	6S	1E	CN 24.9
Russell Siding	31	5S	4E	DTM 17.9
Sand Creek	31	7S	3E	DTI-A 38.8; WAB 65.6
Sand Lake	(now Pentecost)			
Seneca	10	8S	2E	WAB 70.2
Sisson	9	7S	5E	LS-M 22.7
South Adrian	(now Page)			
Stan	14	7S	3E	WAB 61.2
Stevens	31	5S	5E	DTM 10.2
Sutton	16	6S	4E	LS-J 5.0
Tecumseh	28	5S	4E	DTI-A 55.4; DTM 15.6; LS-J 9.0
Tecumseh Jct.	(now Osborn)			
Tecumseh Pit	4	6S	4E	DTI-A 54.1
Tipton	28	5S	3E	DTM 21.8
#Wapano				DTI-A

WB	1	7S	3E	LS-A 328.3 –
				WAB 59.0
Wellsville	12	7S	4E	LS-M 26.1
Weston	17	8S	3E	LS-F 19.1
Wood	29	5S	1E	CN 18.0
Wood	14	8S	5E	LS-A 313.4
Woodstock	(now Cement City on LS-Y)			
#Woodward				DTI-A 48

LIVINGSTON COUNTY

Anderson	17	1N	4E	GTW-A 78.2
Ann Pere	6	2N	5E	AA-A 72.0 –
				PM-D 52.9
Brighton	31	2N	6E	PM-D 45.2
Canwell	8	2N	5E	PM-D 51.0
Chilson	33	2N	5E	AA-A 66.9
#Clarence				PM-D
Cohoctah	11	4N	4E	AA-A 84.5
East Cohoctah	(now Cohoctah)			
Fleming	28	3N	4E	PM-D 57.6
Fowlerville	14	3N	3E	PM-D 62.5
Genoa	15	2N	5E	PM-D 48.5
Glade	36	3N	4E	AA-A 73.9
Green Oak	11	1N	6E	PM-D 40.0
Gregory	21	1N	3E	GTW-A 82.5
Hamburg	23	1N	5E	AA-A 59.4;
				GTW-A 67.4
Hamburg Jct.	(now Lakeland)			
Howell	35	3N	4E	AA-A 73.9;
				PM-D 54.2
Howell Jct.	(now Ann Pere)			
Island Lake	4	1N	6E	PM-D 42.0
Lakeland	22	1N	5E	AA-A 61.8 –
				GTW-A 69.9
Oak Grove	35	4N	4E	AA-A 80.2
Pettysville	16	1N	5E	AA-A 63.3
Pettysville	20	1N	5E	GTW-A 71.5

Pinckney	23	1N	4E	GTW-A 75.0
Rushton	26	1N	6E	GTW-A 61.7
Summit	(now Canwell)			
Whitmore Lake	32	1N	6E	GTW-A 64.6
Whitmore Lake	(also see same, Washtenaw Co.)			

MACOMB COUNTY

Armada	24	5N	13E	GTW-A 7.3
#Beebes	(now Main St.)			
Center Line	21	1N	12E	MC-B 15.8 (new station)
Center Line	33	1N	12E	MC-B 13.7 (old station)
Chesterfield	19	3N	14E	GTW-H 26.6
Depews Siding	20	3N	12E	MC-B 27.4
Double Track Switch	35	1N	12E	GTW-H 11.4
East Detroit	25	1N	12E	GTW-H 12.1
Fraser	5	1N	13E	GTW-H 16.5
Glenwood	(now Warren (old))			
Gravel Pit	5	3N	12E	GTW-A 22.1
#Henderson				GTW
Hoffs Siding	33	2N	12E	MC-B 17.8
Lenox	(now Richmond)			
Main Street	1	4N	14E	GTW-A 0.5
#Measel				GTW-H
Memphis	(see same, St. Clair Co.)			
Milton	8	3N	14E	GTW-H 28.9
Mound Road Yard	33	1N	12E	MC-B 12.5
Mount Clemens	11	2N	13E	GTW-H 22.0
New Baltimore	(now New Haven)			
New Haven	33	4N	14E	GTW-H 32.2
Packard Switch	20	3N	12E	MC-B 26.2
Rays Pit	19	3N	12E	MC-B 27.9
Richmond	1	4N	14E	GTW-A 0— GTW-H

				37.9 — MC-DM
				14.7
Ridgeway (Jct.)	(now Lenox)			
Romeo	2	4N	12E	GTW-A 14.2
Shelby	8	3N	12E	GTW-A 22.3
Spinning(s)	4	1N	12E	MC-B 18.0
Sterling	21	2N	12E	MC-B 20.1
Utica	4	2N	12E	MC-B 23.8
Utica Bend Switch	20	3N	12E	MC-B 26.1
Utica Plank	(now Fraser)			
Warren (old)	4	1N	12E	MC-B 17.1
Warren (new)	21	2N	12E	MC-B 20.7
Washington	33	4N	12E	GTW-A 19.9
Yates	(see same, Oakland Co.)			

MANISTEE COUNTY

Arcadia	10	24N	16W	A&BR 0
#Arendal				M&NE-A 8
B. & D. Camp No. 1	21	22N	16W	M&NE-A 6.1
B. & D. Camp No. 2	(now Lake View Farm)			
#Bark				PM-P
Bear Creek	30	23N	14W	M&NE-A 18.3 — M&NE-3 0
Brethren	16	22N	14W	PM-P 105.2
Brookfield	25	23N	16W	M&NE-O 11.9
Butwell	4	24N	15W	A&BR 8.3
Chief Lake	34	23N	15W	M&NE-A 15.1
Churchills	24	24N	13W	AA-C 262.6
Conger	33	23N	14W	M&NE-3 1.7 — PM-P 108.2
Copemish	18	24N	13W	AA-C 267.6 — A&BR 21.1 — M&NE-A 29.4
Corfu	(now High Bridge?)			
#Desmond				PM

Doubling	(now Dublin)			
Douglas	11	22N	16W	M&NE-A 8.3
Dublin	30	21N	13W	PM-P 94.9
East Lake	7	22N	17W	PM-M 23.7
Filer City	19	21N	17W	M&GR 5.2; M&NE-YM1 2.9
Florence	31	21N	13W	PM-P 94.4
Gilberts	(now Churchills)			
Glovers	(now Glovers Lake)			
Glovers Lake	13	24N	15W	A&BR 12.6
Goodrichs	(now Norwalk)			
#Gustavs				M&NE-R
Harlan	24	24N	13W	AA-C 261.6
#Harts Siding				AA-C
Henry	15	24N	14W	A&BR 17.7 – M&NE-1 2.8 – PM-P 117.0
High Bridge	28	22N	14W	PM-P 101.8
#Hilliards				PM-P
Humphrey	18	24N	14W	A&BR 13.8
Kaleva	21	23N	14W	M&NE-A 19.9 – PM-P 110.1
Lake View Farm	(now Douglas)			
Lemon Lake	1	23N	14W	M&NE-A 25.2
#Little				PM-P
Malcomb	8	24N	15W	A&BR 6.0
Manistee	1	21N	17W	M&NE-A 0 – M&NE-YM1 0; PM-M 26.5
Manistee	11	21N	17W	M&GR 0
Manistee	12	21N	17W	(old) M&NE-YM1 0.5
Manistee Crossing	(now Kaleva)			
#Maple Grove		23N	14W	M&NE-A 23
Marilla	21	23N	13W	M&NE-R 6.8
Marsh	28	21N	16W	M&GR 7.8 – PM-M 19.3
Nelsons Switch	8	24N	13W	M&NE-A 30.8
Newland	22	22N	16W	M&NE-A 6.3

Norwalk	6	22N	15W	M&NE-A 11.8
#Oakhill	24	21N	17W	M&GR 4
Onekama	26	23N	16W	M&NE-O 12.6
Onekama Jct.	1	22N	16W	M&NE-A 9.8 –
				M&NE-O 9.8
Polock Hill	29	22N	16W	M&NE-A 4.8
Pomona	16	24N	13W	AA-C 265.0
River Branch Jct.	22	23N	14W	M&NE-A 21.3 –
				M&NE-R 1.4
Saile	3	24N	15W	A&BR 10.5
#Sands Siding		23N	13W	M&NE-R 9
Sorenson	19	24N	15W	A&BR 4.0
Springdale	19	24N	14W	A&BR 15.0
#State Road		24N	16W	A&BR 1
State Road	34	24N	14W	PM-P 114.0
Stronach	20	21N	17W	PM-M 20.9
#Tuxbury				PM
#Wards		23N	14W	M&NE-A 24
Wealthy	15	22N	16W	M&NE-A 6.6
Wellston	13	21N	14W	PM-P 97.7

MASON COUNTY

Adamsville	(now Fern)			
Amber	15	18N	17W	PM-L 130.8
AuSable River	(now Sauble)			
Batchelor	29	19N	15W	PM-M 4.5
Black Creek	(now Custer)			
Branch	24	18N	15W	PM-L 116.8
Buttersville	22	18N	18W	M&O 0
Canfield Camp	(now Millerton)			
Cemetery	10	18N	18W	L&N 0.2
Conrad	18	16N	17W	PM-L 133.9
Custer	15	18N	16W	PM-L 125.8
Elmton	19	20N	15W	M&GR 16.0

Epworth Heights	4	18N	18W	L&N 1.0
Fern	28	17N	16W	M&O 14.0
Fountain	13	19N	16W	PM-M 8.1
Free Soil	27	20N	16W	PM-M 12.9
Gun Lake Switch	3	19N	16W	PM-M 10.4
Hamlin Lake	27	19N	18W	L&N 4.2
Harding	16	16N	17W	PM-L 131.7
Harleys	(now Riverton)			
Hoags	3	20N	16W	M&GR 11.9
Hoags Siding	(now Hoags)			
Howells	(now Elmton)			
Howells Siding	(now Howells)			
Lincoln Fields	3	18N	18W	L&N 1.5
Ludington	15	18N	18W	PM-L 137.2;
				L&N 0
Ludington Yard	13	18N	18W	PM-L 135.0
Manistee Jct.	(now Merritt)			
Merritt	(now Walhalla)			
Millerton	13	19N	15W	M&GR 22.3
North Hamlin	22	19N	18W	L&N 4.7
Riverton	10	17N	17W	M&O 8.4
Sauble	13	20N	16W	M&GR 14.6
Scottville	18	18N	16W	PM-L 128.7
Tallman	4	18N	15W	PM-M 2.9
#Tomlin				M&GR 14
#12 Mile Siding				PM-L
Walhalla	21	18N	15W	PM-L 120.6—
				PM-M 0
Weimer	27	19N	18W	L&N 3.9
Weldon Creek	13	18N	16W	PM-L 123.1
Wileys	18	17N	16W	M&O 10.7

MECOSTA COUNTY

Barryton	28	16N	7W	PM-JB 11.5
Bell Siding	(now Borland)			
#Bigelows				GR&I-N 288

Big Rapids	11	15N	10W	C&BR 0;GR&I-N 289.9; PM-J 93.6 – PM-R 51.2
Borland	7	13N	9W	GR&I-N 278.1
Byers	31	15N	9W	GR&I-N 285.9 – MEC 0
#Case				GR&I
Chatterton	8	15N	7W	PM-JB 7.8
Chippewa Lake	29	15N	8W	PM-JC 5.2
#Colfax	3	16N	9W	C&BR 6
Crapo	(see same, Osceola Co.)			
#Doyle		16N	10W	GR&I-4
#Hogan				PM-JB
Horsehead Lake	22	15N	8W	MEC 9.5
Hughes	25	15N	8W	PM-JB 3.2
Lower Big Rapids	(now Big Rapids on GR&I-N)			
Marshfield	15	15N	9W	PM-J 87.3
Martiny	33	15N	8W	PM-J 82.6
McKay	19	15N	7W	PM-JB 4.3
Mec	12	14N	8W	PM-J 78.2 – PM-JB 0.7
Mecosta	11	14N	8W	PM-J 78.9
Midland Gravel Co.	35	14N	7W	PM-J 71.1
Millbrook	2	13N	7W	PM-J 70.3
Miller(s)	11	14N	7W	PM-JW 2.3
Moiles	17	15N	7W	PM-JB 6.6
Morley	25	13N	10W	GR&I-N 274.4
Paris	15	16N	10W	GR&I-N 295.4
Rem	16	14N	7W	PM-J 74.6 – PM-JW 0.2
Remus	16	14N	7W	PM-J 74.4
Rodney	24	15N	9W	PM-J 85.2 – PM-JC 0 – MEC 6.2
Rust	24	14N	10W	GR&I-N 282.4
Stanwood	25	14N	10W	GR&I-N 281.0
Stimson Jct.	34	16N	10W	GR&I-N 292.2 – GR&I-4 0

#Stirling				PM
Upper Big Rapids	11	15N	10W	GR&I-N 290.4 —
				PM-J 93.3
Upper Paris	10	16N	10W	GR&I-N 296.6
Winchester		(see Chatterton)		

MIDLAND COUNTY

Alamando	3	15N	2W	PM-L 36.4
Anderson	7	14N	2E	PM-L 22.1
Averill(s)	34	15N	1E	PM-L 25.8
Bay City Road	21	14N	2E	PM-L 19.2
#Bluffs				PM-L
Coal Kilns	2	16N	2W	PM-LG 2.9
Coleman	30	16N	2W	PM-L 39.9 —
				PM-LG 0 —
				PM-LM 0
Dean	27	14N	2E	PM-L 18.2
Dibble	35	14N	2E	PM-L 16.6
Dorr		(now Alamando)		
Hubbard	12	15N	2E	M&H 11.0
Midland	21	14N	2E	PM-L 20.1;
				M&H 0; MC-L
				19.6
North Bradley	12	15N	2W	PM-L 34.2
Sanford	24	15N	1W	PM-L 28.3
Smiths Crossing	1	13N	2E	PM-L 15.4

MISSAUKEE COUNTY

Ardis	2	22N	6W	GR&I-K 22.5
Ardis Jct.	5	22N	6W	GR&I-K 19.1 —
				GR&I-K5 19.1
#Becketts Crossing		22N	8W	C&NE 8
#Blodgett	16	22N	8W	C&NE 6

#Brown				AA-B
Butcher	(see same, Kalkaska Co.)			
#Cranmer		22N	8W	GR&I-K 14
Cummer	1	22N	6W	GR&I-K 24.0
#Dudley				GR&I
Falmouth	6	21N	6W	GR&I-K4 19.9
Freys	(now Veneer Jct.?)			
#Gerrish	9	22N	8W	C&NE 9
#Hecker		22N	7W	GR&I-K4 16
#Herrick				GR&I
#Herrick Jct.				GR&I
#Hoop				PM-K
Jennings	5	22N	8W	GR&I-K2 3.4
#Kokomo	2	22N	8W	C&NE 12
#Koopman		22N	7W	GR&I-K4 17
Lake City	6	22N	7W	GR&I-K3 11.6;
				C&NE 14
Lucas	16	21N	8W	AA-B 220.4
McBain	25	21N	8W	AA-B 216.4
Merritt	5	22N	5W	GR&I-K 25.6
Missaukee(City)	30	23N	6W	GR&I-K5 22.4
Missaukee Park	12	22N	8W	GR&I-K 8.8
Mitchell	(now Jennings)			
#Mitchells Crossing		22N	8W	C&NE 10
Mynnings	8	22N	6W	GR&I-K 18.7
#Reedsburg	25	23N	5W	GR&I-K 30
Round Lake Jct.	18	22N	8W	GR&I-K 4.2 —
				GR7I-K2 0
Sandstown	7	22N	7W	GR&I-K 10.6 —
				GR&I-K3 10.6
#Section 10				GR&I
Stratford	6	24N	5W	PM-K 32.8
Veneer Jct.	14	22N	7W	GR&I-L 15.4 —
				GR&I-K4 15.4
Wagner	16	22N	8W	GR&I-L 6.1
Wagner Lake	(now Wagner)			
#Wardville		23N	5W	GR&I-K 28
Widdicomb	(now Veneer Jct.)			

MONROE COUNTY

Azalia	25	5S	6E	AA-A 26.8
#Azalia				WAB
Briar Hill	10	5S	9E	DTM-M 22.0
Bryar Hill	(on CCS, now Briar Hill on DTM-M)			
#Burns Siding				DTI-?
Carleton	17	5S	9E	DTI-M 24.2 − PRR 116.3 − PM-T 105.2 − (CCS 28.7)
Chapman	20	5S	10E	DTSL 28.5
Clarkesville	(now Rea)			
Cone	19	5S	6E	WAB 42.7
Cousino	35	7S	8E	DTSL 10.9
Diann	30	6S	7E	AA-A 20.5 − DTI-M 40.1
Dundee	18	6S	7E	AA-A 22.8 − DTI-T2 0 − DTM 0
Dundee	19	6s	7E	CCS 43.0
Durban	(see Raisinville)			
Erie	8	8S	8E	PM-T 125.4
Exeter	(now Scofield)			
Federman	5	7S	7E	AA-A 18.6 − LS-M 12.4
#Forks Switch				LS-?
Fix Bros. Siding		6S	9E	MC-T 32.7
France	21	7S	7E	AA-A 14.8
Frenchtown		6S	9E	MC-T 34.1
Grafton	29	5S	9E	PM-T 106.8
Greenings		7S	9E	DTSL 16.2
Hawthorn	26	8S	7E	AA-A 8.3
Ida	3	7S	7E	LS-M 9.9
Lambertville	30	8S	7E	DTI-T 9.5
LaSalle		7S	8E	DTSL 12.7; LS-D 45.4; MC-T 40.1

Lulu	8	7S	7E	AA-A 16.7
#Macon	6	6S	7E	AA-A 24
Maybee	31	5S	8E	DTI-M 31.9
#Meyers				LS-D; MC-T
Milan	2	5S	6E	AA-A 30.2—
				WAB 37.3
				(Milan Jct. on
				AA-A)
Milan	(also see same, Washtenaw Co.)			
Milan Jct.	(Milan on AA-A)			
Monroe		7S	9E	DTSL 17.4;
				LS-D 40.5—
				LS-M 0; MC-T
				35.4
Monroe		7S	9E	PM-T 115.1
Newport	1	6S	9E	DTSL 25.1;
				LS-D 33.1;
				MC-T 27.8
North Raisinville	(now Raisinville)			
Ottawa Lake	19	8S	6E	LS-A 309.1
Ottawa Yard		8S	8E	PM-T 127
Petersburg	4	7S	6E	LS-M 17.0
Petersburg Jct.	10	7S	6E	DTI-M 44.4—
				DTI-T 0—
				DTI-T2 6.9
#Raisin				PM-T
Raisinville	11	6S	7E	DTI-M 34.8
Rea	16	6S	6E	DTM 3.8
Reeves	(now Azalia)			
St. Anthonys	12	8S	6E	DTI-T 6.3
Samaria	10	8S	7E	AA-A 11.5
Scofield	28	5S	8E	DTI-M 29.6
#Seola				AA-A 13
#Shore Line Quarry				DTSL 19
Southport	14	6S	9E	DTSL 23.3
South Rockwood	16	5S	10E	DTSL 30.0;
				MC-T 22.8
Steiner	8	6S	9E	PM-T 110.0
Stony Creek		6S	9E	DTSL 22.1;
				LS-D 37.5;
				MC-T 30.7

Strasburg		7S	8E	LS-M 6.2
#Strongs				DTSL
Strongs Siding	16	5S	10E	LS-D 36.1
Swan Creek	(now Newport)
Temperance	14	8S	7E	AA-A 9.3
#Todds				AA-A
Toledo Jct.		6S	9E	PM-T 111.7 – PM-TZ 0
Vienna	16	8S	8E	DTSL 8.0; LS-D 50.3; MC-T 45.0
Vienna Jct.	32	8S	8E	LS-D 52.9 – MC-T 48.0
Warner		6S	9E	DTSL 19.4; LS-D 39.2; MC-T 34.1; PM-TZ 2
Washington Street		7S	9E	LS-M 0.8
Weeks	(now Samaria)
#Willits				AA-A
Winchester	15	7S	8E	PM-T 119.5

MONTCALM COUNTY

Amble	15	12N	9W	PM-V 77.8
#Belvidere		12N	7W	PM-V
#Blanchards		12N	6W	PM-
#Bushnell				GTW-M
Butternut	8	9N	5W	GTW-M 22.4
Carson City	12	9N	5W	GTW-M 18.9
Cedar Lake	25	12N	6W	PM-V 56.5
Colby	13	10N	7W	PM-J 47.9
#Colwell		11N	9W	PM-I
Conger	12	12N	10W	GR&I-N 271.6
Coral	8	11N	9W	PM-I 60.0
#Dickinsons				GR&I-N 267

Edmore	21	12N	6W	PM-G 59.5 — PM-J 58.7 — PM-V 59.5
#Erwin				GR&I-N
Eureka Place	12	9N	8W	GTW-M 37.9
Fenwick	25	9N	7W	PM-J 39.9
Fish Creek Branch	13	10N	7W	PM-J 47.3
Gowen	18	10N	8W	PM-I 50.8
Graffville				PM-
Greenville	9	9N	8W	GTW-M 40.4
Greenville	15	9N	8W	PM-G 81.4
Hemmingway				PM-J2 1.4
Hiram	15	11N	10W	GR&I-N 264.2
Howard City	26	12N	10W	GR&I-N 268.0 — PM-I 64.3 — PM-V 82.5
#Jackson				GR&I-N
Kaywood	(now Gowen)			
Lakeview	16	12N	8W	PM-V 71.7
Maple Hill	2	11N	10W	GR&I-N 265.9
#Maple Valley	15	11N	9W	PM-I 58
Martha	35	10N	8W	PM-G 77.8
McBrides	9	11N	6W	PM-G 63.5
Millers	9	9N	7W	GTW-M 35.2
Moeller	30	10N	7W	PM-G 75.5
North Greenville	10	9N	8W	PM-G 80.7 — PM-I 45.9 (GTW-M 40.4)
Osin	24	12N	7W	PM-V 62.3
Pierson	27	11N	10W	GR&I-N 262.3
Reynolds	23	12N	10W	GR&I-N 269.0
#Shanty Plains	36	9N	7W	PM-J
Sheridan	36	10N	7W	GTW-M 30.7; PM-J 44.4
Sidney	22	10N	7W	PM-G 72.6
Six Lakes	16	12N	7W	PM-V 65.3
Slaghts Track	20	11N	6W	PM-G 65.7 — PM-J2 0
Stanton	31	11N	6W	PM-G 67.9 — PM-J 50.3
#Summerville				PM-V

#Town Line	18?	12N	7W	PM-V 67
Trufant(s)	26	11N	9W	PM-I 55.9
Vestaburg	28	12N	5W	PM-V 53.1
Vickeryville	12	9N	6W	GTW-M 24.9
#Virgil				GTW-M
#Wagers		10N	7W	PM-J
Wood Lake	(now Hiram)			
#Woods Mill				PM-G
Wyman	4	12N	6W	PM-J 61.9

MONTMORENCY COUNTY

#Anderson				BC-A 50
Atlanta	12	30N	2E	BC-A 52.9
Bigelow	22	30N	1E	MC-MT5 6.8
Big Rock	8	30N	2E	MC-MT5B2 1.1
#Briley				BC-A
Cahoons	24	30N	4E	BC-A 65.9
Camp 21	27	31N	1E	BC-A 43.5
#Camp 25		31N	2E	BC-A 47
Camp 30	9	31N	1E	BC-A 41.9 + 4.0
Camp 29	4	29N	3E	BC-A 58.1 + 6.1
Connor(s)	27	30N	4E	BC-A 64.5
Conners Camp 2	19	31N	2E	D&M-V 28.0
Dana	31	29N	1E	MC-MT 24.3
Davidson Wye Branch Jct.				
	14	30N	1E	MC-MT5 10.3 − MC-MT5B 0
Dobbins	13	30N	3E	BC-A 58.7
Donnelly Branch Jct.	15	30N	1E	MC-MT5 8.5 − MC-MT5A 0
Fitzpatrick	25	31N	1E	BC-A 45.7
Francis	8	30N	2E	MC-MT5B2 1.6
#Galt		31N	1E	BC-A 41
Gibbs	30	31N	1E	BC-A 40.2
Green	27	31N	2E	BC-A 49.5
Hemlock	13	30N	3E	BC-A 58.1

Hillman	23	31N	4E	D&M-H 24.6
Hoey	(now Hemlock)			
Jackson Lake	10	31N	2E	D&M-V 24.1
#Kaybee		31N	1E	BC-A 43
Kevan	19	30N	2E	MC-MT5B 2.3 –
				MC-MT5B1 0
Kingsland	8	30N	3E	BC-A 55.5
#Larson		30N	2E	BC-A 51
Lewiston	27	29N	1E	MC-MT 27.7;
				ASNW-2 30.0
#Lutes		30N	4E	BC-A 61
McPhee	14	32N	2E	D&M-V 20.5
#Meaford		31N	1E	BC-A 46
Rust	16	30N	4E	BC-A 62.7
Stevens	26	31N	1E	BC-A 44.0
Stoddards	18	30N	4E	BC-A
Valentine Lake	(probably same as Jackson Lake)			
Vienna Jct.	28	29N	1E	MC-MT 27.0 –
				MC-MT5 0 –
				MC-MT6 0
Watson	9	30N	3E	BC-A 56.4
Wilson	17	30N	2E	MC-MT5B 4.6 –
				MC-MT5B2 0

MUSKEGON COUNTY

Bailey	11	10N	13W	PM-P 25.7
Berry	32	11N	16W	PM-A 61.6 –
				PM-R 0
Big Rapids Jct.	(now Berry)			
Black Lake	(now Lake Harbor)			
#Brickton				PM
Brunswick	13	12N	15W	PM-R 14.7
Califf	19	11N	16W	PM-A 65.0
Casnovia	24	10N	13W	PM-P 22.5
Cloverville	(now Eggleston)			
County Line	(now Bailey)			
County Line	(now Brunswick)			

Dalton	30	11N	16W	PM-A 63.2
Eggleston	6	9N	15W	GR&I-M 32.7
Emens	23	12N	15W	PM-R 13.4
Evenwood	32	12N	15W	PM-R 10.9
Fruitport	36	9N	16W	PM-AO 25.2
Fruitport Jct.	(now Kanitz)			
Fruitport Jct.	(now Pickand)			
Halls	25	11N	15W	GTW-M 84.2
#Hartman				GR&I-M
Henry Street	1	9N	17W	GTW-YM 3.0
Hines Crossing	26	11N	14W	GTW-M 79.3
Holton	23	12N	15W	PM-R 12.3
#Hume Avenue				GTW-YM
Jefferson Street	30	10N	16W	GTW-M 94.7
Kanitz	33	10N	16W	GR&I-M 36.0 –
				PM-AO 32.6
#Lake				PM-A
Lake Harbor	8	9N	16W	PM-A 52.8
#Lake Side				PM-A 59
Lakewood	12	11N	17W	PM-A 66.3
Linderman	31	12N	15W	PM-R 9.9
Mona Lake	5	9N	16W	PM-A 53.5
Montague	21	12N	17W	PM-A 72.2
Moon	14	10N	13W	PM-P 24.5
Moorland	29	11N	14W	GTW-M 81.6
Muskegon	29	10N	16W	GTW-M 94.6 (at Peck Street)
Muskegon	30	10N	16W	GTW-M 96.0 (old sta.); GR&I-M 39.5; PM-A 56.5
Muskegon Heights	5	9N	16W	GR&I-M 38.0; PM-A 54.0
Nielson	2	11N	17W	PM-A 68.6
North Yard	20	10N	16W	PM-A 57.8 – PM-AO 35.6
Norton	10	9N	16W	PM-AO 30.6
Opdyke	9	9N	15W	GR&I-M 30.5
Pickand	25	9N	16W	PM-AO 26.4 – PM-AZ 46.6 + 3.8

Port Sherman	33	10N	17W	PM-YM 4.0
Ravenna	11	9N	14W	GR&I-M 22.4
Sand Pit	7	10N	16W	PM-A 59.3
Shaw	33	10N	16W	GR&I-M 36.5 — GTW-YM 0.4
Simpson	28	11N	16W	GTW-M 93.4 — GTW-YM 0 — PM-AO 33.4
Slocum	31	11N	13W	GTW-M 77.4
Slocums Grove	(now Slocum)			
Spires	22	11N	16W	PM-R 3.0
Stone Siding	21	9N	16W	PM-A 50.2
Sullivan	11	9N	15W	GR&I-M 27.8
Sweet	(now Lakewood)			
#Third Street				
Toledo Crossing	(now Simpson)			
Trent	(now Moon)			
Twin Lake	12	11N	16W	PM-R 6.4
#Voss				PM-P
Western Avenue	19	10N	16W	GR&I-M 39.3 — PM-YM 0.1; PM-A 56.2
Whitehall	28	12N	17W	PM-A 71.7 (old at 71.4)
#White Lake Jct.		12N	17W	PM-A

NEWAYGO COUNTY

Alderson	3	16N	13W	PM-P 67.5
Alleyton	6	13N	12W	PM-R 29.8
Ashland	36	11N	13W	PM-P 27.7
Bailies	(now Reeman)			
Bakers	14	15N	11W	PM-R 45.5
Bitely	27	16N	13W	PM-P 63.3
Brohman	24	15N	13W	PM-P 57.8
Brookings (Lake)	10	15N	13W	PM-P 60.5
Brooks	12	11N	13W	PM-P 31.4
Brunswick	(see same, Muskegon Co.)			

Camp 8	11	15N	13W	PM-P 60.0
Cardinal Jct.	36	15N	12W	PM-R 38.5
Croton	(now Erwin)			
Diamond Loch	(now Ramona)			
#Dickinson		11N	13W	PM-P
Drew	4	12N	12W	PM-P 40.9
Eastman	22	14N	12W	PM-R 33.7
Erwin	9	12N	12W	PM-P 39.5 –
				PM-P2
Field (Crossing)	11	14N	12W	PM-R 36.0
Fremont	35	13N	14W	PM-R 19.6
Fremont Center	(now Fremont)			
Fremont Lake	3	12N	14W	PM-R 18.2
Gilbert	20	13N	12W	PM-P 43.9
Grant	24	11N	13W	PM-P 29.8
Harroun	15	14N	12W	PM-R 35.2
Hayes Siding	36	15N	12W	PM-R 38.7
Hess Lake	36	12N	13W	PM-P 33.4
Hungerford	15	15N	11W	PM-R 44.2
Jackson Crossing	24	15N	13W	PM-P 57.2
#Jewell				PM-?
Kinney	2	14N	12W	PM-R 37.0
Kopje	14	15N	13W	PM-P 58.6
Lilley	15	16N	13W	PM-P 65.1
Lilley Jct.	15	16N	13W	PM-P 65.5 –
				PM-P4 0
Lumberton	20	15N	11W	PM-R 42.2
Marl Lake	6	12N	12W	PM-P2 2.0
McCool	(now Erwin)			
#McLanes				PM-R
Merritts	26	16N	11W	GR&I-4 5.8
Monroeville	(now Woodville)			
Morgan	(now White Cloud)			
Narrow Gauge Crossing	12	14N	13W	PM-P 53.4
Nassons	10	16N	13W	PM-P 66.6
Newaygo	24	12N	13W	PM-P 36.2
#Newaygo Lakes				PM-?
Norths Siding	1	14N	13W	PM-P 53.9
Norwich	(now Hungerford)			
Otia	(now Brohman)			

Park	35	16N	11W	GR&I-4 6.3?
Park City	2	14N	13W	PM-P 54.3
Pattersons	29	14N	12W	PM-P 49.6
Pickerel Creek	(now Alderson)			
#Progress Dam		14N	12W	PM-R 33
Ramona	13	14N	13W	PM-P 52.2
Ray	29	13N	12W	PM-P 42.4
Reeman	8	12N	14W	PM-R 16.4
Reeves	36	15N	13W	PM-P 55.2
Ryerson	15	13N	13W	PM-R 27.0
Simmonds	25	12N	13W	PM-P 35.3
Sisson	13	16N	13W	PM-P4 2.4
Swains Crossing	2	14N	12W	PM-R 37.9
Traverse Roads	(now Monroeville)			
Trumbulls Siding	14	15N	11W	PM-R 45.9
Uhl	(now Gilbert)			
#Vincent				GR&I-4 8.9
#West Troy				PM-P3 3.9
West Troy Jct.	3	15N	13W	PM-P 61.7 –
				PM-P3 0
White Cloud	5	13N	12W	PM-P 47.2 –
				PM-R 31.0
White River Club	22	14N	12W	PM-R 33.9
Wilcox	2	14N	12W	PM-R 37.4
Woodville	30	15N	11W	PM-R 39.7
Wooster	16	13N	13W	PM-R 25.0
Worcester (Hill)	(now Wooster)			

OAKLAND COUNTY

Amy	(now Auburn)			
Andersonville	27	4N	8E	GTW-D 38.5
Auburn	(now Auburn Heights)			
Auburn Heights	36	3N	10E	GTW-A 31.7
Baileys Wye	35	5N	10E	MC-B 41.8
Bay City Crossing	(now Rochester Jct. on GTW-A)			
Belford	(now Newark)			

Belt Line	3	2N	10E	GTW-D 22.6 —
				GTW-YP 8.9
Birmingham	30	2N	11E	GTW-D 17.8
Birmingham	36	2N	10E	GTW-DO 18.5
Bloomfield Hills	14	2N	10E	GTW-D 21.2
#Boomers				GTW-
Charing Cross	24	2N	10E	GTW-D 19.9
Clarkston	31	4N	9E	GTW-D 35.2
Clyde	10	3N	7E	PM-T 58.2
Cole	(now Randall Beach)			
#Colerain				GTW-D
Davisburg	17	4N	8E	GTW-D 41.5
Drayton Plains	10	3N	9E	GTW-D 31.1
Eames	28	4N	10E	GTW-P 6.2
Ferndale	27	1N	11E	GTW-D 10.9
Goodison(s)	28	4N	11E	MC-B 34.9
Highland	27	3N	7E	PM-T 61.3
Holly	34	5N	7E	GTW-D 46.5 —
				PM-T 50.1
Lake Orion	2	4N	10E	MC-B 40.3
Leonard	11	5N	11E	GTW-P 21.3
Lincoln	5	2N	8E	PM-T 70.6
M.A.L. Crossing	32	3N	10E	GTW-A 35.3 —
				GTW-D 25.2
M.A.L. Jct.	34	3N	10E	GTW-A 33.6 —
				GTW-YP 7.5
Milford	11	2N	7E	PM-T 65.1
Newark	3	5N	7E	PM-T 45.0
New Hudson	3	1N	7E	GTW-A 55.1
Northville	(see same, Wayne Co.)			
Novi	22	1N	8E	PM-T 74.5
Oakwood				
Boulevard	32	2N	11E	GTW-D 14.3
Orchard Lake	15	2N	9E	GTW-A 40.0
Orion	(now Lake Orion)			
Oxford	22	5N	10E	GTW-P 13.9 —
				MC-B 43.6
Pleasant Ridge	21	1N	11E	GTW-D 12.0
P.O.N. Jct.	17	3N	10E	GTW-P 2.6 —
				GTW-YP 2.5

Pontiac Yard	29	3N	10E	GTW-D 26.9
Randall Beach	9	4N	10E	GTW-P 9.2
Rochester	11	3N	11E	MC-B 30.9
Rochester	15	3N	11E	GTW-A 26.3
Rochester Jct.	14	3N	11E	GTW-A 25.2—
				MC-B 30.0
Rose Center	22	4N	7E	PM-T 54.8
Royal Oak	5	1N	11E	GTW-D 13.2—
				GTW-DO 13.2
Rudds	12	4N	10E	MC-B 38.7
Shoup	21	5N	11E	GTW-P 18.3
Slaters Pit	35	2N	7E	GTW-A 53.8
South Grand Blanc	(now Belford)			
South Lyon	20	1N	7E	AA-S 60.4;
				GTW-A 59.0—
				PM-D 36.1
Springfield	(now Andersonville)			
Sylvan Lake	1	2N	9E	GTW-A 37.5
Thomas	4	5N	10E	MC-B 47.5
Urbanrest	(now Ferndale)			
Walled Lake	35	2N	8E	GTW-A 47.6
Waterford	4	3N	9E	GTW-D 33.3
West Pontiac	11	3N	9E	GTW-D 30.3
Windiate	5	3N	9E	GTW-D 34.3
Wixom	31	2N	8E	GTW-A 50.7—
				PM-T 70.4
Yates	13	3N	11E	MC-B 28.6

OCEANA COUNTY

Barnett	(now Shelby)			
Bender	6	14N	17W	PM-A 88.1
Blackmarrs	16	13N	17W	PM-A 79.8
Bunker Lake	16	13N	17W	PM-A 79.5
Charcoal Kilns	24	15N	18W	PM-AH 92.2
Cockell	20	15N	17W	PM-AH 93.9
Collins	25	15N	18W	PM-A 90.7
Cooks Switch	4	13N	17W	PM-A 81.5

Crossmans	7	14N	17W	PM-A 87.7
East Golden	36	15N	17W	PM-A 89.3
Fisher Camp	(now Lake)			
Ford	28	14N	17W	PM-A 83.3
Gale	6	15N	15W	M&O 31.3
Goodrich	29	16N	15W	M&O 29.2
Greenwood	(now Rothbury)			
Hart	14	15N	18W	PM-A 93
Hart	17	15N	17W	PM-AH 95.2
#Lake	30?	16N	15W	M&O 22
#Maple	30?	14N	15W	M&O 35.5
Mears	23	15N	18W	PM-A 91.8 –
				PM-AH 91.8
New Era	33	14N	17W	PM-A 82.1
Old South Branch	(now Peachville)			
Peachville	13	16N	16W	M&O 19.6
Pentwater	14	16N	18W	PM-A 99.0
Rankin	8	14N	17W	PM-A 87.2
Rothbury	21	13N	17W	PM-A 78.4
Shelby	17	14N	17W	PM-A 86.2
#Slaght				PM-A
South Branch Camp	(now Old South Branch)			
Stetson	(now Walkerville)			
Walkerville	5	15N	15W	M&O 24.5
#Water Tank				M&O

OGEMAW COUNTY

Ambroses	2	23N	1E	MC-MS 7.1
Beaver Lake	29	23N	1E	MC-M 60.9 –
				MC-MS 0
Bohnet	34	23N	1E	MC-M 58.4
Bush Lake	26	21N	3E	D&M-A2 2.6
Chicago Siding	18	21N	2E	MC-ME 2.6
Cranage	10	22N	1E	MC-M 56.5
Damon	5	24N	2E	ASNW-a 22.1
Edwards Lake	22	21N	1E	MC-ME 6.4
Georges Lake	19	21N	2E	MC-ME 3.3

Georgetown	(now Greenwood)			
Goodar	3	24N	4E	D&M-B2A 22.7
Greenwood	35	21N	2E	MC-M 44.7
Hauptman	32	22N	2E	MC-M 50.3 – MC-M7 0
Ice Tracks	18	21N	1E	MC-ME 2.9
Lane	(now Lupton)			
Loranger	16	21N	2E	MC-M 47.8 – MC-ME 0
Lupton	36	24N	3E	D&M-B 27.0
Maltbys	21	24N	4E	D&M-B 22.2
#Millers Mill				D&M-B
Ogemaw	15	22N	1E	MC-M 56.1
Ogemaw Springs	(now Ogemaw)			
Piper	12	23N	1E	MC-MS 6.1
Prescott	27	21N	3E	D&M-A 11.8
Rose City	31	24N	3E	D&M-B 31.8
#Rowena				MC-M
Sages Lake	2	23N	1E	MC-MS 8.0
#Slayton				MC-MS
Smith Jct.	24	24N	4E	D&M-B 19.2 – D&M-B2 19.2
South Branch	24	24N	4E	D&M-B2 19.7 – D&M-B2A 19.7
Summit	35	21N	2E	MC-M 43.9
Welch	(now Loranger)			
West Branch	30	22N	2E	MC-M 52.7
#Woodrow		24N	2E	ASNW-2
Wrights	(now Loranger)			

OSCEOLA COUNTY

#Allens				GR&I-N 322
Anderson	33	20N	9W	M&GR 57.8 – M&GR-3 57.8
Ashton	4	18N	10W	GR&I-N 309.6
Brazil	16	17N	7W	PM-L 82.6

#Carlsons				GR&I
Chippewa	11	17N	7W	PM-L 68.2
#Compton				GR&I
Crapo	34	17N	10W	GR&I-N 298.2
Crocker	25	20N	8W	M&GR 66.9
Dennis	29	20N	8W	M&GR 63.9
Dewings	34	19N	10W	GR&I-N 311.6
Dighton	28	20N	9W	M&GR 60.9 –
				M&GR-2 60.9
Duroy	6	20N	7W	AA-B 212.9
Evart	3	17N	8W	PM-L 75.9
#Gorham				AA-B
#Hartwick				M&GR-2 69
#Hayes				GR&I
#Headland				PM-?
Hersey	24	17N	10W	PM-L 85.7
Hewitts	(now Hewitts Lake)			
Hewitts Lake	33	20N	10W	M&GR 52.0
#Hoods				GR&I-N 323
#Jacksons				GR&I
Keegan	4	17N	10W	GR&I-N 303.9
#Langworthy		19N	10W	M&L
#Larsen		19N	10W	M&GR 50
LeRoy	13	19N	10W	GR&I-N 315.2
#Leyburns				GR&I-N 304
#Logwood				GR&I
#Lyons				GR&I
Manley	4	17N	7W	PM-L 70.3
Marion	27	20N	7W	AA-B 208.6;
				M&GR 71.7
Milton Jct.	(now Orono)			
Mitchells	21	17N	10W	GR&I-N 301.0
#Newbergers				GR&I-N 319
Noble	11	17N	9W	PM-L 80.9
Orient	(now Sears)			
Orono	21	18N	10W	GR&I-N 307.6 –
				GR&I-3 0
Osceola Jct.	6	20N	9W	GR&I-N 323.4 –
				GR&I-2 0
Park Lake	7	20N	7W	AA-B 212.7
#Potters				GR&I-N 299

Reed City	9	17N	10W	GR&I-N 302.7 — PM-L 89.2
#Richs				GR&I-N 322
Riverbank	6	19N	10W	M&GR 48.7
#Rolfe		20N	9W	M&GR 59
Rose Lake		19N	9W	M&GR-3 59.9
#Rosenbergs				GR&I
Sears	5	17N	7W	PM-L 71.9
#South Allens				GR&I-N 318
Sutliffs	4	20N	10W	GR&I-2 3.9
Tustin	25	20N	10W	GR&I-N 319.8 — M&GR 54.6
Wings Jct.	12	17N	9W	PM-L 79.8

OSCODA COUNTY

Big Creek	8	25N	1E	ASNW-1 30.5
#Church		25N	3E	ASNW-1 14
Comins	22	28N	3E	ASNW-A 50.6 — ASNW-3 0 — ASNW-4 0
Dew	1	27N	3E	ASNW-A 47.0
Fairview	11	27N	3E	ASNW-2 13.5
#Fitzpatrick				ASNW-4A
#Flat Lake				ASNW
Hardy	1	28N	3E	ASNW-4 4.2
#Hicks		25N	1E	ASNW-1 26
Hill(s)	8	28N	3E	ASNW-3 3.9
Imlay	7	25N	4E	ASNW-1 7.9
#Kane				ASNW-2
#LeLone		28N	3E	ASNW-4A
Luzerne	26	26N	1E	ASNW-1 35.6
#Lymburn				ASNW-2
#Maple Grove				ASNW-2
Marsh	21	28N	3E	ASNW-3 1.6
McCollum(s)	11	27N	4E	ASNW-A 42.8
McKinley	15	26N	4E	ASNW-AO 37.5 — ASNW-1

				0 — ASNW-2B
				3.3 + 2.7
Millen	8	27N	4E	ASNW-A 45.8 —
				ASNW-2
				43.7 + 0.7
Potts		(now McKinley)		
#Red Oak		28N	2E	ASNW-2
#Snyder		27N	4E	ASNW-2
#Tong				ASNW-2
Town Line	6	27N	3E	ASNW-2 18.0
Twin Lake Jct.	13	26N	4E	ASNW-AO
				35.8 — ASNW-2
				1.7
#Wiggins		28N	3E	ASNW-A 49

OTSEGO COUNTY

#Anderson				BC-A
Arbutus Beach	4	29N	3W	MC-M 113.5
Bagley		(now Sallings)		
Bank 6	5	32N	1W	MC-MP 7.6
Barn Branch		(now Nizer)		
#Bear Lake	1	29N	1W	ASNW-2;
				MC-MT6 5.5
#Beehan				BC-A 38
Bradford (Lake)		(now Wrights Lake)		
#Brothers				GR&I
Buells	15	32N	3W	MC-M 129.0 —
				MC-M6 0
Cameron	36	31N	4W	BC-A 20.3
#Camp 21				BC
#Camp 22				BC
C.B. Jct.	10	29N	1W	MC-MT2 7.9
Chamberlin	29	30N	1W	MC-MB 12.5 —
				MC-MT2 11.4
#Corbin				BC
Cornwells	3	32N	1W	MC-MP 14.2
Crowley	24	30N	2W	MC-MB 9.8

Elmira	19	31N	4W	GR&I-N 400.1
#Fairbanks				MC
Fayette	28	29N	4W	D&C 8.2
Gaylord	4	30N	3W	BC-A 23.2; MC-M 119.2
Hadley	(now Bagley)			
Hallock	15	31N	4W	BC-A 16.9
Hamilton	(now Cameron)			
Harold	3	31N	3W	MC-M 124.8
Huntworth	19	31N	4W	GR&I-N 400.7
Jennings Branch Jct.	26	31N	2W	MC-MB3 5.6— MC-MB3A 0
Johannesburg	20	30N	1W	MC-MB 13.8— MC-MT2 12.7
Johannesburg Jct.	22	30N	2W	MC-MB 7.2— MC-MB2 0
Johnston	27	31N	1W	BC-A 36.9
Leonard Branch Jct.	21	31N	2W	MC-MB3A 2.5— MC-MB3A1 0
Logan	(now Rogers)			
Manistee River	30	29N	4W	D&C 14.9
Marion	15	31N	4W	BC-A 15.9
#Marl		31N	1W	BC-A 36
Martindale	32	31N	1W	MC-MB3 9.2
McGraw Jct.	28	30N	2W	MC-MB 5.8— MC-MB3 0
Mosher	17	31N	4W	BC-A 14.8
#Nizer		31N	1W	BC-A 39
New East Branch	32	29N	4W	D&C 13.6
North Elmira	18	31N	4W	BC-A 13.2— GR&I-N 401.5
Nugent	29	30N	1W	MC-MB 12.7
Oak Grove	28	30N	3W	MC-M 115.1
Otsego	(now Otsego Lake)			
Otsego Lake	8	29N	3W	MC-M 111.8
Pratts	16	29N	1W	MC-MT2 6.6
#Rogers				MC-M 126
Sallings	28	30N	3W	MC-M 115.4— MC-MB 0
Shultz	19	31N	2W	BC-A 33.3
Sparr	32	31N	2W	BC-A 28.8

Trombley	30	30N	2W	MC-MB 4.2
#Tyrus				MC
Vanderbilt	22	32N	3W	MC-M 127.7
Wah Wah Soo	28	30N	3W	MC-M 114.7
Waters	29	29N	3W	MC-M 109.0
Water Tank	31	29N	4W	D&C 14.1
Wrights Lake	(now Waters)			
Yuill	(now Harold)			
Yuill	24	31N	4W	BC-A 18.1

OTTAWA COUNTY

Agnew	26	7N	16W	PM-A 36.5
Bakers	21	8N	16W	PM-A 43.4
Beech Tree	9	7N	16W	PM-A 39.6
Berlin	(now Marne)			
Blendon	21	6N	15W	PM-AO 6.6
Bottje	33	8N	16W	PM-A 41.5
#Bushkill				PM-A
Cemetery Crossing	14	8N	16W	GTW-D 184.8
Conklin	32	9N	13W	GR&I-M 17.2
Coopersville	23	8N	14W	GTW-D 172.6
Cronje	21	5N	15W	PM-A 24.5 –
				PM-AM 0
Dennison(s)	17	8N	14W	GTW-D 175.5
Farmers	12	6N	16W	PM-A 32.6
Ferrysburg	16	8N	16W	PM-A 44.8 –
				GTW-D 187.1
#Fort Howard				PM-AM 1
Grand Haven	20	8N	16W	GTW-D 188.3;
				PM-A 44.0
Harlem	32	6N	15W	PM-A 29.1
Harrisburg	5	9N	13W	GTW-M 74.6
Herrington	23	8N	13W	GR&I-M 11.6
Holland	28	5N	15W	PM-A 23.0 –
				PM-C 25.3
Hudson	(now Hudsonville)			
Hudsonville	29	6N	13W	PM-C 11.8

Jenison(s)	13	6N	13W	PM-C 7.2
Jennisonville	(now Jenison)			
Johnsville	(now Agnew)			
Kirk (Jct.)	9	8N	16W	PM-A 46.8 – PM-AZ 46.8
#Macatawa	33	5N	16W	PM-AM
Macatawa Jct.	(now Cronje)			
Marble	35	7N	16W	PM-A 34.9
Marne	35	8N	13W	GTW-D 166.6
Mill Point	20	8N	16W	GTW-D 187.0 + 1.7
New Holland	33	6N	15W	PM-AO 4.1
North Holland	5	5N	15W	PM-A 28.0
Nunica	14	8N	15W	GTW-D 179.5; PM-AO 19.9
Oconto	15	7N	16W	PM-A 38.5
Olive	(now Olive Center)			
Olive Center	10	6N	15W	PM-AO 8.2
Ottawa	3	6N	15W	PM-AO 9.7
Ottawa Beach	33	5N	16W	PM-AM 6.1
Penn Jct.	1	7N	13W	GR&I-M 9.0 – GTW-D 165.3
Pigeon (River)	(now Farmers)			
Reno	22	8N	13W	GR&I-M 12.9
Robinson(ville)	15	7N	15W	PM-AO 13.3
Rosymound	4	7N	16W	PM-A 41.0
Sheldon	(now Bakers)			
Spoonville	34	8N	15W	PM-AO 17.2
Spring Lake	15	8N	16W	GTW-D 186.4
Veneklassen	23	5N	15W	PM-C 22.4
Vriesland	2	5N	14W	PM-C 16.3
Walker	36	8N	13W	GR&I-M 10.0 – GTW-D 165.3 + 0.8
Waverly	21	5N	15W	PM-A 23.6 – PM-AO 0 – PM-C 24.5
West Chester	(now Conklin)			
West Olive	12	6N	16W	PM-A 32.9
#Zams Spur				GTW-D
Zeeland	18	5N	14W	PM-C 20.7

PRESQUE ISLE COUNTY

#Austins Siding		34N	3E	D&M-N 164
Bell	23	33N	8E	D&M-Q 17.6
Big Cut	19	34N	4E	D&M-N 158.6
Black Lake	7	35N	2E	D&M-K 5.2
Black Lake Jct.	6	34N	2E	D&M-N 170.8 —
				D&M-K 0
#Blond		33N	3E	D&M-V 8
Bunton	28	34N	4E	D&M-N 155.9
Calcite	23	35N	5E	D&M-R 12.0
Case	13	34N	2E	D&M-N 166.1
#Cedar				D&M-?
Crawford (Quarry)	(now Calcite)			
#Daust				D&M-?
Hoffman	(now Metz)			
Hurst	27	33N	4E	D&M-V 6.0
Kely Island Quarry	2	33N	8E	D&M-Q 20.4
LaRocque	36	34N	4E	D&M-N 152.6 —
				D&M-V 0
				(P.O. Hawks)
Liske	20	34N	6E	D&M-R 5.5
#Male Spur				D&M-R
May Lake Jct.	14	33N	4E	D&M-V 4.0
Metz	3	33N	5E	D&M-V 148.5
Millersburg	15	34N	3E	D&M-N 161.6
Nowicki	1	33N	5E	D&M-N 147.0
Onaway	6	34N	2E	D&M-N 170.4
Orchard	32	34N	6E	D&M-R 3.0
#Pack Siding		33N	3E	D&M-V 11
Polaski	25	33N	6E	D&M-N 140.4
Posen	9	33N	6E	D&M-N 143.5
Providence	16	34N	3E	D&M-N 162.5
Rainy Lake	16	33N	3E	D&M-V 13.3
Rogers City	15	35N	5E	D&M-R 14.8
Rogers City Jct.	8	33N	6E	D&M-N 144.7 —
				D&M-R 1.2
#Sobieski				D&M-N
South Rogers City	33	34N	5E	D&M-N 149.7

#Spur No. 1   D&M-?
Vincent   (now Posen)

ROSCOMMON COUNTY

#Archill				MC-M7
#Barker City				MC-M7
Boyces	10	21N	3W	MC-M7 24.5
#Edna	15	22N	3W	MC-M7
#Fortesque				MC-M7
Geels	6	23N	1W	MC-M 69.4
Hodgemans	8	24N	2W	MC-M 76.2 –
				MC-M5 0
#Lone Bridge				MC
Michelson	19	23N	4W	GR&I-K 31.6
Moore	26	24N	2W	MC-M 71.6
Nolan	19	21N	1W	MC-M7A
				14.5 + 1.5
Roscommon	6	24N	2W	MC-M 77.1
St. Helen	22	23N	1W	MC-M 64.5
Tierney	16	23N	1W	MC-M 66.1
#Williams Jct.				MC

SAGINAW COUNTY

Alicia	17	10N	4E	GTW-S
				27.9 + 6.3
Arndt	34	12N	5E	PM-Q 5.0
Arthur	15	12N	6E	PM-S 9.3
Birch Run	29	10N	6E	PM-T 15.5
Blackmar	2	10N	5E	PM-T 11.3
Brewer	29	12N	5E	PM-Q 2.8
Brewster Siding	25	12N	4E	GTW-S 38.6
Bridgeport	16	11N	5E	PM-T 6.3
Buena Vista	25	12N	5E	MC-BS 14.4

Burt	29	10N	5E	GTW-S 25.4
Calvin	35	12N	3E	PM-V 9.9
Carrollton	7	12N	5E	GTW-S 41.8;
				MC-S 103.4
Centre Street	35	12N	4E	PM-YSS 3.5
Chesaning	16	9N	3E	MC-S 78.1
County Line	33	10N	6E	PM-T 18.0
Court Street	26	12N	4E	MC-S 100.0
Court Street W.S.	23	12N	4E	PM-YSB 2.6
Creen	(now Greens on PM-S)			
Crow Island	7	12N	5E	PM-B 2.1
Donald	17	12N	5E	PM-S 1.5
Drissell(s)	(now Lawndale)			
East Saginaw	(now Saginaw on PM)			
Eaton	(see same, Gratiot Co.)			
Fergus	20	10N	3E	MC-S 82.9
Fifield	33	13N	5E	PM-B 4.8
Fitch	(see same, Bay Co.)			
Fordney	34	12N	4E	MC-S
				98.9 – PM-YSB
				3.9
Fosters	5	10N	5E	GTW-S 29.7
Frankenmuth	(now Gera)			
Frankentrost	29	12N	6E	MC-BS 12.0
Freeland	16	13N	3E	PM-L 11.0
Garfield	17	11N	3E	MC-S 89.5
Genesee Avenue	(now Saginaw on MC-S and			
	GTW-S)			
Genesee Avenue	30	12N	5E	PM-YSS 0.7
Gera	3	12N	6E	PM-Q 11.1
Graham	33	12N	3E	PM-V 13.4
Gratiot Road	27	12N	4E	PM-YSB 3.4
Graylock	36	11N	2E	PM-V 11.4
Greene	(now Merrill)			
Greens	13	12N	5E	PM-S 4.8
Groveton	28	10N	3E	MC-S 81.6
Harger	29	12N	5E	MC-BS 17.7
Hemlock	28	12N	2E	PM-V 17.3
#Howry				PM-S
Hoyt	29	12N	5E	MC-BS
				18.1 – MC-Q
				2.2 – PM-T 2.2

#Jamestown Mine				PM
Jefferson Avenue	25	12N	4E	PM-YSS 1.7
Kulmback	31	12N	6E	PM-Q 7.3
Lawndale	32	13N	4E	PM-L 5.9
Loop Line Switch	8	12N	5E	PM-B 1.5
Manning	18	12N	6E	PM-S 6.8
McClures	29	13N	5E	GTW-S 44.6
McClures	30	13N	5E	MC-S 106.4
Melbourne	21	13N	5E	GTW-S 46.4
Mentz	36	12N	3E	PM-V 9.3
Merrill	26	12N	1E	PM-V 22.3
Mershon	13	12N	4E	PM-L
				0.7 – PM-YSB
				0 – PM-YSW
				0 – PM-YSZ
				0 – GTW-S
				40.6 – MC-S
				102.2
Michigan Avenue	34	12N	4E	PM-YSB 4.1
Moiles Siding	29	10N	5E	GTW-S 26.3
#Mun(h)all				MC
MX	24	12N	4E	GTW-S
				39.1 – MC-BS
				20.2
North Saginaw	(now Saginaw on MC-S)			
Oakley(s)	36	9N	2E	MC-S 74.2
Orville	19	11N	5E	GTW-S 32.9
Paines	31	12N	4E	MC-S
				95.6 – PM-V
				7.7
Pine Grove	(now Groveton)			
Potters	25	12N	1E	PM-V 20.4
Prairie Farm	(now Alicia)			
Prairie Farm Jct.	17	10N	5E	GTW-S 27.9
#Riverside Mine				
Saginaw	18	12N	5E	PM-B 0 – PM-L
				0 – PM-S
				0 – PM-T 0
Saginaw	24	12N	4E	GTW-S 39.9;
				MC-S 101.5
Saginaw City	(now Court Street)			

Saginaw City Jct.	(now Hoyt)			
Saginaw E.S.	24	12N	4E	GTW-S 39.2; MC-BS 20.2
Saginaw Jct.	29	12N	5E	PM-Q 2.6 – PM-T 2.6 – PM-YSS 0
Saginaw Yard	25	12N	4E	GTW-S 37.5
St. Charles	5	10N	3E	MC-S 85.7
Sand Ridge	34	12N	3E	PM-V 11.2
S. B. Jct.	24	12N	4E	MC-BS 20.7 – MC-S 101.2
Sheridan Avenue	25	12N	4E	GTW-S 37.8 – (PM-YSS 1.5)
Shields	7	12N	5E	MC-S 103.2
Smiths	13	10N	5E	PM-T 13.1
South Saginaw	26	12N	4E	PM-YSS 2.8
Standard Mine	5	11N	5E	PM-T 4.1
State Road	23	12N	4E	PM-YSB 1.5
Stephen	14	12N	5E	PM-S 3.9
Swan Creek	3	11N	3E	MC-S 92.5
Swan Creek	34	12N	3E	PM-V 10.6
Taymouth	(now Burt)			
Tittabawassee (Jct.)	(now Paines)			
Uncle Henry Mine	18	12N	6E	PM-S 6.1
Veenfleits	25	12N	6E	MC-BS 8.3
Verne	17	10N	5E	GTW-S 27.5
Verne Mine Jct.	(now Prairie Farm Jct.)			
#Ward				PM-V
Washington Avenue	13	12N	5E	PM-L 0.1 – PM-B 0.1
Washington Avenue	24	12N	4E	MC-BS 20.3
Washington Avenue	25	12N	4E	PM-YSS 1.9
Zilwaukee	5	12N	5E	GTW-S 43.5; MC-S 105.1; PM-YSZ 1.4

ST. CLAIR COUNTY

Abbottsford	30	7N	16E	PM-Q 77.7
Adair	2	4N	15E	MC-DM 8.0
Algonac		2N	16E	AT 7.1
Allenton	28	6N	13E	PM-NA 29.0
Almont Jct.	18	6N	17E	PM-NA 4.7 – GTW-H 54.7
Atkins	10	7N	16E	PM-N 11.6
Avoca	10	7N	15E	PM-Q 73.5
#Baird				DCS 87
Balkwell	11	7N	16E	PM-N 10.4
Balmers	(now Saginaw Jct.)			
Belle River	25	4N	16E	PHD 16.2
Berville	35	6N	13E	PM-NA 25.6
Blaine	21	8N	16E	PM-N 15.3
Broadbridge		3N	16E	AT 1.9
Brockway Center	(now Yale)			
Bruce	30	7N	16E	PM-Q 78.8
Burns	19	6N	16E	PM-NA 10.6
Butlins	4	4N	16E	MC-DM 4.7
Canal Bridge	27	7N·	17E	PM-N 3.9
Capac	28	7N	13E	GTW-C 309.3
Carl(e)ton	11	4N	16E	MC-DM 2.3
Columbus	10	5N	15E	GTW-H 44.9
#Cornell	9	6N	16E	GTW-C 327½
Doyle	31	6N	14E	PM-NA 23.3
Eighty Foot Grade	(now Balkwell)			
Emmett	36	7N	14E	GTW-C 317.9
Fargo	25	8N	15E	DCS 84.8; PM-NZ 17.3
Farrs	(now Fargo)			
Fort Gratiot	35	7N	17E	GTW-C 337.6 – GTW-H 59.5
Gardendale	23	7N	17E	PM-N 6.1
Goodells	2	6N	15E	GTW-C 322.9
#Goodyear Siding				MC-DM 6
Grand Trunk Jct.	(now Tunnel Jct.)			

Grant Center	(now Blaine)			
Gratiot Center	17	7N	17E	PM-N 6.9
#Gravel Siding				PM-NZ 15
Green Corners	29	8N	15E	PM-NZ 20.5
Harker Street	34	7N	17E	PM-N 2.2
Hickey	(now Columbus)			
Jeddo	9	8N	16E	PM-N 17.7
Kimball	21	6N	16E	PM-NA 8.5
#Kingsley		7N	16E	PM-N 11
Lamb	20	6N	15E	PM-NA 15.8
Lutz Siding	18	8N	15E	PM-NZ 22.0
Marine City	12	3N	16E	AT 0 − PHD 19.1
#Martin				PM-NA 22½
Marysville	29	6N	17E	PHD 3.4
Memphis	35	6N	14E	PM-NA 19.7
Merrillsville	3	8N	14E	PM-Q 64.8
Military Street	15	6N	17E	PM-Q 89.1
North Street	12	7N	16E	PM-N 8.9
Peat Siding	19	7N	13E	GTW-C 306.5
#Pilgrim Siding				GTW-C
Pine Grove Avenue	3	6N	17E	PM-N 1.5
Poplar Street	3	6N	17E	PM-N 1.6
Port Huron	16	6N	17E	GTW-C(new) 333.9 − PM-Q 88.2;GTW-C(old) 335.5; PHD 0; PM-N 0 − PM-Q 90.1
Pound Hill	14	6N	16E	PM-NA 6.4
Ruby	7	7N	16E	DCS 89.0
Roberts Landing				AT 3.8
Saginaw Jct.	(now Zion)			
St. Clair		5N	17E	PHD 11.3
St. Clair Springs		5N	17E	MC-DM 0
#Sanborn				GTW-C 323 3/4
Shanahan	36	6N	14E	PM-NA 18.7
16th Street	16	6N	17E	GTW-C 334.3; PM-Q 88.3
Smith	(now Allenton)			
Smiths Creek	31	6N	16E	GTW-H 48.6

South St. Clair		5N	17E	MC-DM 0.8 (−PHD 12.3)
Sunnyside	6	6N	16E	GTW-C 325.6
Sweet Siding	18	6N	17E	PM-NA 4.9
Tappan	18	6N	17E	GTW-C 332.1−GTW-H 55.6−PM-NA 4.0−PM-Q 86.1−DCS 99.2
Tenth Street	15	6N	17E	PM-Q 88.7
Thomas Street	3	7N	17E	PM-N 1.3
Thornton	(now Sunnyside)			
Tunnel Jct.	(now Tappan)			
Tunnel Yard		6N	17E	GTW-C 333.3
Twelfth Street	3	7N	17E	PM-N 1.8
Upton Works	16	6N	17E	PM-Q 87.9
Wadhams	2	6N	16E	DCS 95.9; PM-Q 82.9
Wales	22	6N	15E	PM-NA 14.1
Westover	7	6N	17E	DCS 98.7; PM-Q 85.6
West Tappan	10	6N	16E	GTW-C 329.0
Yale	11	8N	14E	PM-NZ 24.9−PM-Q 66.1
Zion	4	7N	16E	PM-N 12.8−PM-NZ 12.8

ST. JOSEPH COUNTY

Burr Oak	23	7S	9W	LS-A 402.2
Centerville	24	6S	11W	MC-A 64.9
Chamberlains	6	5S	12W	GTW-C 140.3
Colon	11	6S	9W	MC-A 54.3
Colon Junction	(now Fairfax)			
Constantine	24	7S	12W	LS-G 3.9

Corey	(see same, Cass Co.)			
Douglass	7	7S	10W	LS-A 413.1
Fabius	33	6S	12W	MC-A 74.8
Factoryville	12	5S	9W	MC-K 23.1
Fairfax	16	6S	9W	MC-A 56.3 – MC-K 30.8
Fawn River	10	5S	11W	LS-A 416.8
Findley	5	7S	9W	LS-S 36.5 – MC-K 35.1
Florence	6	7S	11W	LS-G 7.3
Flowerfield	6	5S	11W	LS-G 19.9
Gravel Pit	12	5S	9W	MC-K 21.6
Klinger Lake	12	8S	11W	LS-A 414.1
Klingers	(now Klinger Lake)			
Leesburg	(now Chamberlains)			
Leonidas	22	5S	9W	MC-K 25.9
Lockport	(now Three Rivers on MC-A)			
Locks	(now Burr Oak)			
Mendon	27	5S	10W	GR&I-S 164.1
Moorepark	19	5S	11W	LS-G 16.4
North Sturgis	36	7S	10W	GR&I-S 150.6
Nottawa	27	6S	10W	GR&I-S 157.9
Nottawa	(also now Wasepi on MC-A)			
Oakwood Crossing	12	8S	11W	LS-A 415.0
Parkville	(now Moorepark)			
Perrin	12	7S	10W	GR&I-S 154.7
Portage Lake	5	5S	10W	GR&I-S 168.1
RK	1	8S	10W	GR&I-S 149.4 – LS-A 408.6 – LS-S 29.7
Red Rock	(now RK)			
Sturgis	1	8S	10W	GR&I-S 149.0; LS-A 408.3; LS-S 29.3
Three Rivers	18	6S	11W	LS-G 11.4
Three Rivers	19	6S	11W	MC-A 70.1
Three Rivers Jct.	29	6S	11W	LS-G 9.6 – MC-A 68.8 + 1.7

VE	19	6S	11W	LS-G 10.8 – MC-A 70.1
Wasepi	15	6S	10W	GR&I-S 159.5 – MC-A 61.2
White Pigeon	12	8S	12W	LS-A 420.1 – LS-G 0
White Pigeon Jct.	11	8S	12W	LS-A 421.2 – LS-G 0.7 + 0.9

SANILAC COUNTY

Amadore	21	9N	16E	PM-N 21.0
Anderson	(now Applegate)			
Applegate	25	11N	15E	PM-N 32.4
Berkshire	35	12N	14E	PM-NS 3.8
Bridgehampton	20	12N	15E	PM-N 41.2
Brockton	(now Hemans)			
Brotherton	18	13N	15E	PM-N 49.0
Brown City	18	9N	13E	PM-Q 54.2
Carsonville	3	11N	15E	PM-N 37.6
Cash	(now Watertown)			
Cedardale	(now Cooley Road)			
Cooks	10	10N	14E	DCS 66.0
#Cooley Road				PM-N 50.3
Croswell	29	10N	16E	PM-N 26.6
Decker	21	12N	12E	DCS 46.8
Deckerville	31	13N	15E	PM-N 46.3
#Deisinger Siding				PM-N 40½
Downing	(now Downington)			
Downington	6	12N	15E	PM-N 45.3
Elmer	21	12N	13E	DCS 52.9
#Erb		9N	15E	DCS 80
#Farmers				PM-N
Greenleaf	8	14N	12E	GTW-B 7.4
#Hazelwood		12N	13E	DCS 56

Hemans	18	12N	12E	DCS 44.8
Kerrwood	12	9N	14E	DCS 74.3
Lewis Siding	5	10N	16E	PM-N 30.7
Marion	12	13N	14E	PM-N 49.3
Marlette	5	10N	12E	PM-Q 45.2
McGregor	18	12N	15E	PM-N 43.2
Melvin	30	9N	14E	PM-Q 60.9
Minden City	12	14N	14E	PM-NH 4.2
#Odlam		9N	16E	PM-N 28
Packs Mills	14	11N	15E	PM-N 34.6
#Packs Siding	14	11N	15E	PM-N 34.8
Palms	36	14N	13E	PM-N
				52.3 – PM-NH
				0
Peck	34	10N	14E	DCS 70.2
Poland	33	12N	15E	PM-N
				39.0 – PM-NS
				0
Reagan	9	10N	12E	PM-Q 46.2
Roseburg	30	9N	15E	DCS 77.2
Sandusky	5	11N	13E	DCS 58.7
Sandusky	32	12N	13E	PM-NS 7.1
Scranton	32	12N	15E	PM-NS 1.6
Snover	19	12N	13E	DCS 50.9
Stillson	10	10N	14E	DCS 66.9
Tyre	1	14N	13E	PM-N 59.9
Valley Center	27	9N	13E	PM-Q 58.2
Walkers	20	11N	14E	DCS 61.7
Watertown	32	11N	14E	DCS 64.3
Wilbur Road	(now Bridgehampton)			
Wilson	15	10N	12E	PM-Q 48.4
Yorks	(now Valley Center)			

SHIAWASSEE COUNTY

Bancroft	35	6N	3E	GTW-C 248.5
Bennington	5	6N	2E	MC-S 58.6
Burton	13	7N	1E	GTW-D 84.5

Byron	14	5N	4E	AA-A 88.9
Carland	25	8N	1E	AA-B 115.7
Corunna	28	7N	3E	AA-A 104.0;
				GTW-D 75.5
Corunna Coal Mine	(see Kerby)			
Dewey	11	7N	2E	MC-S 65.6
Durand	22	6N	4E	AA-A 95.5 –
				GTW-C 253.3 –
				GTW-D
				67.0 – GTW-S
				0
East Durand	22	6N	4E	GTW-C 255.4
Emergency	22	6N	4E	AA-A 94.8
Faben	24	7N	2E	AA-A 106.7
Hazel Green	(now Henderson)			
Henderson	14	8N	2E	MC-S 70.2
#Kelly Siding				GTW-D
King	14	7N	2E	AA-B 108.8
Kerby (Mine)	13	7N	3E	GTW-D
				75.3 + 2.7
Laingsburg	28	6N	1E	MC-S 52.1
Lennon	24	7N	4E	GTW-S 6.3
Maple River Pit	3	6N	2E	MC-S 60.4
Morrice	12	5N	2E	GTW-C 242.2
Mungerville	(now Burton)			
Owosso	24	7N	2E	AA-A&B 107.1;
				GTW-D 78.5;
				MC-S 63.6
Owosso Jct.	24	7N	2E	AA-B 107.8 –
				GTW-D
				79.2 – MC-S
				63.4
Perry	16	5N	2E	GTW-C 240.0
Pitt	23	6N	4E	AA-A 93.9 –
				GTW-D 65.5
San	29	7N	3E	AA-A 104.8 –
				GTW-D 76.5
Shaftsburg	25	5N	1E	GTW-C 235.7
Six Mile Mine	18	8N	3E	AA-A 106.0 + 7.1
Vernon	7	6N	4E	AA-A 98.7;
				GTW-D 70.2

#Woodhull		5N	1E	GTW-C
York	16	6N	4E	AA-A 96.2

TUSCOLA COUNTY

Abke	15	14N	9E	MC-BC 23
Akron	3	13N	8E	DCS 19.2
Akron	34	14N	8E	PM-S 24.7
#Akron Coal Mine		14N	8E	DCS 18
Ashmore	10	14N	9E	MC-BC 25.4
Atwood	22	13N	9E	MC-BC 16.1
Bank Sand	32	12N	8E	MC-BC 2.6
#Berlin				MC-B
Bloomfield	11	13N	8E	DCS 20.7
Bradley (Farm)	(now Bradleyville)			
Bradleyville	27	14N	7E	DCS 13.4
Bruce	(now Deford)			
Caro	3	12N	9E	DCS 28.3; MC-BC 13.7
Caro Jct.	7	11N	8E	MC-B 86.5 − MC-BC 0.4
Cass City	33	14N	11E	GTW-P 74.4 − GTW-B 0
Colling	22	14N	9E	MC-BC 22.1
#Corsan				PM-Q
County Line	(now Robinson)			
#Cramptons				MC-B
#Crossman				MC-BC
Dayton	16	12N	10E	DCS 34.8
Deford	32	13N	11E	GTW-P 68.6
Denmark Jct.	28	12N	7E	MC-B 91.0 − MC-BS 4.8
Dewar	4	12N	7E	PM-S 14.3
Downing	31	14N	8E	DCS 16.5
Duro	10	14N	9E	MC-BC 24.1
Fairgrove	17	13N	8E	PM-S 21.6
Fostoria	26	10N	9E	PM-F 24.1
Frank	19	11N	9E	PM-Q 25.5

Gagetown	1	14N	10E	GTW-P 80.0
Gilford	34	13N	7E	PM-S 16.7
Gravel Pit	15	13N	9E	MC-BC 17.1
#Gravel Pit				DCS 24
Great Lakes Sand	15	11N	8E	PM-Q 22.1
Haines	11	11N	7E	PM-Q 17.2
#Handy				PM-S
Harbin	31	11N	10E	PM-Q 32.9
Hutchinson	34	14N	9E	MC-BC 21.0
Juniata	19	11N	9E	PM-Q 25.4
Karr	(now Ashmore)			
Kemps	24	15N	8E	PM-S 33.2
Kingston	32	12N	11E	GTW-P 61.7
Kintner	25	13N	7E	PM-S 19.0
#Lockwood				DCS
Markell		10N	9E	PM-F
Masoner	10	13N	9E	MC-BC 18.1
Mayville	25	11N	9E	PM-Q 31.2
McHale	15	11N	8E	PM-Q 21.6
Millington	16	10N	8E	MC-B 79.6
Mitchells	13	13N	8E	DCS 21.7
Montei	24	13N	8E	DCS 22.8
Patterson	3	13N	9E	MC-BC 19.9
Peninsular Street	3	12N	9E	MC-BC 12.7 –
				(DCS 28.3
				adjacent)
Perkin(s)	32	12N	8E	MC-BC 3.1
#Pleasant Hill				DCS 25
Polmantier	13	14N	11E	GTW-B 4.8
Purdy	10	13N	9E	MC-BC 19.0
Quanicassee	29	14N	7E	DCS 11.4
Reese	7	12N	7E	MC-B 94.5 –
				PM-S 12.5
Richville	29	12N	7E	MC-BS 6.5
Robinson	1	14N	9E	MC-BC 26.6
Ross Crossing	14	12N	8E	MC-BC 7.2
#Sanson				GTW-P
Seeley		12N	9E	DCS 33
Sharpville	25	14N	7E	DCS 15.4
Silver Creek	(now Silverwood)			
Silverwood	35	11N	10E	PM-Q 36.7

#Smiths				MC-B
Stewarts	34	10N	9E	PM-F 22.1
Stone	8	12N	7E	PM-S 13.7
Tuscola	8	11N	7E	PM-Q 14.9
Unionville	36	14N	8E	PM-S 31.0
V	7	11N	8E	MC-B 86.0 –
				PM-Q 19.4
Van Patten	4	12N	7E	PM-S 15.4
Vassar	7	11N	8E	MC-B 86.2;
				PM-Q 19.2
Wahjamega	17	12N	9E	MC-BC 9.4
Wampson	15	11N	8E	PM-Q 22.5
Watrousville	22	12N	8E	MC-BC 5.4
Wells	(now Wellsford)			
#Wellsford		12N	10E	DCS 37
Wilmot	17	12N	11E	DCS 39.6 –
				GTW-P(new)
				64.9;
				GTW-P(old)
				65.5
Woodman	(now Woodway)			
Woodway	23	14N	8E	PM-S 27.4

VAN BUREN COUNTY

Bangor	12	2S	16W	PM-C 60.6
Barrison	16	3S	14W	PM-H 27.5
Bear Lake Mills	(now Berlamont)			
Benway	16	3S	14W	PM-H 27.3
Berlamont	13	1S	15W	MC-H 25.0
Bloomingdale	17	1S	14W	MC-H 23.0
Breedsville	29	1S	15W	PM-C 57.7
Browns Mills	(now Maple Forest)			
Cableton	10	1S	17W	PM-H 1.0
Columbia	10	1S	15W	MC-H 27.7
Covert	14	2S	17W	PM-H 8.0
Decatur	20	4S	14W	MC-C 168.3
Deerfield	(now McDonald)			

#Emanuel				KLSC-P 0
Fruitland	22	1S	17W	PM-H 2.8
Geneva	(now Locata)			
Gobles	25	1S	14W	MC-H 18.5
Gobleville	(now Gobles)			
Grand Junction	8	1S	15W	MC-H 29.2 —
				PM-C 53.8
Gross	13	2S	16W	PM-C 61.7
Harrison	25	1S	13W	MC-H 12.3
Hartford	16	3S	16W	PM-C 68.8 —
				PM-H 15.8
Hills Siding	10	2S	17W	PM-H 7.0
Horner	8	1S	15W	PM-C 54.8
Kendall	27	1S	13W	MC-H 14.9
Kibbie	5	1S	16W	MC-H 35.0
Kirby	13	3S	15W	PM-H 25.0
Kirk	19	3S	16W	PM-C 71.4
Lacota	2	1S	16W	MC-H 32.0
Lake Cora	18	3S	14W	PM-H 25.7
Lawrence	10	3S	15W	PM-H 22.2
Lawton	32	3S	13W	KLSC 16.0 —
				MC-C 160.6 —
				PM-H 34.0
Lawton Track Pan	1	4S	14W	MC-C 163.3
Maple Forest	6	1S	15W	MC-H 30.3
Mattawan	13	3S	13W	KLSC 11.7
Mattawan	14	3S	13W	MC-C 156.4
McDonald	27	2S	16W	PM-C 64.8
Mentha	25	1S	13W	MC-H 12.8
Millers	(aka Benway)			
Newbre	22	3S	13W	KLSC 13.9
Packard	(now Roosevelt Hills)			
Paw Paw	13	3S	14W	PM-H 30.5
Paw Paw	(also original name for Lawton on MC-C)			
Pine Grove (Mills)	29	1S	13W	MC-H 17.5
Roosevelt Hills	34	1S	17W	PM-H 5.3
#Sand Lake				KLSC
#Severns		1S	13W	MC-H 14
South Haven	3	1S	17W	PM-H 0; MC-H 39.6

#Thomas		2S	16W	PM-C 62
Toquin	31	2S	16W	KLSC-P 0 —
				PM-H 11.4
White Oaks	1	4S	14W	MC-C 163.0
Wildeys	17	3S	14W	PM-H 26.8
Wildeys	(original location now Lake Cora)			

WASHTENAW COUNTY

Ann Arbor	28	2S	6E	MC-E 37.3
Ann Arbor	29	2S	6E	AA-A 45.2
Barton	4	2S	6E	AA-A 50.4
Bell	21	2S	6E	AA-A 46.9
Bridgewater	1	4S	4E	LS-Y 17.3
Chelsea	12	2S	3E	MC-E 54.1
#Chelsea Track Pan				MC-E
#Davidson				MC-E 52
Delhi	2	2S	5E	MC-E 42.6
Delhi Mills	(now Delhi)			
Dexter	32	1S	5E	MC-E 46.8
Dicksons	(now Salem)			
Ferry	32	2S	6E	AA-A 44.5
Fosters	7	2S	6E	MC-E 40.1
Four Mile Lake	9	2S	4E	MC-E 51.3
Geddes	36	2S	6E	MC-E 33.3
#Harrisons				LS-Y 5
Hogan	20	4S	4E	LS-J 16.5
Kinnear	9	2S	5E	MC-E 45.2
Kirby	(now Osmer)			
Leland		1S	6E	AA-O 52.4 —
				AA-S 52.4
#Lowell				MC-E
Manchester	2	4S	3E	LS-J 21.3; LS-Y
				24.3
Manchester Jct.	3	4S	3E	LS-J 22.0 — LS-Y
				25.4
Milan	35	4S	6E	AA-A 31.5
Milan	(also see same, Monroe Co.)			

#Nora		4S	6E	AA-A 35
Northfield	(now Kirby)			
Osmer	4	2S	6E	AA-A 50.9
Pittsfield	(AA-A name for Pittsfield Jct.)			
Pittsfield Jct.	21	3S	6E	AA-A 40.4 —
				LS-Y 7.1
River Raisin	17	4S	4E	LS-J 17.3
Salem	11	1S	7E	PM-D 30.9
Saline	36	3S	5E	LS-Y 11.1
Scio	9	2S	5E	MC-E 44.3
Shanghai Pit	31	2S	7E	MC-E 31.8
Sylvan	21	2S	3E	MC-E 58.1
Urania	3	4S	6E	AA-A 36.5
White Star Track	16	2S	6E	AA-A 47.9
Whitmore Lake	5	1S	6E	AA-A 56.9
Whitmore Lake	(see same, Livingston Co.)			
Whittaker	16	4S	7E	WAB 31.5
Wiard	10	3S	7E	MC-E 27.6
Willis	12	4S	7E	WAB 28.6
Willow Run	11	3S	7E	MC-E 26.6
Worden	25	1S	7E	AA-S 54.9
Ypsilanti	4	3S	7E	MC-E 29.4 —
				LS-Y 0
Ypsilanti Jct.	(now Pittsfield Jct.)			

WAYNE COUNTY

Allen Park				DTI-D 9.1
Allen Road				MC-DD 3.0
Ash	34	4S	9E	PRR 119.2
Avery Ave.				GTW-H 2.3
Barrett Track	29	3S	9E	PM-T 95.2
Bay City Jct.				MC-E 2.2 —
				MC-B 2.2
Beaubien Street				GTW-H 3.8 —
				LS-D 4.4 —
				MC-B 5.9
Beaufait Station				MC-YDB 4.2

Beck	21	1S	8E	PM-D 27.0
Beech	30	1S	10E	PM-D 15.9
Belden	(now Willow)			
Belleville	28	3S	8E	WAB 23.8
Belt Line Jct.				GTW-H 5.1 –
				MC-B 7.2 –
				MC-YDB 0
#Bennett(s Siding)				DTI
Benson Yard				MC-YDB 3.1
Berlin Yard	(now Benson Yard)			
Birrell	29	1S	10E	PM-D 15.1
Boulevard				MC-YDB 1.7
Boulevard Switch				GTW-D 4.0
Brownstown	8	4S	10E	PRR 125.0
Canton	18	2S	9E	PM-T 86.5
Champlain Street				MC-YDB 4.0
Chandler				CCS 17.5 – LS-D
				22.4
Chene Street				MC-YDB 0.1
Chrysler Center				GTW-D 6.1
Cicotte Street				PRR 133.9
Clay Avenue				GTW-D 4.3
Conners Grove	3	1S	12E	GTW-H 9.2
Coolidge				PRR 135.6 –
				(WAB 6.5)
County House	(now Eloise)			
Curtis Siding	34	3S	10E	DTI-D 4.4
D. & I. Jct.	22	4S	10E	DTI-M 15.2 –
				DTI-D 0
D. & M. Jct.				GTW-D 3.2 –
				LS-D 3.2
Dearborn				MC-E 10.2
Dearborn Jct.				MC-E 9.6 –
				MC-DD 6.0
Dearoad				DTSL 46.1
Delta Switch				MC-T 5.8
Delta Yard				MC-T 5.9
Dehoco	21	1S	8E	PM-D 27.7
Delray				DTI-M 0.5 –
				DURS 4.5 –
				MC-T 5.3 –

				MC-DD 0 –
				LS-D 10.2 –
				PM-D 4.5 –
				WAB 4.4 –
				WAB-W 2.5
Denton(s)	5	3S	8E	MC-E 24.8
Dequindre Street				GTW-D 0.7 –
				MC-YDM 1.3
Detroit				MC-E (2nd) 0;
				MC-E (3rd)
				1.4; FSUD 0;
				GTW-D 0
East Yard				GTW-H 6.6
Ecorse				DTI-M 3.8;
				DTSL 43.4;
				LS-D 14.3 –
				MC-T 8.9
Ecorse Jct.				DTSL 47.0 –
				PRR 137.1 –
				WAB 5.6
				(River Rouge
				on DTSL)
Edison				DTSL 34.7
Eight Mile Road	3	1S	12E	GTW-H 10.1
#8-Mile Siding				GTW-D 8
Elm	25	1S	9E	PM-D 18.0
Elmwood	(now Norton)			
Eloise	26	2S	9E	MC-E 15.2
Eureka				PRR 128.2
Exposition Switch				MC-T 5.6
#Fairview Station				DT
15th Street				MC-E 1.2
Fishers	(now Beech)			
Flat Rock	31	4S	10E	DTI-M 18.2 –
				(CCS 23.1)
FN				DTI-M 11.1 –
				DTSL 37.3 –
				LS-D 20.8 –
				MC-T 15.5
				(Trenton Jct.
				on DTSL only)

Ford				DTI-M 8.5
Ford Jct.				DT 9.3 –
				GTW-D 7.2
Fordson				DT 0 – MC-E 5.7
Fordson Yard				DTI-D 15.3 –
				PM-D 6.9
Forest Lawn	16	1S	12E	DT 12.7 –
				GTW-H 7.2 –
				MC-B 9.2 –
				MC-YDE 0
Fort Street				PM-D 5.5
French Landing	24	3S	11E	WAB 21.3
Fullerton	30	1S	11E	PM-DW 5.2 –
				PRR-UB 3.0
Fullerton Yard				PRR-UB 2.5
Garfield				PRR 133.0
Gibralter				MC-T 19.9
Gillen Yard	(see Eight Mile Road)			
Grand River				GTW-H 1.9 –
Avenue				MC-B 4.0
Gratiot Avenue				GTW-D 1.7;
				LS-D 1.7;
				MC-YDB 2.5
Greenfield	30	1S	11E	PM-DW 5.9
Grosse Isle				MC-TG 2.4
Grosse Isle Shops				MC-TG 1.8
Hand	8	3S	10E	WAB 12.4
Harper Avenue				MC-YDB 1.0
Harper Yard				MC-YDB 1.3
Highland Park				GTW-D 6.6
Holden Road				GTW-H 3.0
Hospital Spur	11	1S	8E	PM-T 79.6
Huron	(now Rockwood on LS-D)			
Inkster	25	2S	9E	MC-E 13.6
Jefferson Avenue				DTI-M 0.7;
				GTW-D 0.9
Jerome Parki	(now Highland Park)			
Junction Yard				MC-E 4.0
Kenwood				GTW-D 5.5
#Kings Yard				GTW-H
Kirby Avenue				MC-B 4.2

Koenig Spur	29	1S	10E	PM-D 15.3
Lake Shore Jct.	(see D. & M. Jct. on GTW-D)			
Lincoln Park				PRR 134.4
Lincoln Yard				PRR 134.4
Livernois Avenue				MC-E 3.3
Livonia	(now Stark)			
Lurmet	4	4S	10E	PRR 126.5
Mack Road				MC-YDB 2.9
Masson	12	1S	11E	GTW-D 8.0
McKinneys	(now Elm)			
Meldrum Avenue				MC-YDB 4.4 — MC-YDM 0
Melvindale				DTI-D 12.4 — (MC-DD 3.0)
#Meyers Jct.				PM-D
Michigan Avenue	19	2S	11E	DT 0.6 — PM-D 7.7
Michigan Avenue				GTW-H 0.5
Mill				DTI-M 4.8
#Mill Street				MC-T
Milwaukee Jct.				GTW-D 4.1 — GTW-H 4.6 — MC-B 6.7
Mount Olivet	10	1S	12E	GTW-H 8.3
Mulkey Avenue				MC-E 5.5
#Nallville				GTW-H
New Boston	8	4S	9E	PM-T 97.9
Nolan Yard	3	1S	12E	GTW-H 9.1
Norris	9	1S	12E	MC-B 10.5
North Detroit	9	1S	12E	MC-B 10.3
Northville	3	1S	8E	PM-T 78.5
North Yard	16	1S	12E	DT 12.2 — MC-B 9.5
Norton	25	1S	9E	PM-D 16.9
Oak	27	1S	10E	PM-D 13.1 — PM-DW 7.9
Oakwood				WAB 7.0
Oakwood Jct.				DTI-D 10.7 — WAB 8.7
Palmer Avenue				MC-YDB 1.8

Penford	27	3S	10E	DTI-D 6.0 – PRR 129.4
Pleasant Street	(now YD)			
Plymouth	23	1S	9E	PM-D 24.5; PM-T (old) 82.5)
Plymouth Jct.	23	1S	9E	PM-D 24.6 – PM-T (new) 82.0
#Preston				WAB
Redford	(now Redford Jct.)			
Redford Jct.	(now Oak)			
River Rouge				DTI-M 2.8; DTSL 47.0 – (WAB 5.6); LS-D 11.4 – MC-T 6.7
Rockwood				DTSL 30.7; LS-D 27.5 – MC-T 22.2
Romulus	17	3S	9E	PM-T 93.8 – WAB 19.0
Rougemere				PM-D 6.6
Rouge Yard				DTI-D 13.6
Russell Street				GTW-H 4.4
#St. Paul Avenue				MC-YDB
#Salt Wells				WAB 7
Schaeffer (Tower)				DTI-D 13.5 – MC-DZ 3.1
Secords	3	3S	8E	MC-E 22.8
17th Street				DURS 1.2 – FSUD 1.2
Sheldon	34	2S	8E	MC-E 22.2
Short Cut				DTI-M 1.6
Sibley				DTI-M 10.3; DTSL 38.9; LS-D 19.9 – MC-T 14.0
6th Street				FSUD 0.1
Slocum Jct.				CCS 17.1 – DTSL 35.8 –

				MC-T 17.1—
				MC-TG 0.1
South Yard				DTI-M 3.2;
				MC-T 3.8
Springwells				MC-E 2.5
Stark	28	1S	9E	PM-D 20.3
State Fair	2	1S	11E	GTW-D 9.3
Stock Yards				MC-TG 1.4
Stony Island				MC-TG 3.1
Strongs Siding				LS-D 28.5
Sunnyside				MC-TG 0.9
Third Street				(see Detroit, 2nd on MC-E)
Thomas Road				MC-DD 4.2
Town Line				MC-E 7.4—
				MC-DZ 4.2
Town Line				(on PM now Greenfield)
Transit Jct.				(now Meldrum Avenue)
Trenton	19	4S	11E	DTI-M 12.1;
				DTSL 36.8;
				LS-D 21.3—
				MC-T 16.0
Trenton Jct.				(now FN except on DTSL)
Trumbull Avenue				GTW-H 2.7
Turkey	21	1S	8E	PM-D 27.5
12th Street				GTW—H 2.4
20th Street				MC-E 1.6
24th Street				GTW-H 1.1
Victoria Avenue				DTSL 46.8—
				MC-DZ 0.6
Vinewood Avenue				GTW-H 0.7—
				LS-D 7.2—
				MC-B 3.1
Waltz	32	4S	9E	PM-T 102.4
Warrens Yards	4	2S	11E	DT 2.5
Waterford	14	1S	8E	PM-T 80.1
Waterloo Street				MC-YDB 3.4
Wayne	33	2S	9E	MC-E 17.7; (on
				PM-T at
				Wayne Jct.)
Wayne Jct.	32	2S	9E	MC-E 18.2—
				PM-T 90.2

West Chicago Blvd.	33	1S	11E	DT 4.1 —
				PM-DW 3.2
West Detroit				GTW-H 0 —
				LS-D 8.2 —
				MC-E 2.9 —
				MC-T 2.9 —
				PM-DW 0 —
				WAB-W 0
West End Avenue				DTI-M 0 (called Detroit, also);
				DURS 4.0
#Whitewood				GTW-D
Willow	29	4S	9E	PM-T 101.2
Woodmere				MC-T 4.90
Woodward Avenue				GTW-H 3.6 —
				LS-D 4.7 —
				MC-B 5.6
Wyandotte				DTI-M 7.4;
				DTSL 41.1;
				LS-D 17.0 —
				MC-T 11.7
YD				LS-D 11.8 —
				MC-T 6.5 —
				MC-DZ 0

WEXFORD COUNTY

Arcadia	32	24N	12W	AA-C 259.2
#Ash				M&NE-R
Bagnall	34	24N	12W	AA-C 257.7
Baxter	4	24N	10W	M&NE-R 31.4
#Blodgett		22N	9W	C&NE 6
Bonds	5	22N	9W	GR&I-N 337.8
Bonds Mill	29	23N	9W	GR&I-N 339.9
Boon	24	22N	11W	AA-C 237.8
Buckley	5	24N	11W	M&NE-R 23.8
Bunyea	28	22N	10W	AA-C 234.0

Cadillac	4	21N	9W	AA-B and AA-C 227.0; C&NE 0; GR&I-N 331.8
Claggetts	10	23N	12W	AA-C 256.3 – M&NE-R 15.1
Clam Lake	(now Cadillac)			
#Clarks		24N	9W	GR&I-N 347
CN	4	21N	9W	AA-B 226.5 – GR&I-N 331.8
#Cutlers				AA-C
#Dakes Mill				M&NE-R
Derry(s)	10	22N	12W	AA-C 246.6
Diggins	30	22N	10W	AA-C 236.3
Duforts	16	22N	11W	AA-C 242.1
#Fairitys				M&NE-R
Fays	32	24N	12W	AA-C 259.6
#Gardiner				AA
#Gasser				AA
Gilbert	20	23N	9W	GR&I-N 341.1
Glengarry	2	23N	12W	M&NE-R 16.8
#Hacker				GR&I-4
Haire	29	24N	9W	GR&I-N 347.4
Haring	16	22N	9W	GR&I-N 335.4
Harlan	(see same, Manistee Co.)			
#Harmons Mill		23N	12W	M&NE-R 13
Harrietta	18	22N	11W	AA-C 244.1
Harts	30	24N	12W	AA-C 260.1
#Haskins		22N	9W	GR&I-N 334
#Henderson				GR&I
Hobart	30	21N	9W	GR&I-N 325.9
#Hoxeyville	36	21N	12W	GR&I-2
Lanka				GR&I
Linden	(now Haring)			
#Long Lake		21N	9W	GR&I-K6 0.7
Long Lake Jct.	11	21N	9W	GR&I-K 2.7 – GR&I-K6 0
Manton	9	23N	9W	GR&I-N 344.0
McPherson	15	22N	11W	AA-C 240.8
Mesick	12	23N	12W	AA-C 254.1
Metheany	33	24N	9W	GR&I-N 345.8

Millersville	29	22N	10W	AA-C 235.3
#Miners Rollway		23N	12W	M&NE-R 12
Missaukee Jct.	16	22N	9W	GR&I-N 336.0 —
				GR&I-K 0
North Yard	33	22N	9W	GR&I-N 333.1
Perues	21	23N	12W	AA-C 251.1
#Round Lake	12	22N	9W	GR&I-K
#Rumbo				M&NE-R
Saunders	11	22N	12W	AA-C 246.2
#Seamans				GR&I-?
Selma	32	22N	10W	AA-C 228.2
Sherman	(now Mesick)			
Springville	(now Bagnall)			
Summit	(now Hobart)			
Umatilla	(now Boon)			
#Valda				GR&I
#Walls		24N	12W	M&NE-R 18
Wexford	(on M&NE-R now Buckley; on			
	GR&I-N now Bonds)			
Williams	11	22N	11W	AA-C 239.8
Yuma	34	23N	12W	AA-C 249.1

PART THREE:

Railroad Lines and Stations, Upper Peninsula, Michigan

DIRECTORY OF RAILROAD LINES

B&S	Blaney & Southern	
	Blaney Jct.-northward	
CNW	Chicago & North Western	
CNW-A	Green Bay, Wisc.-Escanaba	
CNW-B	Escanaba-Ishpeming	
CNW-BC +	Cascade Jct.-Palmer-Ishpeming, plus branch	
CNW-BO	Old line at Negaunee	
CNW-BS +	Swanzy-Princeton, plus branch	
CNW-C	Watersmeet-Choate, plus branches	
CNW-E	Escanaba-Antoine	
CNW-F +	Narenta-Felch, plus branches	
CNW-G	Ishpeming-Martins Landing	
CNW-I +	Stager-Amasa, plus branches	
CNW-I2	Mastodon-Dunn Mine	
CNW-I3	Great Western-Mansfield Mine	
CNW-M	Milwaukee-Watersmeet-Hurley	
CNW-M2 +	Connorsville Branch, plus branches	
CNW-M3	Cisco Lake Branch	
CNW-M4	Ethelwood Branch	
CNW-M5	Beaton Branch	
CNW-M6	Gogebic Branch	
CNW-M7 to CNW-M13	Other branches near Ironwood and Bessemer	
CNW-R +	Clowry-Republic, plus branches	
CNW-S	Green Bay-Saunders	
CNW-V	Winde-Ladoga	
CNW-W	Powers-Watersmeet	
CNW-WG	Hazel-Gibbs City	
CNW-WN	Quinnesec-Niagara	
CNW-W2 to CNW-W8	Other branches near Iron Mountain	
CNW-W9 to CNW-W16	Other branches near Iron River	

CR	Copper Range
CR-A	McKeever-Houghton-Calumet
CR-B	Baltic Branch
CR-C	Calumet Jct.-Gay
CR-E	Edgemere Branch
CR-F	Mill Mine Jct.-Freda
CR-G	Greenland Branch
CR-K	Coles Creek Branch
CR-L	Laurium Branch
CR-M	Mohawk Branch
CR-O	Mill Mine Jct.-Ricedale (via old main line)
CR-R	Redridge Branch
CR-S	Atlas-Senter
DSSA	Duluth, South Shore & Atlantic
DSSA-A +	St. Ignace-East Yard, plus branch
DSSA-B	East Yard-Ewen
DSSA-BB	Blueberry Mine Branch
DSSA-BC1&2	Champion Mine Branches
DSSA-BG	Greenwood Mine Branch
DSSA-BH	Ohio Mine Branch
DSSA-BM	Imperial Mine Branch
DSSA-BO	Old main line, Negaunee-Winthrop Jct.
DSSA-BW	Winthrop Mine Branch
DSSA-B2 to DSSA-B13	Other branches
DSSA-C	Ewen-Marengo Jct.
DSSA-CB	Bessemer Branch
DSSA-CW	White Pine Branch
DSSA-H +	Nestoria-Houghton, plus branch
DSSA-M	East Yard-Negaunee via Marquette & Western
DSSA-M +	Branches in Negaunee and Ishpeming
DSSA-P	Palmer Branch
DSSA-Q	Marquette docks
DSSA-R +	Republic Branch, plus branches
DSSA-S +	Sault Ste. Marie-Soo Jct., plus branch
E&LS	Escababa & Lake Superior

E&LS	Wells-Channing
E&LS-E	Escanaba Branch
E&LS-N	North Escanaba Branch
E&LS 2 to 7	Other branches
GB	Garden Bay
	Cooks-Van Harbor
H&TL	Hecla & Torch Lake
	Red Jacket Mine-Torch Lake Mills
KC	Keweenaw Central
KC	Calumet Jct.-Mandan
KC-2	Crestview Branch
KC-3	Lac la Belle Branch
LS&I	Lake Superior & Ishpeming
LS&I-A	Munising-Princeton
LS&I-A +	Other branches
LS&I-B	West Yard-Big Bay
LS&I-E	Stillman-Sunrise Landing
LS&I-E +	Other branches
LS&I-M	Lawson-West Yard
LS&I-O	Old main line, Eagle Mills-Ishpeming Yard
LS&I-O +	Other branches
LS&I-R	Republic Branch
LS&I-S	Presque Isle-Duncan
LS&I-S +	Other branches
LS&I-T	Tilden Mine Branch
MAN	Manistique
	Grand Marais-Curtis
M&LS	Manistique & Lake Superior
M&LS	Manistique Wharf-Doty
M&LS +	Other branches
MILW	Chicago, Milwaukee, St. Paul & Pacific
MILW-A	Green Bay-Champion
MILW-A2 to MILW-A8	Other branches

MILW-C	Kelso Jct.-Iron River
MILW-CF	Crystal Falls Branch
MILW-C2 to MILW-C9	Other branches
MILW-M	Menominee Branch
MILW-O	Channing-Ontonagon
MILW-O +	Other branches
MR	Mineral Range
MR-C +	Lake Jct.-Calumet-Mohawk, plus branches
MR-H +	Hancock-Lake Linden, plus branches
MR-L	Belt Line Jct.-Laurium
MR-M +	Houghton-Calumet, plus branches
MR-S +	Keweenaw Bay-Riddle Jct., plus branches
ONT	Ontonagon
	Ontonagon-Iron River Jct.
SOO	Soo Line
SOO	Minneapolis-Sault Ste. Marie
SOO-A	Rapid River-Eben Jct.
SOO-B	Bessemer Branch
SOO +	Other branches
W&M	Wisconsin & Michigan
W&M	Peshtigo-Iron Mountain
W&M-S	Aragon Mine Branch
W&M-W	Constine (Wisc.) Branch
W&M +	Other branches

ALGER COUNTY

Acker Mill	10	45N	20W	LS&I-A2 2.5
#Ackers				LS&I-A 10
#Addis	33	45N	20W	LS&I-A 11
#Alder				LS&I
#Ames	2	45N	19W	LS&I-E
Anna River	(now Hallston on DSSA-A)			
AuTrain	32	47N	20W	DSSA-A 125.0
#Baldy				LS&I
Beaver	14	48N	14W	MAN-A 12.3
Bennett	25	48N	14W	MAN-A 14.4
#Bing		46N	18W	LS&I-E 10
#Birdseye				LS&I-E 4
#Block				LS&I
#Blueberry				LS&I
Boucha	35	47N	17W	LS&I-E 21.1
#Boven				LS&I
#Brabant				LS&I-E3 5
Brownstone	25	47N	21W	DSSA-A 127.4
Calciferous	35	46N	21W	LS&I-A 15.5
Camp 15	8	47N	17W	LS&I-E4 5.3
#Carons				SOO
#Cavite		46N	13W	LS&I-E 6
Chapman	18	46N	17W	LS&I-E 15.2 —
				LS&I-E3 0
Chatham	6	46N	21W	LS&I-A 17.3
#Cico				LS&I-E
Coalwood	31	46N	19W	LS&I-E 1.5
Deerton	15	47N	22W	DSSA-A 135.7
Dewey	32	46N	20W	LS&I-A 12.2
Dieming	33	46N	22W	LS&I-A 23.8
Diffin	15	44N	22W	CNW-V 19.0
Dixon	31	46N	20W	LS&I-A 14.0
Dorsey	32	46N	22W	LS&I-A 25.1

Doty	22	46N	18W	LS&I-E 11.5 — M&LS 38.3
#Doublejack				LS&I-E
#Doubling				SOO-A
#Ducey				DSSA
East Bay	4	49N	13W	MAN-A 1.7
Eben Jct.	30	46N	21W	LS&I-A 19.7 — SOO-A 379.6
#Edmund				LS&I-E
Ethel	10	46N	18W	LS&I-E2 1.8
Evelyn	22	46N	18W	DSSA-A 108.4 — LS&I-E 11.7
Farm	12	48N	14W	MAN-A 10.4
Ferguson	25	46N	22W	LS&I-A 21.0
#Field		46N	20W	LS&I-A 8
#Finns				LS&I
#Fish Hatchery				LS&I
#Gibbs		46N	18W	DSSA-A 107
#Glasier				LS&I
#Gogarnville				DSSA
Grand Marais	6	49N	13W	MAN-A 0
Grand Marais Jct.	23	48N	13W	MAN-A 13.4
#Grey				LS&I
Haggins	34	47N	17W	LS&I-E 20.5
#Hale				LS&I
Hallston	15	46N	19W	LS&I-A 3.8
Hallston	(now Munising Jct. on DSSA-A)			
Hanley	36	46N	19W	LS&I-E 7.1
Hartho	14	46N	18W	LS&I-E 12.4
#Howard				LS&I-A 9
Hyde	31	46N	20W	LS&I-A 12.5
#Ivy				LS&I-A
#Jenks				LS&I
#Jenney		45N	19W	M&LS-3
Jeromeville	(now Shingleton)			
Juniper	29	46N	18W	LS&I-E 8.9
Kellan	25	46N	20W	LS&I-A 7.6
Ladoga	21	45N	22W	CNW-V 24.4
Leroux	25	47N	17W	LS&I-E 22.0
#Lloyd				LS&I-E
#Lorna				LS&I-A

Louds (Spur)	7	45N	21W	SOO-A 376.0
Masters	5	47N	17W	LS&I-E 17.8
#Meadow				LS&I-E
Merriam	17	46N	19W	LS&I-A 5.1
Metser	22	46N	17W	LS&I-E3 3.3
Miller	(see Spur 35)			
Munising	2	46N	19W	LS&I-A 0
Munising	(now Wetmore on DSSA-A)			
Munising Jct.	17	46N	19W	DSSA-A 116.7 − LS&I-A 5.3 + 0.4
Myren	33	47N	17W	LS&I-E 19.8 − LS&I-E4 0
#Myrtle				LS&I
#Nettles				LS&I
Onota	13	47N	22W	DSSA-A 133.7
#Paige		46N	21W	LS&I-A 19
Percy	13	46N	18W	LS&I-E 14.2
#Peterson				LS&I
Petrel	26	46N	17W	LS&I-E3 5.2
Railo	36	46N	20W	LS&I-A 8.7
#Reedsboro		46N	18W	DSSA-A 106
Ridge	12	46N	20W	DSSA-A 119.2
#Roberts				LS&I
Rock River	(now Rockton)			
Rockton	22	47N	21W	DSSA-A 129.4
#Roscoe				LS&I-E 5
Rumely	26	46N	22W	LS&I-A 22.5
#Samson				LS&I ?
Sand River	(see same, Marquette Co.)			
#Seamark				LS&I-E
Shingleton	31	46N	17W	DSSA-A 104.6; M&LS 34.6
Slapneck	35	46N	21W	LS&I-A 15.2
Spur 35		46N	17W	M&LS 35
Spur 139-T	7	47N	22W	DSSA-A 139.4
Spur R-370	7	44N	21W	SOO-A 370.1
Star Siding	35	46N	17W	DSSA-A 100.9
Stillman	36	46N	20W	LS&I-A 8.4 − LS&I-E 0
Summit	30	49N	13W	MAN-A 7.8

Sunrise Landing	29	48N	14W	LS&I-E 39.2
#Tanning	11	46N	21W	LS&I-A 1
Tioga	14	47N	22W	DSSA-A 134.8
#Train Falls				LS&I-A 13
Traunik	30	45N	21W	SOO-A 372.8
Trenary	19	44N	21W	SOO-A 368.0
#Underwood				DSSA-A
Vail	35	46N	20W	LS&I-A 9.8—
				LS&I-A2 0
Valley	20	46N	19W	LS&I-A 6.4
Van Meer	8	46N	17W	LS&I-E 16.9
Vida	31	46N	20W	LS&I-A 13.9
West AuTrain	31	47N	20W	DSSA-A 126.0
#West Percy				LS&I
Wetmore	13	46N	19W	DSSA-A 112.5
#White City				LS&I-A 10
Whitefish	9	47N	22W	DSSA-A 137.4
Whitefish Tank	31	46N	22W	LS&I-A 26.6
Wilcox	34	47N	20W	DSSA-A 123.0
Williams Crossing	28	47N	17W	LS&I-E4 1.1
#Wrights				LS&I
#Zervel				LS&I

BARAGA COUNTY

Arnheim	10	52N	33W	DSSA-H 32.4
Assinins	15	51N	33W	DSSA-H 24.6
#August				ONT? DSSA?
Baraga	33	51N	33W	DSSA-H 21.9
#Bashore				MR-S
Beaufort	22	48N	31W	DSSA-B 196.2
Beaufort Mine	22	48N	31W	DSSA-BH 1.0
Bellaire	(now Froberg)			
#Bess				DSSA
#Birch				DSSA
#Bode				DSSA-B
#Bonne				DSSA-B
Bovine Siding	16	50N	33W	DSSA-H 14.5

#Bennans				DSSA
Cliffs Siding	13	46N	32W	DSSA-B 200.2
Covington	22	48N	34W	DSSA-B 215.0
#Foy				DSSA-B
Froberg	12	51N	34W	MR-S 5.1
Giddings	(see same, Houghton Co.)			
Hamar (Siding)	14	51N	34W	MR-S 6.7
Herman	1	49N	33W	DSSA-H 8.9
#Hutula				DSSA-B
Imperial Mine	25	48N	31W	DSSA-BM 0.5
Imperial Mine Jct.	24	48N	31W	DSSA-B 194.2 –
				DSSA-BM 0
Iron Bridge	9	51N	33W	DSSA-H 26.2
#Keeler				DSSA-B
Kelsey	32	52N	33W	MR-S 2.3
Keweenaw Bay	27	52N	33W	DSSA-H 28.2 –
				MR-S 0
King Lake	23	48N	33W	DSSA-B 208.1
#Kuro				MR-S
L'Anse	8	50N	33W	DSSA-H 17.0
Leo	(now Spur 216)			
#Mission				DSSA
#Mullen				DSSA
Murphy	24	48N	34W	DSSA-B 213.3
#Nelsons Spur No. 1				MR-S
#Nelsons Spur No. 2				MR-S
Nestoria	12	48N	32W	DSSA-B 200.9 –
				DSSA-H 0
Newton	22	52N	33W	DSSA-H 30.1
Norwood Mine	(now Ohio Mine (new))			
Ohio Mine (new)	22	48N	31W	DSSA-BH 0.7
Ohio Mine (old)	22	48N	31W	DSSA-BH1 0.5
Ohio Mine Spur	22	48N	31W	DSSA-B 195.8 –
				DSSA-BH 0
#Opal				DSSA
#Palmer		50N	33W	DSSA-H 11
#Papin				MR-S
#Paquette				DSSA
Pelkie	16	51N	34W	MR-S 8.8
Perch	35	48N	35W	DSSA-B 221.5
#Perch Creek		47N	35W	MILW-O 355.5?

Portland Mine	26	48N	31W	DSSA-BH2 0.7
#Redruth	18?	48N	31W	DSSA-B
#Robinson				DSSA-B
#Shirley				DSSA
#Spruce				DSSA
Spur 201	11	48N	32W	DSSA-B 201.6
Spur 203	15	48N	32W	DSSA-B 203.0
Spur 205	17	48N	32W	DSSA-B 205.2
Spur 208	26	48N	33W	DSSA-B 208.5
#Spur 212				DSSA-B 212
Spur 216	21	48N	34W	DSSA-B 216.4
Spur D-5	16	49N	32W	DSSA-H 5.7
Spur D-14	16	50N	33W	DSSA-H 14.6
Spur D-15	9	50N	33W	DSSA-H 15.5
Spurr	24	48N	31W	DSSA-B 194.4 –
				DSSA-B7 0
Spurr Mine	24	48N	31W	DSSA-B7 0.4
Sturgeon	2	48N	32W	DSSA-H 1.3
Summit	17	49N	32W	DSSA-H 7.3
Tama Siding	(now Spur D-5)			
Taylor (Jct.)	34	50N	33W	DSSA-H 12.3 –
				DSSA-H2 0
Taylor Mine	9	49N	33W	DSSA-H2 2.3
Three Lakes	17	48N	31W	DSSA-B 198.0
#Tibbets				DSSA-B 217
Tioga	(now Spur 205?)			
Titan Mine	21	48N	31W	DSSA-BH 1.3
#Treado				DSSA-B
Tunis	25	47N	35W	MILW-O 354.5
Vermilac	29	48N	33W	DSSA-B 211.0
Watton	19	48N	34W	DSSA-B 218.5
Webster Mine	26	48N	31W	DSSA-BH2 1.0
Wetmore Mine	(now Imperial Mine)			

CHIPPEWA COUNTY

Alberta	(now Fibre)
Alexander	(now Cordell)

#Algonquin	11	47N	1W	DSSA-S
Bay Mills	29	46N	2W	DSSA-S2 2.4
Bay Mills	(now Brimley)			
#Bradkins		45N	7W	DSSA-A 37
#Breshme		45N	7W	DSSA-A 38
Bridge	25	46N	7W	DSSA-S 39.9
Brimley	4	46N	2W	DSSA-S 12.2 –
				DSSA-S2 0
Calco	23	46N	6W	DSSA-S 34.4
#Cana	8	44N	6W	DSSA-A 30
#Chesebrough	7	44N	6W	DSSA-A 30½
Coles	(see Calco)			
Cordell	19	44N	4W	SOO 458.1
Cottage Park	7	45N	1W	SOO 379.6
Dafter	22	46N	1W	SOO 483.2
#Dell	31	44N	5W	DSSA-A 26
Dick	22	44N	5W	SOO 455.1
Dorgans	12	46N	3W	DSSA-S 14.6
Dryburg	15	44N	3W	SOO 466.7
Eckerman	22	46N	6W	DSSA-S 35.2
#Elbon	15	46N	3W	DSSA-S 17
#Ferguson				DSSA-S
Fibre	18	44N	3W	SOO 464.0
Gladys	31	47N	1W	DSSA-A 7.7
Haff	21	44N	5W	SOO 453.8
Hendrie	27	45N	7W	DSSA-A 36.6
Hulbert	26	46N	7W	DSSA-A 40.9
#Iroquis		46N	4W	DSSA
Johnsonburg	14	46N	3W	DSSA-S 16.1
#Kane				DSSA-S
#Keme	7	44N	6W	DSSA-A 31
Kinross	23	45N	2W	SOO 475.6
Kinross Air Base	30	45N	2W	SOO 476.2 + 2.3
#Leland		46N	1W	SOO
Lyonton	21	46N	6W	DSSA-S 36.9
Natpo	31	45N	7W	DSSA-S 44.5
#Nolan				DSSA-S
Peshims	7	45N	7W	DSSA-A 40.0
Pine River	(now Rudyard)			
Poleco	27	46N	7W	DSSA-S
Raco	19	46N	3W	DSSA-S 19.9

Rexford	29	46N	4W	DSSA-S 25.0
#Rifle Range				DSSA
Rudyard	6	44N	2W	SOO 470.5
St. Marys Transfer	1	47N	1W	DSSA-S 0.8 –
				SOO 493.3
Sault Ste. Marie	6	47N	1W	DSSA-S 0 – SOO
				494.1
Scotts Quarry	29	44N	4W	SOO 458.1 + 0.5
Seewhy	30	46N	6W	DSSA-S 38.2
South Shore Jct.	(now St. Marys Transfer on SOO)			
Spur 27	25	46N	5W	DSSA-S 27.5
Spur 42	27	46N	7W	DSSA-S 41.8
#Spur 444				SOO 444
Spur 447	29	44N	6W	SOO 447.3
Spur 458	20	44N	4W	SOO 458.1
Spur 459	20	44N	4W	SOO 459.1
#Spur 467				SOO 467
Spur 477	24	45N	2W	SOO 476.8
Stevensburgh	(now Dafter)			
Strongs	29	46N	5W	DSSA-S 31.8
Superior	(now Brimley)			
Superior Jct.	1	47N	1W	DSSA-S 0.5
Trout Lake	23	44N	6W	DSSA-A 27.6 –
				SOO 449.7
Weller	24	46N	4W	DSSA-S 21.0
Wellsburg	16	46N	3W	DSSA-S 18.0
#Wenzels	13	44N	4W	SOO 463
Wilwin	7	44N	6W	DSSA-A 32.1

DELTA COUNTY

Alecto	18	39N	24W	CNW-F 4.7
Bark River	7	38N	24W	CNW-A 103.2
Barkville	(also known as Bark River)			
Bay Siding	31	40N	22W	CNW-B 119.9
Beaver	6	41N	22W	CNW-B 131.6
#Bichler		39N	23W	E&LS-E
Brampton	21	41N	22W	CNW-B 127.3

Campbell	24	42N	23W	CNW-B 134.3
Centerville	(now Lathrop)			
Chaison	7	40N	22W	CNW-B 123.7
Chandler	16	40N	23W	E&LS 9.7
Chandlers Falls	25	40N	23W	E&LS 5.0
#Cliffs				SOO
Cornell	31	41N	24W	E&LS 13.9
Days River	(now Brampton)			
Ducettes Spur	20	43N	21W	SOO-A 362.1
Ensign	36	41N	21W	SOO 354.3
Escanaba	29	39N	22W	CNW-B 114.5 + 0.3 (1st sta.)
Escanaba	30	39N	22W	CNW-B 114.9 (2nd sta.); E&LS-E 3.8
Escanaba	25	39N	23W	CNW-A 114.5 (3rd sta.)
#Farrell Spur		41N	18W	SOO 368
Felch Jct.	(now Tesch)			
Ferry	(now Wilson)			
Flat Rock	7	39N	22W	CNW-B 117.7
Flatrock Switch	12	39N	23W	E&LS 1.5 − E&LS-E 0
Ford River	36	39N	24W	CNW-A 108.2
Friday	12	42N	22W	CNW-V 7.3
Garden	17	39N	18W	GB 12.9
Garth	33	41N	21W	SOO 350.3 + 1.8
Gladstone	21	40N	22W	SOO 342.7
Gladstone Crossing	(now Lambert)			
#Gladstone Wharf				SOO
Grant	(now Marrengers)			
Gravel Pit	8	41N	21W	SOO-A 351.0
Groos	1	39N	23W	E&LS 2.0 − E&LS-N 0
#Haggersons Spur		39N	24W	SOO 329
Hendricks	6	41N	24W	E&LS 22.2
Hendricks Tank	8	41N	24W	E&LS 21.0
#Hoops Spur		43N	21W	SOO-A
Isabella	2	41N	19W	SOO 366.8
Kingsley	25	41N	23W	E&LS 16.0

Kipling	10	40N	22W	SOO 344.8
#Lamay(s)				E&LS 15
Lambert	25	40N	23W	E&LS 5.3
Larch	6	39N	22W	CNW-B 118.2;
				SOO 339.4
Larsons Spur	6	43N	23W	CNW-B 144.9
Lathrop	6	43N	23W	CNW-B 144.3
LeBresh Spur	26	42N	22W	CNW-V 4.4
#Lefebvres				E&LS 9
Maple Ridge	34	43N	23W	CNW-B 139.1
Maplewood	8	41N	21W	SOO-A 351.4
Marrengers	8	40N	23W	E&LS 10.8
Mason	(now West Gladstone)			
Masonville	31	41N	21W	SOO 347.9
McLaughlin	26	40N	18W	GB 5.9
#McQueens Spur		39N	23W	SOO 333
#Miners				SOO-A
Nahma Jct.	1	40N	20W	SOO 362.2
Narenta	34	39N	24W	CNW-A 106.2 —
				CNW-F 0
Newhall	23	39N	24W	SOO 330.5
New Minneapolis	(now Isabella)			
North Escanaba	19	39N	22W	CNW-B 115.7 —
				CNW-E 0
North Escanaba	12	39N	23W	E&LS-N 1.0 —
				SOO 337.9
North Wye	18	39N	22W	CNW-B 115.9
No. 6 Ore Yard	23	39N	23W	CNW-E 1.7
#Odetts Spur				SOO-A
Ogontz	35	41N	20W	SOO 360.1
#Ore Scale	20	39N	23W	CNW-E
Osier	13	43N	22W	CNW-V 12.2
Perkins	(on CNW-B now Winde)			
Perkins	4	41N	22W	CNW-V 1.3
Petersons	28	39N	24W	CNW-F 1.4
Pine Ridge	29	39N	23W	CNW-A 110.1
Portage	20	39N	23W	CNW-E 5.1
Rapid River	29	41N	21W	SOO 348.8 —
				SOO-A 348.8

Rapid Siding	(now Rapid River)			
Roberts Siding	36	41N	18W	GB 1.1
Rock	3	42N	23W	CNW-B 138.3
Russell	23	41N	18W	SOO 372.6
St. Jacques	36	41N	20W	SOO 360.4
Salva	1	40N	24W	E&LS 12.5
Schaffer	20	39N	24W	CNW-F 3.7
Setif	28	41N	21W	SOO 350.3
Siding No. 1	19	39N	23W	CNW-E 5.9
Siding R-358	30	43N	21W	SOO-A 358.6
South Wye	(now Escanaba-3rd sta.)			
Spur R-355	20	42N	21W	SOO-A 354.6
#Spur 357				SOO 357
#Spur R-359				SOO-A 359
#Spur R-362				SOO-A 362
#Spur R-363				SOO-A 363
#Spur R-367				SOO-A 367
#Spur 370				SOO 370
#Spur 371				SOO 371
Station 51	35	40N	18W	GB 7.4
Sturgeon River	6	40N	19W	SOO 362.8
Ten Mile Spur	(now Siding R-358)			
Tesch	28	39N	24W	CNW-E 10.8 – CNW-F 2.6 – SOO 327.8
Trombley	14	42N	23W	CNW-B 136.1
Vans Harbor	7	39N	18W	GB 13.7
Van Winkle	33	41N	18W	SOO 369.4
Wells	18	39N	22W	E&LS 0
West Gladstone	18	40N	22W	CNW-B 121.2
#West Point		41N	18W	SOO 374½
White	(now Woodlawn)			
White Fish River	28	41N	21W	SOO 349.8
Winde	8	41N	22W	CNW-B 130.6 – CNW-V 0
Woodlawn	22	41N	24W	E&LS 18.5 – E&LS-2 0

DICKINSON COUNTY

Alfred	35	43N	27W	E&LS 38.5
Antoine	30	40N	30W	CNW-E 52.6 — CNW-W 29.9
#Antoine Mine	20	40N	30W	MILW
Appleton Mine	13	39N	29W	CNW-E 39.2 — CNW-E2 0
Appleton Mine	7	39N	29W	CNW-E2 0.8
Aragon Jct.	24	39N	28W	W&M 62.1 — W&M-S 0
Aragon Mine	8	39N	29W	CNW-W4 0.6; W&M-S 5.5
Bergam	12	39N	28W	W&M 64.1 — W&M 3 0
#Bjorkman				MILW
Bradley Mine	25	40N	31W	MILW-A2 0.5
Breen Mine	22	39N	28W	CNW-W at Waucedah
#Brier Hill Mine				?
#Bryden		43N	28W	E&LS 46
#Callah				W&M
Calumet Mine	8	41N	28W	CNW-F2 3.4
Carys Spur	16	42N	30W	MILW-A 307.2
Channing	8	43N	30W	MILW-A 315.3 — MILW-O 315.3 — (E&LS 63.5)
Chapin Mine	(now Bradley Mine)			
Clano	15	39N	29W	W&M-S 3.0
Clifford Mine	17	40N	30W	MILW-A4 1.5
Cuff Siding	21	40N	30W	CNW-E 50.0
Cundy (Mine)	3	40N	30W	W&M 71.9
Curry (Mine)	9	39N	29W	CNW-W 20.1
Cyclops Mine	8	39N	29W	CNW-W5 0.7
East Norway	4	39N	28W	W&M-W2A 0.3
East Vulcan Mine	11	39N	29W	CNW-W2A 0.3
Felch	33	42N	28W	CNW-F 35.0
Few Mine	6	39N	29W	W&M 69.5

Floodwood	12	44N	30W	MILW-A 323.0
Ford Siding	(now Channing)			
#Ford Spur				MILW-A
Foster City	7	41N	27W	CNW-F 30.1
Fumee	1	39N	30W	CNW-W 23.1
#Golden		43N	30W	E&LS 59
Granite Bluff	22	41N	30W	MILW-A 300.2
Groveland	(now Randville)			
Groveland Jct.	3	41N	30W	MILW-A 303.4 – MILW-A5 0
Groveland Mine	31	42N	29W	MILW-A5 3.5; MILW-A6 3.7
Hamlin	33	39N	28W	W&M 58.8
Hardwood	9	41N	27W	CNW-F 28.0
Henderson	20	43N	28W	E&LS 49.3
Hewitt Mine	(now Millie Mine)			
Holmes	(now Sagola)			
Hylas	15	41N	27W	CNW-F 26.2
Indiana Mine	27	40N	30W	CNW-E 48.8
Iron Mountain	31	40N	30W	CNW-W 28.9; MILW-A 291.2 – (W&M 76.3)
Johnson Spur	(now Henderson)			
Kates	(see same, Marquette Co.)			
Kelvin	23	39N	29W	W&M-S 2.0
#King				CNW-E
#LaCourts Spur				MILW-A
Lindsley	32	43N	27W	E&LS 41.9
Loop Line Jct.	21	40N	30W	CNW-E 50.5 – CNW-W8 3.5
Loretto	13	39N	28W	W&M 63.6
Loretto	18	39N	28W	CNW-W 15.4
Loretto Mine	7	39N	28W	CNW-E 39.3 + 1.2
#McRae		43N	27W	E&LS 41
Merriman	28	41N	30W	MILW-A 298.6
Metronite Quarry	26	42N	28W	CNW-F3 1.4
Metropolitan	31	42N	28W	CNW-F 36.5
Millie Mine	31	40N	30W	CNW-W7 2.7
Munro Mine	6	39N	29W	W&M 68.9
Norway	5	39N	29W	W&M 67.9

Norway	8	39N	29W	CNW-W5 20.9
Norway Mine	5	39N	29W	CNW-W5 0.9
O'Callaghan	13	39N	29W	W&M 62.8
O'Callaghan (Mills) Spur	13	39N	29W	W&M-3 1.0
#Ornum				W&M
Pewabic Mine	32	40N	30W	CNW-W7 2.2
Quinnesec	3	39N	30W	CNW-W 24.6— CNW-WN 0; W&M 71.8
Quinnesec Jct.	19	40N	30W	MILW-A 292.8— MILW-A3 0
Quinnesec Mine	34	40N	30W	CNW-W ?; MILW-A3A 5.4
Ralph	22	43N	28W	E&LS 46.6
Randville	33	42N	30W	MILW-A 304.5— MILW-A6 0
Randville Mine	31	42N	29W	MILW-A6 4.1
River Siding	31	42N	29W	MILW-A6 4.1
Ruprechts	20	39N	28W	CNW-W 14.3
#Russell				E&LS 44
Sagola	29	43N	30W	MILW-A 311.5
Sawyer Lake	28	44N	30W	MILW-A 319.2
Siding No. 5	2	39N	29W	CNW-E 41.6
South Norway	8	39N	29W	W&M-S 5.0
Spruce	35	42N	28W	CNW-F 33.0— CNW-F2 0— CNW-F3 0
#Spur 221				MILW-A 221
Sturgeon	18	39N	28W	CNW-E 38.3
Sumac	20	39N	28W	CNW-E 36.8
Summit	26	39N	28W	CNW-W 10.8
Traders Jct.	18	40N	30W	MILW-A 293.6— MILW-A4 0
Traders Mine	(now Clifford Mine)			
Turner	11	43N	29W	E&LS 52.7
Turner Jct.	15	43N	29W	E&LS 53.8
Verona Mine	11	39N	29W	CNW-W2A 0.9
Vista	29	39N	28W	W&M 60.4
Vivian Mine	34	40N	30W	MILW-A3A 6.2

Vulcan	10	39N	29W	CNW-W 18.6
Vulcan Mine	10	39N	29W	CNW-W2 0.7
#Wann				W&M
#Ward		43N	28W	E&LS 45
Waucedah	22	39N	28W	CNW-W 12.1
Wells Spur	3	39N	29W	CNW-E 42.2
West Chapin Mine	25	40N	31W	MILW-A2 1.6
West Vulcan Mine	9	39N	29W	CNW-W3 0.5

GOGEBIC COUNTY

Abitosse	35	48N	46W	DSSA-C 292.1
Anvil Mine	14	47N	46W	CNW-M9 0.9
Ashland Mine	22	47N	47W	SOO-B2 0.4 + 0.4
Asteroid Mine	13	47N	46W	CNW-M 340.3
Aurora Mine	23	47N	47W	SOO-B2 3.2
Beaton	17	45N	40W	CNW-M 300.2 –
				CNW-M5 0
#Bernard				DSSA-C
Bessemer	10	47N	46W	CNW-M 343.7;
				DSSA-CB 2;
				SOO-B 443.5
Bessemer Jct.	34	48N	46W	DSSA-C 293.7 –
				DSSA-CB 0
Black Siding	31	46N	41W	CNW-M 307.4
Blemers	17	45N	40W	CNW-M 299.3
Brotherton Mine	9	47N	45W	CNW-M2B 0.2
#Camp Francis				DSSA
#Carlson				CNW
Castile Mine	10	47N	45W	CNW-M2B 0.9
Chicago Mine	9	47N	45W	CNW-M2A 0.7
Cisco Lake	33	45N	41W	CNW-M3 5.3
Colby Mine	16	47N	46W	SOO-B3 0.4;
				SOO-B4A 1.5
Connorville	16	48N	45W	CNW-M2 7.7
Crozer	18	45N	38W	CNW-W 99.5
Croziers Mill	13	45N	39W	CNW-R 3.6
Davis Mine	(now New Davis Mine)			

#Defer				DSSA
Duke	23	48N	44W	DSSA-C 280.0
Dunham	14	46N	44W	CNW-M 326.8
East Norrie Mine	23	47N	47W	SOO-B2 3.4
#Erickson				DSSA
Ethelwood	7	47N	43W	CNW-M4 8.7
Eureka Mine	13	47N	46W	CNW-M 341.0; CNW-M13 1.1
Everest	13	46N	41W	CNW-M 308.0
Fisk Mine	9	47N	45W	CNW-M2A 0.4
#Foster				DSSA
Geneva Mine	18	47N	46W	CNW-M10A 1.0
Gogebic	25	46N	42W	CNW-M 309.8
Gogebic Jct.	30	46N	41W	CNW-M 308.9 − CNW−M6 0
Hartleys	16	46N	44W	CNW-M 328.9
Ironton Mine	17	47N	46W	CNW-M10 0.8 + 0.6
Ironwood	22	47N	47W	CNW-M 350.0; SOO-B 437.2
Jackpot Mine	16	47N	46W	CNW-M10 1.7
Jack Spur	(now Spur 280)			
Junet	(now Spur 301)			
Keweenaw Mine	11	47N	46W	CNW-M9 0.8; SOO-B 445.3
#Kilton				DSSA
Lake Street	22	47N	47W	CNW-M 349.3 − SOO-B 443.5
Manley Siding	2	47N	45W	CNW-M2 2.9
Marenisco	16	46N	43W	CNW-M 322.2 − CNW-M4 0
#Massie				DSSA-C
Meteor Mine	11	47N	45W	CNW-M2B 2.5
#Midway				DSSA-C
Mikado Mine	18	47N	45W	CNW-M8 1.2
Montreal	33	48N	47W	DSSA-C 300.4
New Davis Mine	9	47N	46W	CNW-M10A 0.7 + 0.3
Newport	34	46N	42W	CNW-M 311.9
Newport Mine	24	47N	47W	CNW-M12 2.8
Norrie Mine	22	47N	47W	SOO-B2 3.9
North Bessemer	33	48N	46W	DSSA-C 295.0

North Ironwood	35	48N	47W	DSSA-C 299.2
North Newport	13	47N	47W	CNW-M11 1.4
Pabst Mine	28	47N	47W	CNW-M13 2.3
Palms Mine	14	47N	46W	SOO-B3A 3.5
Pilgrim Mine	18	47N	45W	CNW-M8 0.4
Planter	31	48N	45W	DSSA-C 289.6
Plymouth Mine	(now Pilgrim Mine)			
Puritan Mine	17	47N	46W	CNW-M10A 2.0
Ramsay	13	47N	46W	CNW-M 341.2
Ross Siding	30	47N	44W	CNW-M 332.9
Royal Mine	18	47N	46W	CNW-M10A 2.5
Ruby Mine	(now Puritan Mine)			
#Siding 339		47N	45W	CNW-M 339
Siemens	18	47N	46W	CNW-M 346.3;
				SOO-B 440.9
Sillberg	36	48N	47W	DSSA-C 297.8
Spur 280	24	48N	44W	DSSA-C 279.8
Spur 287	26	48N	45W	DSSA-C 286.3
Spur 301	33	48N	47W	DSSA-C 301.3
State Line	32	44N	39W	CNW-M 283.6
Stickley	11	45N	41W	CNW-M 303.1–
				CNW-M3 0
Sunday Lake Mine	10	47N	45W	CNW-M2B 0.5
Sylvania	19	45N	39W	CNW-M 295.2
Tamarac(k)	23	45N	38W	CNW-W 95.2
Thayer	5	45N	41W	CNW-M 306.8
Thomaston	34	48N	45W	DSSA-C 287.6
Tilden Mine	15	47N	46W	SOO-B4 0.4
Tobin Siding	23	47N	45W	CNW-M 335.4
Tula	21	48N	44W	DSSA-C 282.0
Turtle	(now Stickley)			
#Twecoma				CNW
Vaughn Mine	23	47N	47W	SOO-B2 3.0
Vernona	18	47N	45W	CNW-M 339.7
Wakefield	16	47N	45W	CNW-M 338.0–
				CNW-M2 0
Wakefield Mine	17	47N	45W	CNW-M7 1.7
Watersmeet	28	45N	39W	CNW-M 292.2–
				CNW-R 0–
				CNW-W 102.9
Water Tank	(now Bessemer Jct.)			

Wellington	3	45N	43W	CNW-M 318.0
Winona Mine	17	47N	46W	CNW-M10 1.4
Wisconsin Mine	(now Davis Mine)			
Yale Mine	16	47N	46W	SOO-B3A 0.3 + -0.2

HOUGHTON COUNTY

Ahmeek Mill	12	55N	33W	MR-H 8.5
#Alahola				MR
Allouez	5	56N	32W	KC 4.4; MR-C 18.2
Allouez Mine	(see same, Keweenaw Co.)			
Alston	33	51N	35W	MR-S 15.6
Anthony	2	47N	36W	DSSA-B 227.8
Arcadian Jct.	(now St. Marys Jct.)			
Arcadian Mine	20	55N	33W	MR-P2 1.5
Atlantic	8	53N	34W	CR-A 37.1
Atlas	23	55N	34W	MR-M 4.2 − MR-M3 0
Atlas	27	55N	34W	CR-A 47.1 − CR-S 0
Baltic	21	53N	34W	CR-B 1.6
Baltic Jct.	20	53N	34W	CR-A 34.7 − CR-B 0
Beacon Hil	25	55N	36W	CR-F 10.0
Belt Line Jct.	14	56N	33W	MR-C 14.9 − MR-L 0
#Berglands Mill Track				MILW-O 364
Boston	(now Siding M-7)			
Boston Jct.	7	55N	33W	MR-H 7.4 − MR-M8 0
#Boyds				MILW-O 371
#Britton Spur	(alternate name for Pori?)			
#Brotherton				MILW-O
Calumet	14	56N	33W	CR-A 59.2 − KC 0; MR-M 13.0 (old); MR-C 14.7 (new)

Calumet Jct.	13	56N	33W	CR-A 57.2 – CR-C 0 – CR-L 57.2 – (KC 1.7)
#Calumet Mine	23	56N	33W	H&TL
Centennial Mine	18	56N	32W	MR-L 1.4 + 0.3
Chassell	32	54N	33W	DSSA-H 40.5
Clark	(now Spur H-3)			
Cole Creek	33	53N	34W	CR-K 2.0
Copper City	5	56N	32W	CR-C 3.3 – (KC 4.8)
Copper Range Jct.	27	55N	33W	MR-H 5.1 – CR-S 0.1
#Corbett				MR
Crystal Lake	2	47N	36W	DSSA-B 276.9
#Danielson				DSSA
Dollar Bay	33	55N	33W	CR-A 45.9; MR-H 3.7
Dollar Bay Dock	33	55N	33W	MR-H4 0.7
Donken	31	53N	35W	CR-A 21.0
#Dow				DSSA
#Drew				MR-S
Dupont Jct.	27	55N	33W	MR-H 5.0 – MR-P 5.1
East Houghton	36	55N	34W	DSSA-H 48.0
#Eddys Spur				CR
Edgemere	19	55N	35W	CR-E 1.2
Edgemere Jct.	19	55N	35W	CR-F 9.6 – CR-E0
Elm River	12	52N	36W	CR-A 19.1
Faleston	(now Lake Roland)			
#Farm				DSSA-H
Findley Jct.	20	49N	37W	MILW-O 378.4
#Fouchette				DSSA-H
#Fox				MILW-O
Franklin	(on MR-H now Atlas)			
Franklin Jct.	(now Franklin)			
Franklin Junior Mine	8	55N	34W	MR-M8 0.6
Franklin Mine	24	55N	34W	MR
Freda	25	55N	36W	CR-F 10.7
Freda Park	25	55N	36W	CR-F 11.4

Frost (Jct.)	25	49N	37W	MILW-O 373.7
#Garon				DSSA-H
#Glanville				DSSA-H
#Globe				CR
#Green		55N	33W	CR-A 44
Grove	6	55N	32W	CR-A 52.2
Grover(ton)	12	55N	33W	MR-H 8.7
Hancock	35	55N	34W	CR-A 42.5;
				MR-H 1.3
Hancock	(see also Lake View)			
Hazel	27	51N	35W	MR-S 13.4
Hecla Mine	23	56N	33W	H&TL 1.0 + 0.6
Highway	4	55N	33W	MR-M 9.3
#Hillier				MR-S
Houghton	36	55N	34W	CR-A 42.1;
				DSSA-H
				48.6 − MR-M 0
Houghton Falls	36	56N	33W	H&TL 3.7
Hubbell	6	55N	32W	MR-H 9.1
Hubbell	12	55N	33W	CR-A 51.2
#Jones Spur				MILW-O
Kearsarge	12	56N	32W	MR-H3 2.6
Kenton	11	47N	37W	DSSA-B 233.4
#Kirby				DSSA-B
Kitchi	5	47N	36W	DSSA-B 230.0
Klingville	33	53N	33W	DSSA-H 34.7
Lake Gerald	11	52N	36W	CR-A 18.6
Lake Jct.	23	55N	33W	MR-H 7.2 −
				MR-C 7.2
Lake Linden	6	55N	32W	CR-A 52.8
Lake Linden	7	55N	32W	MR-H 9.7
Lake Roland	22	52N	36W	CR-A 15.9
Lake View	35	55N	34W	MR-M 1.0
(Hancock)				
#Lakewood		53N	35W	CR-A 24
LaSalle Jct.	4	55N	33W	MR-M 9.0 −
				MR-M9 0
#LaSalle Mine				MR-M9
Laurium	24	56N	33W	CR-L 59.1;
				MR-L 3.0
#Legris				CR

Linwood	7	55N	32W	MR-H 9.3
#Maki				MR-S
Mason	26	55N	33W	CR-A 48.1;
				MR-H 6.5
#Mayflower		56N	32W	CR-A
#Mays				MR-H
Messner	13	53N	34W	CR-O 32.7
Midway	1	55N	33W	MR-C 10.0
Mill Mine Jct.	8	53N	34W	CR-A 35.6—
				CR-F 0—
				CR-O 34.3
Mills	13	55N	33W	CR-A 50.0;
				MR-H 7.7
#Monroe Jct.				H&TL 4^1/$_2$
#Morrisons Spur				CR
Motley	30	51N	36W	MR-S 24.2
#Nestor Crossing		47N	35W	MILW-O 278
#New Arcadian Mine				MR-P2
Nisula	31	51N	35W	MR-S 17.9
North Kearsarge	5	56N	32W	KC-3.4
North Kearsarge Mine	5	56N	32W	MR-C5 0.5
North Tamarack Mine	11	56N	33W	MR-C3 1.8
Obenhoff	1	54N	35W	CR-F 2.8
Opechee	(now Osceola)			
Osceola	26	56N	33W	MR-M 11.5;
				MR-C 12.8
Osceola Mine	27	56N	33W	MR-C1 0.8
Otter	33	51N	36W	MR-S 22.2
Painesdale	31	53N	34W	CR-A 31.6
Painesdale Jct.	(now Mill Mine Jct.)			
#Perch Creek Spur				MILW-O
#Phillips		56N	31W	CR-C
Pilgrim	5	54N	33W	DSSA-H 45.7
Point Mills	10	55N	33W	MR-P 8.8
Point Mills Jct.	(now Atlas on CR-A)			
Pori	5	49N	37W	MILW-O 381.8
Portage Coal Dock	32	55N	33W	MR-H 3.2
#Prickett				MILW-O
#Pryor				MR-H

#Quincy Mills				MR-H
Quincy Mine	26	55N	34W	MR-M3 1.8
#Quinn				DSSA-H
Red Jacket	14	56N	33W	MR-M2 1.3
Red Jacket Mine	14	56N	33W	H&TL 0
Redridge	29	55N	35W	CR-R 0.9
Redridge Jct.	20	55N	35W	CR-F 7.6 − CR-R 0
Ricedale (new)	3	52N	34W	CR-A 27.9 −
				CR-O 27.9
Ricedale (old)	35	53N	34W	CR-O 29.2
Ripley	36	55N	34W	CR-A 43.4;
				MR-H 1.3
Robinson		(now Chassell)		
#Rubicon				MR-S
St. Marys Jct.	8	55N	33W	MR-M 7.0 −
				MR-P 0
Salmon Trout	3	54N	35W	CR-F 5.4
#Samach				MR-S
Senter	1	54N	33W	CR-S 3.2
Shops	35	55N	34W	CR-A 41.4
Shore Line Jct.	35	55N	34W	MR-M 0.4 −
				MR-H 0.4 −
				(CR-A 42.5)
Siding M-7	7	55N	33W	MR-M 7.0
Sidnaw	5	47N	35W	DSSA-B 223.8 −
				MILW-O 362.4
#Smelter				CR
South Kearsarge	7	56N	32W	KC 2.0;
				MR-M3A 0.7
South Kearsarge Mine	7	56N	32W	MR-C4 0.7
South Lake Linden	6	55N	32W	CR-A 51.4
South Lake Linden		(on MR-H, now Grover)		
South Range	17	53N	34W	CR-A 34.5
Spur 237	8	47N	37W	DSSA-B 237.4
#Spur 269				MILW-O 353
#Spur 275				MILW-O 359
#Spur 277				MILW-O 361
#Spur 283		48N	36W	MILW-O 367
#Spur 284		48N	36W	MILW-O 368
#Spur 288				MILW-O 372

#Spur 293		49N	37W	MILW-O 377
#Spur 294				MILW-O 378
#Spur 297				MILW-O 381
#Spur 298				MILW-O 382
Spur D-38	5	53N	33W	DSSA-H 39.3
Spur D-39	5	53N	33W	DSSA-H 39.5
Spur H-3	33	55N	33W	MR-H 3.6 —
				MR-H4 0
Stackpole	28	52N	36W	CR-A 15.3
#Stantons Spur				MILW-O 372
Stanwood	20	55N	35W	CR-F 8.4
Stonington	20	53N	35W	CR-A 23.4
Swedetown	23	55N	34W	MR-M 3.7
Tamarack	23	56N	33W	MR-C 14.2
Tamarack Mine	14	56N	33W	MR-C3 0.3
Tecumseh Mine	34	56N	33W	MR-M10 0.3
Toivola	8	53N	35W	CR-A 25.3
Torch Lake Jct.	23	56N	33W	MR-M 13.0
Torch Lake Mills	7	55N	32W	H&TL 5.6
Trimountain	29	53N	34W	CR-A 32.6
Twin Lakes	22	52N	36W	CR-A 16.7
Upper Mills	13	55N	33W	MR-C 7.9
West End Bridge	36	55N	34W	MR-M 0.3 —
				(CR-A 42.3)
White	36	51N	36W	MR-S 19.0
Winona	29	52N	36W	CR-A 13.6
Wolverine	8	56N	32W	KC 2.4
Wolverine Mine	7	56N	32W	MR-C4A 0.6
Woodside	33	55N	33W	CR-A 46.5;
				MR-H 4.4
Yandell	7	56N	32W	CR-C 0.6

IRON COUNTY

Alpha	13	42N	33W	CNW-I2 4.5
Amasa	4	42N	33W	CNW-I 23.8;
				MILW-O 335.5
Amasa-Porter Mine	22	44N	33W	MILW-O2 1.0

Amasa-Porter Mine Jct.	14	44N	33W	MILW-O 332.2 – MILW-O2 0
Andersons Spur	8	44N	35W	CNW-WG 5.8
Armenia Mine	23	43N	32W	CNW-I3A 0.9 + 0.7; MILW-C2A 0.1 + 0.2
Armstrong	32	42N	33W	CNW-W 54.7
Atkinson	(now Gibbs City)			
Baker Mine	31	43N	34W	CNW-W10E
Balkan Mine	13	42N	33W	CNW-I2 4.4
Balsam	13	44N	33W	MILW-O 330.9 – CNW-I 18.7
Baltic Mine	7	42N	34W	CNW-W10A 0.5
Basswood	19	44N	36W	CNW-W 81.3
Bates Interchange	31	43N	34W	CNW-W10 2.9 – MILW-C 23.7
Bates Jct.	32	43N	34W	MILW-C 22.9 – MILW-C8 0
Bates Mine	19	43N	34W	MILW-C8 2.7
#Bates Yard				MILW-C
Beechwood	1	43N	36W	CNW-W 75.9
Bengal Mine	36	43N	35W	CNW-W10D 0.8
Berkshire Mine	6	42N	34W	CNW-W10C 0.4
Beta Mine	26	43N	35W	CNW-W14 0.2
Beyersdorf Spur	9	44N	37W	CNW-W 88.0
#Blixt Spur				MILW-C
Book Mine	12	42N	33W	CNW-I2 5.5
Bristol Mine	10	43N	32W	MILW-C7 2.3
#Brule				CNW
Buchholz Mine	27	43N	35W	CNW-W14 0.6
Cadiz	22	42N	34W	CNW-W 59.3 – CNW-W9 0
Cardiff Mine	22	43N	35W	MILW-C8A 5.7
#Carpenter Jct.	26	43N	33W	MILW-C 8.4 – MILW-C6 0
Carpenter Mine	31	43N	32W	MILW-C6A 1.0
Caspian	1	42N	35W	CNW-W 65.6
Caspian Mine	1	42N	35W	CNW-W16 0.8

Chatham Mine	35	43N	35W	CNW-W12 0.8
Chicagon	25	43N	34W	MILW-C 16.3
Chicagon Mine	26	43N	34W	CNW-W9 7.1;
				MILW-C5 0.8
Clairs Mine	(now Bristol Mine)			
Cortland Mine	34	43N	35W	CNW-W11 1.6
Crystal Falls	29	43N	32W	CNW-I 8.6;
				MILW-CF 6.8
Crystal Falls Jct.	19	43N	32W	MILW-C 5.6 −
				MILW-CF 5.6
Crystal Falls Mine	22	43N	32W	MILW-C3 0.9
Davidson No. 1 Mine	23	43N	35W	CNW-W13A 1.3
#Davidson No. 2 Mine				
Davidson No. 3 Mine	14	43N	35W	MILW-C8 4.3
DeGrass Mine	7	42N	34W	CNW-W10A 1.5
Diana	1	45N	34W	MILW-O 344.5
Dober No. 2 Mine	1	42N	35W	CNW-W16 0.2
Dufeck Spur	5	44N	37W	CNW-W 89.5
Dunn Mine	1	42N	33W	CNW-I2 7.1
Elmwood	10	44N	37W	CNW-W 86.7
Fairbanks Mine	20	43N	32W	MILW-C4 1.5
Fogerty Mine	1	42N	35W	CNW-W16 1.5
Forbes Mine	14	43N	35W	MILW-C8 4.8
Fortune Lake	27	43N	33W	MILW-C 9.4
Fortune Lake Mine	24	43N	33W	MILW-C 7.7
Genesee Mine	30	43N	32W	MILW-C7 1.4
Gibbs City	8	44N	35W	CNW-WG 6.4
Gibson Mine	15	44N	33W	MILW-O3 0.7
Gratton (Spur)	1	43N	32W	MILW-O 322.8
Great Western	21	43N	32W	CNW-I 10.9
Great Western Jct.	15	43N	32W	MILW-C 3.4 −
				MILW-C4 0
Great Western Mine	21	43N	32W	MILW-C4 1.0
Hazel	1	43N	36W	CNW-W 75.1 −
				CNW-WG 0

Hemlock	(now Basswood)			
Hemlock Mine	(Amasa on CNW-I)			
Hiawatha No. 1				
Mine	35	43N	35W	CNW-W12
				0.7 + 0.3
Hiawatha No. 2				
Mine	2	42N	35W	CNW-W12 0.3
Hilltop Mine	22	43N	32W	MILW-C3 0.5
Hollister Mine	13	43N	32W	CNW-I3A 1.4;
				MILW-C2A1.4
Homer Mine	23	43N	35W	MILW-C8A 5.5
Hope Mine	27	43N	32W	MILW-C2 2.7
Iron River	26	43N	35W	CNW-W 67.7;
				MILW-C 26.0
Iron River Jct.	(now Stager)			
James Mine	(see Osana Mine)			
#Johnson Spur				MILW-O
Judson Mine	13	42N	33W	CNW-I2 4.0
Kelso Jct.	1	43N	32W	MILW-O 323.1 −
				MILW-C 0
Kiernan Spur	10	43N	31W	MILW-O 319.4
Kimball Mine	29	43N	32W	CNW-I4 1.0 + 0.4
Lamont Mine	20	43N	32W	MILW-C4 1.6
Lee Peck Jct.	14	43N	32W	CNW-I3A 2.0 −
				MILW-C 1.8 −
				MILW-C2 0
Lee Peck Mine	26	43N	32W	MILW-C2 2.2
Lincoln Mine	21	43N	32W	MILW-C4 1.3
Lloyds Spur	2	44N	37W	CNW-W 85.1
Mansfield Mine	17	43N	31W	CNW-I3 15.7
Mastodon	19	42N	32W	CNW-I 1.9 −
				CNW-I2 1.9
Mastodon Mine	(at site of Aplha)			
#Maywood				CNW
McDonald Mine	23	43N	32W	CNW-I3A 0.9 + 0.3;
				MILW-C2A
				0.6
McGills Mine	1	42N	35W	CNW-W16 0.9
McGoverns	33	42N	33W	CNW-W 53.7
#McLane				DSSA-A
#McLeans Spur				MILW-O

McRaes Spur	27	44N	36W	CNW-W 79.0
#Mentzers Spur				MILW
Michigan Mine	9	44N	33W	MILW-O4 0.6
Mitchell Spur	30	44N	32W	MILW-O 329.1
Minckler Mine	23	43N	35W	CNW-W13B2 0.6
Monitor Mine	(now Lamont Mine)			
Monogahela Mine	31	43N	32W	MILW-C6 2.1
Nanaimo Mine	26	43N	35W	CNW-W14 0.3
Naults	35	42N	33W	CNW-W 51.2
Net River	25	46N	34W	MILW-O 346.3
North Hiawatha Mine	35	43N	35W	CNW-W12 1.0
Odgers Mine	30	43N	32W	MILW-C7 1.9
Osano Mine	23	43N	35W	CNW-W13B1 0.4
#Paines		44N	36W	CNW-W 80
Paint River	(now Elmwood)			
Paint River Mine	(see Fairbanks Mine)			
Palatka	12	42N	35W	CNW-W 64.5
Panola	8	42N	32W	CNW-I 4.8
Park Siding	14	46N	34W	MILW-O 348.5
#Paulsens Spur				MILW-C
Pentoga	25	42N	34W	CNW-W 56.5
#Ponca				MILW-O 325
Porter Mine	(see Amasa-Porter Mine)			
Purcell Mine	14	43N	35W	MILW-C8 5.4
Ravenna Mine	19	43N	32W	CNW-I5 10.7
Richard	1	42N	34W	MILW-C 17.9
Riverton Mine	36	43N	35W	CNW-W16 0.1
Rogers Mine	29	43N	34W	CNW-W10 4.3
Saunders	(now Scott Lake)			
Scott Lake	20	42N	34W	CNW-W 61.5 – CNW-S 0
Shafer Mine	31	43N	32W	MILW-C7 0.8
Sherwood Mine	23	43N	35W	CNW-W13B3 0.3
Siding No. 2	(now Ponca)			
Siding No. 3	(now Diana)			
Spies Mine	24	43N	35W	MILW-C8 3.5 + 0.5
#Spur F22				MILW-C 22
#Spur F23				MILW-C 23
#Spur F27				MILW-C 27

#Spur 232			MILW-O 232
Spur 234	1	43N 31W	MILW-O 317.4
Spur 247	14	44N 33W	MILW-O 331.8
Spur 255	20	45N 33W	MILW-O 337.9
#Spur 256			MILW-O 340
#Spur 259			MILW-O 342
Spur 265	(see Park Siding)		
Stager	31	42N 33W	CNW-W 47.1 –
			CNW-I 0
Stambaugh	35	42N 35W	CNW-W 66.8
Stambaugh	36	42N 35W	MILW-C 25.6
Stambaugh Mine	25	43N 35W	CNW-W15 0.3
Sunn Spur	24	43N 34W	MILW-C 14.7
Tobin Mine	31	43N 32W	MILW-C7 1.0
Toleens (Spur)	(now Spur 234)		
Triangle Spur	33	45N 33W	MILW-O 336.9
Tully Mine	36	43N 35W	MILW-C9 0.4
#Union Mine			CNW-I?
Victoria Mine	(see Hilltop Mine)		
Virgil Mine	24	43N 35W	MILW-C8
			3.7 + 0.6
Warner Mine	9	44N 33W	MILW-O3 1.1
Warner Mine Jct.	15	44N 33W	MILW-O 332.6 –
			MILW-O3 0
Wauseca Mine	23	43N 35W	CNW-W13B2 0.5
#Wells Spur			MILW-C
Wickwire Mine	35	43N 35W	CNW-W12 1.4
Worthing	31	43N 34W	CNW-W10 2.4 –
			MILW-C 24.4
Youngs Mine	12	42N 35W	CNW-W10A 0.3
Youngstown Mine	19	43N 33W	CNW-I5 10.5
Zimmerman Mine	12	42N 34W	CNW-W10A 1.3

KEWEENAW COUNTY

Ahmeek	32	57N 32W	MR-C 19.1
#Ahmeek Jct.			MR
Allouez	(see same, Houghton Co.)		

Allouez Mine	32	57N	32W	MR-H3 3.7 + 0.7
Central	23	58N	31W	KC 18.1
Cliff	36	58N	32W	KC 12.5
Crestview	19	58N	31W	KC-2 2.0
Crestview Jct.	31	58N	31W	KC 13.8 – KC-2 0
Delaware	15	58N	30W	KC 23.0
Fulton	33	57N	32W	CR-C 0.4
Gay	30	56N	30W	CR-C 31.9
Gratiot Mine	27	57N	32W	KC 7.8 + 0.8
Hebards	6	56N	31W	CR-C 23.4
Lac la Belle	32	58N	30W	KC-3 5.6
Lac la Belle Jct.	14	58N	30W	KC 24.6 – KC-3 0
Mandan	17	58N	29W	KC 26.5
Mohawk	27	57N	32W	CR-M 1.4 – (KC 7.5 + 0.7)
Mohawk	28	57N	32W	KC 7.0; MR-C 20.7
Mohawk Mine	27	57N	32W	KC 7.3 + 0.7 – (CR-M 1.4); MR-C 21.3
Nichols	33	57N	32W	CR-C 18.8 – CR-M 0 – KC 5.4
Ojibway	14	57N	32W	KC 9.7
Ojibway Mine	14	57N	32W	KC 9.7 + 1.2
#Phillips				CR-C
Phoenix	32	58N	31W	KC 14.3
Phoenix Mine	30	58N	31W	KC-2 0.9
Snowshoe	21	56N	31W	CR-C 28.4
Traverse	17	56N	31W	CR-C 26.5
Wyoming	14	58N	30W	KC 23.7

LUCE COUNTRY

#Bonifas				DSSA-A
Danaher	34	46N	12W	DSSA-A 71.7
#Deer Park				DSSA
Dollarville	27	46N	10W	DSSA-A 60.3

East Branch	33	46N	12W	DSSA-A 73.2
Edjon	26	46N	9W	DSSA-A 52.5
Laketon	36	46N	12W	DSSA-A 70.2
Lencel	28	46N	9W	DSSA-A 55.4
McMillan	33	46N	11W	DSSA-A 67.2
McPhee	28	46N	9W	DSSA-A 54.8
Natalie	32	46N	10W	DSSA-A 62.0
Newberry	25	46N	10W	DSSA-A 58.5
Peroid	27	46N	9W	DSSA-A 53.9
Sage	33	46N	8W	DSSA-A 49.6
Soo Jct.	35	46N	8W	DSSA-A 42.9 — DSSA-A 46.6
Spur 75	31	46N	12W	DSSA-A 75.4

MACKINAC COUNTY

Allenville	4	40N	4W	DSSA-A 10.1
#Berst				DSSA-A
#Bissell				DSSA-A
#Bovee		43N	11W	SOO 416
#Browns Spur				SOO-4
#Burma				DSSA-A
Caffey	33	44N	7W	SOO 441.5
Carruthers Spur	(now Spur 409)			
#Cisco		43N	11W	SOO 417
Connors Spur	15	43N	10W	SOO 423.4
Corinne	31	43N	11W	SOO 414.3
Curtis	13	44N	12W	MAN-B 49.3
Diller	17	44N	12W	MAN-B 44.3
#Dunleith				SOO 425
Engadine	16	43N	10W	SOO 422.0
Fiborn (Quarry)	15	44N	7W	DSSA-A 33.8 + 3.1
Fiborn Jct.	1	44N	7W	DSSA-A 33.8
Garnet	33	44N	8W	SOO 435.7
Gilchrist	11	43N	9W	SOO 431.5
Gould City	28	43N	11W	SOO 415.9
Graylock	14	43N	10W	SOO 424.0

Greene	13	42N	5W	DSSA-A 13.9
#Haslemere		43N	11W	SOO 418
Hendricks Quarry	6	44N	8W	SOO-4 11.3
Hubbell	(now Rexton)			
Hunt Spur	18	42N	12W	SOO 407.0
Jacob City	(now Moran)			
#Johnson				DSSA
#Kemp				DSSA-A
Kennedy	(now Engadine)			
Kenneth	28	43N	5W	DSSA-A 19.6
Lewis	(now Caffey)			
#Marstone				DSSA-A
Meads Quarry	(now Hendricks Quarry)			
Mille Coquins	12	43N	10W	SOO 425.1
Moran	32	42N	4W	DSSA-A 11.0
#Murray				DSSA
Naubinway Jct.	16	43N	9W	SOO 428.7
#Nero				DSSA-A
Nogi	11	42N	4W	DSSA-A 16.1
Ozark	8	43N	5W	DSSA-A 22.9
Palms	34	43N	5W	DSSA-A 18.5
#Perrons Spur				SOO 420
Pike Lake	2	42N	12W	SOO 411.2
#Quinn				DSSA-A
#Reavie				DSSA-A 4
Rexton	36	44N	8W	SOO 439.0 –
				SOO-4 0
#Rugsten				DSSA
St. Ignace		40N	3W	DSSA-A 0
#Spur 407	(alt. name for Huntspur?)			
Spur 409	9	42N	12W	SOO 409.3
#Spur 410				SOO 410
#Spur 416		43N	11W	SOO 416
#Spur 428		43N	9W	SOO 428
#Spur 433				SOO 433
#Spur 438				SOO 438
#Spur 439				SOO 439
#Spur 442				SOO-4
#Spur 444				SOO 444
#Spur 444				SOO-4
Statts Spur	(now Gould City)			
Swift	24	43N	11W	SOO 419.4

Welch	(now Garnet)			
West Yard		40N	3W	DSSA-A 1.0
Wilman	16	44N	11W	MAN-B 52.1
#Yatton				SOO 413

MARQUETTE COUNTY

Adams Mine	6	47N	26W	LS&I-S2 0.5
Albion Mine	19	47N	27W	CNW-BC2 2.9
Alder	(now Ransom)			
Allen Mine	8	47N	26W	CNW-BX4 0.6
American Mine	32	48N	28W	CNW-G 188.5
American Mine Jct.	(now Blueberry Mine Jct.)			
Anderson	12	45N	24W	LS&I-A 33.3
Antlers	2	50N	27W	LS&I-B 21.4
Archibald Mine	(site now of Gwinn Mine)			
Arnold	12	42N	26W	E&LS 30.6
#Ash				LS&I
Athens	6	47N	26W	LS&I-O 68.2 — LS&I-02 0
Athens Mine	6	47N	26W	LS&I-02 0.5
Austin (Mine)	20	45N	25W	LS&I-A 43.6
Austin Jct.	3	43N	26W	E&LS-4 7.0 — E&LS-4A 0
Bagdad	24	48N	26W	DSSA-B 160.4
Bagdad Jct.	24	48N	26W	DSSA-B 159.8 — LS&I-S 63.0
Bancroft	20	48N	25W	DSSA-B 156.9
Barnes	1	47N	28W	LS&I-S 78.4
Barnes-Hecker Mine	2	47N	28W	LS&I-SB 0.4
Barnum Mine	9	47N	27W	LS&I-S5A 0.7
Barnum Mine	(at Barnum Siding on DSSA-B)			
Barnum Siding	9	47N	27W	DSSA-B 170.2
#Basil		47N	24W	LS&I-M 44

#Bayshore			MILW
#Beaver			CNW
Bennett Mine	(now New Richmond Mine)		
Bessie Mine	35	48N	29W	DSSA-B11 1.1
Bessie Mine Jct.	2	47N	29W	DSSA-B 181.1 — DSSA-B11 0
Big Bay	15	51N	27W	LS&I-B 27.4
Big Creek	16	47N	24W	LS&I-M 44.5
Birch	29	50N	26W	LS&I-B 15.8
Blueberry Mine	3	47N	28W	CNW-G 187.5 — DSSA-BB 3.3
Blueberry Mine Jct.	8	47N	28W	DSSA-B 178.9
Boston Jct.	(now Blueberry Mine Jct.)		
Boston Mine	32	48N	28W	DSSA-B5 2.1
Brasted Mine	21	47N	27W	DSSA-W1A 0.7
Breitung Mine	6	47N	26W	LS&I-O 68.8 + 0.2 — CNW-BO 175.6
Breitung-Hematite Mine	(now Breitung Mine)		
Brotherton Mine	(now Stegmiller Mine)		
#Browns Crossing			DSSA-B 187
Bruce	26	48N	25W	DSSA-B 159.7
Buckroe	2	49N	26W	LS&I-B 12.4
Buffalo Mine	5	47N	26W	DSSA-M5 0.2
Bunns	9	51N	27W	LS&I-B 28.0
#Burtis			LS&I-B
Cambria Mine	35	48N	27W	DSSA-M3 0.8; LS&I-SA2 1.3
Cambria-Jackson Mine	36	48N	27W	LS&I-SA2A 0.3
Camp 4	33	47N	23W	LS&I-M 38.0 + 2.2
#Camp 7			E&LS
Camp 8	14	43N	26W	E&LS-4B 2.0
Carlshend	7	45N	23W	LS&I-A 31.9
Carp	5	47N	26W	DSSA-B 164.9
Carp Furnace	26	47N	25W	LS&I-M 49.4
Cascade Jct.	30	47N	25W	CNW-B 169.2 — CNW-BC
Cascade Mine	(now Palmer Mine)		

Cedar Bank	14	45N	24W	LS&I-A 34.4
Champion	32	48N	29W	DSSA-B 185.7 – MILW-A 346.3 – (CNW-R8 via MILW)
Champion Jct.	32	48N	29W	DSSA-B 185.2 – DSSA-BCl 0 – MILW-A 345.8
Champion Mine	31	48N	29W	DSSA-BCl 1.6; DSSA-BC2 1.4; MILW-A8 2.0
Chase Mine	3	47N	28W	LS&I-BC 0.8
Cheshire Jct.	(now Swanzy)			
Cheshire Mine	(now Princeton Mine)			
Chicago Mine	7	47N	26W	LS&I-O3 1.2
Chocolay	(now Lakewood on DSSA-A)			
Clarksburg	7	47N	28W	DSSA-B 180.0
Cleveland Hematite Mine	2	47N	27W	DSSA-M2 1.8
Cleveland Mine	10	47N	27W	DSSA-O 169.0
Cliffs Mine	9	47N	27W	LS&I-S 73.3
Clowry	26	48N	29W	CNW-G 191.7 – CNW-R 191.7
Coal Dock	24	47N	25W	LS&I-M 51.5
Columbia Mine	(now Kloman Mine)			
Copps Spur	2	47N	28W	CNW-G 186.0 – LS&I-S 79.8
Crescent	13	47N	25W	LS&I-M 52.1
Cyr	34	45N	24W	CNW-B 151.5
Cyr Mine	35	45N	25W	LS&I-A2 1.3
Davis Mine	7	47N	26W	LS&I-O4 0.9
Dead River	13	48N	26W	LS&I-S 61.5
#Deer Lake				LS&I
Della	31	49N	25W	LS&I-B 7.2
Detroit Mine	3	47N	27W	DSSA-M2 2.1
Dewey	25	42N	25W	E&LS 24.4
Dexter Jct.	16	47N	28W	DSSA-B 177.2 – DSSA-B9 0
Dexter Mine	3	47N	28W	DSSA-B9 2.6
Dey Mine	(part of Dexter Mine)			

Diorite	32	48N	28W	CNW-G 188.4—
				DSSA-BB 1.8
Dishneau	26	48N	30W	DSSA-B 188.6
Dishno	23	48N	30W	CNW-G 197.8
#Dorias				DSSA
Dow	11	47N	25W	LS&I-M 53.7
Dukes	35	46N	23W	LS&I-M 29.5
Duncan	36	48N	29W	CNW-G 190.3—
				LS&I-R 84.1—
				LS&I-S 84.1
Eagle Mills	34	48N	26W	DSSA-B 162.9
Eagle Mills	35	48N	26W	LS&I-O 65.1—
				LS&I-S 65.1
Eagle Mills Transfer	34	48N	26W	LS&I-S 65.9
East Cambria Mine	35	48N	27W	LS&I-SA2 1.0
East Champion Mine	31	48N	29W	DSSA-BC1 1.0
East Chicago 40 Mine	(see Chicago Mine)			
East New York Mine	2	47N	27W	CNW-G 178.7
East Yard	26	48N	25W	DSSA-A 154.5—
				DSSA-B 154.5
#Emil				LS&I
Emmet	(now Lawson)			
Empire Mine	19	47N	26W	CNW-B2A 1.2;
				DSSA-P 3.9
Engine Works	14	47N	25W	LS&I-M 52.5
Erie Mine	21	47N	30W	DSSA-R2 4.2
Excelsior Mine	6	47N	27W	CNW-GX2 2.0
Finnegan	33	48N	26W	LS&I-S 67.2
Firmin	15	45N	24W	LS&I-A 35.2
Fitch Mine	24	47N	28W	DSSA-WGA 1.3
#Flynn				LS&I-M
Forestville	8	48N	25W	LS&I-S 57.6
Forsyth	(now Little Lake)			
Foster Mine	23	47N	27W	CNW-BC4 4.6
Francis Mine	27	45N	25W	LS&I-A2 4.8
#Fredeen No. 1				LS&I-M 41
Gardner Mine	35	45N	25W	LS&I-A2 2.0

#Gene				LS&I-A
Gentian	32	47N	25W	CNW-B 167.6
#Gillespie				LS&I
Gleason	10	43N	26W	E&LS-4 6.7
#Gleasons				DSSA
#Goodman				LS&I
#Goodrich				DSSA
Goose Lake	23	47N	26W	CNW-B 171.3
Gordon	7	47N	23W	DSSA-A 145.0
Granite	29	47N	29W	CNW-R 198.5
Granot	33	50N	26W	LS&I-B 14.7
Green Garden	25	47N	24W	LS&I-M 40.7
Greenwood	15	47N	28W	DSSA-B 176.2
Greenwood Mine	14	47N	28W	DSSA-BG 0.8
Greenwood Mine Jct.	13	47N	28W	DSSA-B 175.0 — DSSA-BG 0
Gwinn	21	45N	25W	LS&I-A 43.0
Gwinn Mine	28	45N	25W	LS&I-AG 0.5
Hard Ore Mine	10	47N	27W	LS&I-S5 0.3
Hartford Mine	36	48N	27W	DSSA-M3A 0.2
Harvey	6	47N	24W	LS&I-M 47.1
Harvey	30	47N	25W	CNW-B 167.9
Helena	11	44N	24W	CNW-B 149.2
Hematite Mine	10	47N	27W	LS&I-S5 0.5
#Hill Top				MILW
#Himrod Mine	7	47N	26W	
Hogan Ore Yard	33	48N	26W	DSSA-B 164.4
#Hoist				LS&I
Holmes Mine	9	47N	27W	DSSA-B 171.0; CNW-BC 13.6
#Holyoke				LS&I
Homeier	36	51N	27W	LS&I-B 23.2
Humboldt Jct.	1	47N	29W	DSSA-B 181.5 — DSSA-R 0
Humboldt Mine	11	47N	29W	LS&I-R 88.5
#Iris				LS&I
Iron Mountain Mine (now Lake Sally Mine)				
Iron Street Crossover	1	47N	27W	DSSA-B 166.9 — DSSA-BO 166.9 — DSSA-M 13.6

Iron Stret Jct.	1	47N	27W	CNW-B; 177.3 – DSSA-B 167.2
Iron Valley Mine	6	47N	26W	DSSA-M8 0.5
Isabella Mine	29	47N	26W	CNW-BC 5.0
Ishpeming	10	47N	27W	CNW-B 179.7 – CNW-G 79.7 – DSSA-B 169.6; LS&I-S 72.8; DSSA-BO 169.2 (old)
Ishpeming Yard	2	47N	27W	LS&I-S 71.6
Jackson Mine	1	47N	27W	CNW-B3 0.8
#Jean				LS&I-B
Johnsons Siding	19	48N	29W	CNW-G 195.7
Jopling	(now Copps Spur)			
Kates Lake	34	45N	27W	E&SL-4 17.5
#Kerkelas Spur		46N	30W	MILW-A
Keystone Mine	(now East Champion Mine)			
#Kilns				DSSA
Kloman Mine	6	46N	29W	DSSA-R2 9.3
#Knox				E&LS
Kruse Mine	(see Rolling Mill Mine)			
Lake Angeline Mine	15	47N	27W	CNW-BC 13.8; DSSA-M3 0.6;LS&I-S5 0.8
Lake Sally Mine	14	47N	27W	CNW-B2 5.4
Lake Superior Mine	9	47N	27W	CNW-G 183.1
Lakewood	6	47N	24W	DSSA-A 150.6; LS&I-M 47
Larsons Spur	(see same, Delta Co.)			
Lawson	2	45N	23W	LS&I-A 27.8 – LS&I-M 27.8
#Lefke				LS&I
#Lena				LS&I
Lillie Mine	35	48N	27W	DSSA-M3 1.0
Little Lake	20	45N	24W	CNW-B 155.3 – LS&I-A 37.9
Lloyd Mine	6	47N	27W	LS&I-SC 0.2

#Longwood			LS&I
Long Siding	3	48N	25W	LS&I-B 3.9
Longyear	24	47N	25W	LS&I-M 51.7
Low Moor	8	47N	28W	DSSA-B 178.3
#Lucky Star			LS&I
Lucy Mine	(see McOmber Mine)		
Maas Mine	31	48N	26W	LS&I-S 69.2
#Mack			LS&I-A
Mackinaw Mine	35	45N	25W	LS&I-A2 1.8
Magnetic Mine	20	47N	30W	DSSA-R2 15.9
Maitland Mine	30	47N	26W	CNW-BC 5.8
#Maney			LS&I-B
Mangum	24	47N	24W	LS&I-M 41.5
Mangum Mill	24	47N	24W	LS&I-M 41.8
#Marcus			LS&I
#Marigold			LS&I
Marquette	23	48N	25W	DSSA-B 155.0; LS&I-M 51.0
Marquette Scales	22	48N	25W	DSSA-B 155.8
#Martin		45N	24W	LS&I-A 35
Martins Landing	19	48N	29W	CNW-G 196.3
Mary Charlotte Mine	7	47N	26W	CNW-O 175.0
Mather Mine A	2	47N	27W	LS&I-SA 1.7
Mather Mine B	1	47N	27W	LS&I-SB 0.3
Mashek	7	42N	25W	E&LS 29.7— E&LS-3.0
#McDermitts			E&LS
McFarland(s)	25	44N	24W	CNW-B 146.7
McOmber Mine	6	47N	26W	CNW-B3 0.3
#McReavey			LS&I
Michigamme	19	48N	30W	CNW-G 201.9; DSSA-B 193.2
Michigamme Mine	19	48N	30W	DSSA-B 192.5; (CNW-G 200.4)
Midway	33	47N	29W	DSSA-R 5.2
#Millers Spur			E&LS
Milwaukee Jct.	(now Republic Jct.)		
Milwaukee Mine	7	47N	26W	LS&I-O4 0.7

Mineral Branch	8	47N	26W	CNW-B 174.6 — CNW-B2 0
Mitchell Mine	21	47N	27W	DSSA-W 1.6
Morgan	26	48N	26W	DSSA-B 162.0
#Morgan Heights				DSSA-B
Morris Mine	1	47N	28W	LS&I-SC 0.6
Mour	26	51N	27W	LS&I-B 24.2
National	14	47N	25W	LS&I-M 52.2
National Mine	21	47N	27W	CNW-BC 11.8
Negaunee	6	47N	26W	CNW-BO 176.7 (old); DSSA-M 13.2 (old); (new) CNW-B 174.6 + 2.4 — DSSA-B 166.1; LS&I-S 70.0
Negaunee Mine	6	47N	26W	DSSA-M4 0.8
New Dalton	17	46N	23W	LS&I-M 35.8
New England Mine	20	47N	27W	DSSA-B4 2.1
#New Furnace		47N	25W	LS&I-M 54
New Richmond Mine	27	47N	26W	CNW-BC 3.4 + 0.4
New Swanzy	17	45N	25W	CNW-BS 3.9; LS&I-A 42.4
New York Mine	3	47N	27W	CNW-B 179.2
New York Hematite Mine	6	47N	26W	CNW-B 176.3 + 0.2
Northampton Mine	30	48N	29W	DSSA-B6 2.1
North Jackson Mine	1	47N	27W	DSSA-M2B 0.2
North Lake	6	47N	27W	LS&I-S 76.7
Northland	5	42N	26W	E&LS 36.0 — E&LS-4 0
Northwestern Mine	(now Francis Mine)			
Ogden Mine	13	47N	27W	CNW-B2 3.4
Old Richmond Mine	28	47N	26W	CNW-BC 4.2
Ontonagon Jct.	(now Winthrop Jct.)			
#Oro		45N	25W	LS&I-A 44
Palmer	29	47N	26W	CNW-BC 5.3

Palmer Mine	(now Old Volunteer Mine)			
Parker Spur	14	44N	24W	CNW-B 148.8
Partridge	9	47N	26W	CNW-B 173.7
Pascoe Mine	29	48N	29W	DSSA-B6A 0.4
Penegor Spur	36	48N	29W	CNW-G 190.5
#Petrie				LS&I-B
Pickerel Lake	24	49N	26W	LS&I-B 8.8
Pinehill	13	48N	26W	LS&I-S 63.9
Pine Street	14	47N	25W	LS&I-M 52.7
Pioneer Mine	4	47N	26W	DSSA-M5 0.6
Plains	3	45N	25W	CNW-B 159.9
#Popple				LS&I
#Powder Hill				LS&I
Powell		50N	26W	LS&I-B 16
Power	11	47N	25W	LS&I-M 54.2
Presque Isle	2	48N	25W	LS&I-P 0.9
Princeton	18	45N	25W	CNW-BS 4.9—
				LS&I-A 45.8
Princeton No. 1 Mine	(at Princeton)			
Princeton No. 2 Mine	20	45N	25W	CNW-BSB 0.8
Prison	36	47N	25W	LS&I-M 28.6
Queen	4	47N	26W	LS&I-O 67.5—
				LS&I-S3 0
Queen Mine	5	47N	26W	LS&I-S3 0.3
#Rabro				LS&I
#Raish				LS&I
Ransom	26	51N	27W	LS&I-B 24.8
Reade	10	42N	26W	E&LS 33.4
#Reichels Mill				LS&I
Republic	7	46N	29W	CNW-R 203.7;
				DSSA-R 8.8;
				MILW-A 337.1
Republic Jct.	5	46N	29W	CNW-R 201.1—
				DSSA-R 6.7—
				MILW-A
				339.2—
				LS&I-R 93.6

Republic Mine	8	46N	29W	CNW-R2 0.9; DSSA-R 9.5; DSSA-R2A 1.0; LS&I-R 95.4; MILW-A7 0.8
#Richard				MILW
Riverside Mine	35	47N	30W	DSSA-R2A 0.6
Robbins Spur	18	47N	27W	DSSA-B 171.6
Rolling Mill Mine	7	47N	26W	DSSA-B3 1.5— (LS&I-S3 via DSSA)
Ross	21	43N	26W	E&LS-4 3.8— E&LS-4B 0
Saginaw Mine	19	47N	27W	CNW-BC2 3.1; DSSA-B4 2.5
St. Lawrence	6	47N	27W	CNW-G 183.1
Salisbury Mine	15	47N	27W	DNW-BC3 0.8
Sand River	12	47N	23W	DSSA-A 139.9
Sands	16	46N	25W	CNW-B 163.7
Schneider	11	47N	25W	LS&I-M 54.0
Selma	28	46N	23W	LS&I-M 31.1
Shenango Mine	(now Mitchell Mine)			
Siding 145	(see Gordon)			
Sigan	9	45N	23W	LS&I-A 30.0
Skandia	19	46N	23W	LS&I-M 33.9
Smith Mine	18	45N	25W	CNW-BS 5.0
Smith Mine Jct.	(now Swanzy)			
South Buffalo Mine	5	47N	26W	DSSA-M6 0.6
South Jackson				LS&I-O 70.0
South Main Jct.	1	47N	27W	DSSA-B 167.8
#Spears				LS&I-M
Spur 181	1	47N	29W	DSSA-B 181.3
#Spur 233½				MILW-A 316½
#Spur 248				MILW-A 331
#Spur 250		46N	30W	MILW-A 333
#Stack				CNW
Star West Mine	28	47N	26W	CNW-BC 4.5
Stegmiller Mine	20	45N	25W	LS&I-A 45.4
Stephenson Mine	20	45N	25W	CNW-BSB 1.3

#Stimson				DSSA
Stoneville	18	47N	27W	DSSA-B 173.6
Street Railway	11	47N	25W	LS&I-M 53.8
Sugarloaf	4	48N	25W	LS&I-B 5.4
#Superior		48N	25W	LS&I-M 53
Swanzy	13	45N	25W	CNW-B 157.6 –
				CNW-BS
#Taylors				CNW
Tilden Mine	26	47N	27W	LS&I-T 2.2
#Tylers				MILW-A
Union Park	2	47N	27W	DSSA-B 168.2 –
				DSSA-O 167.9
Van Iderstine	7	48N	25W	LS&I-S 60.3
#Valley Mill				DSSA-B
Vick	3	45N	23W	LS&I-A 28.9
Volunteer (New) Mine	25	47N	27W	DSSA-P 5.6
Volunteer (Old) Mine	(now Palmer Mine)			
Wabik	5	47N	29W	CNW-R 195.2 –
				MILW-A 345.1
Washington Mine	11	47N	29W	DSSA-B11 0.5
Watson	22	42N	25W	E&LS 26.2
Watson Mine	32	47N	26W	CNW-BC 4.6 + 0.5
West Branch	28	44N	26W	E&LS-4 10.3
West End Mine	31	47N	26W	CNW-BC 6.0
West Ishpeming	9	47N	27W	CNW-G 180.3
West Republic Mine	7	46N	30W	DSSA-R2A 1.0
West Yard	3	48N	25W	LS&I-B 3.7 – LS&I-M 54.7 – LS&I-P 0 – LS&I-S 54.7
Wheeling Mine	(now Davis Mine)			
#White				E&LS
Whitman	35	48N	26W	LS&I-M 65.1

Winthrop Jct.	16	47N	27W	CNW-BC 13.3 –
				CNW-BC3 0 –
				DSSA-B
				171.4 –
				DSSA-BO
				171.0 –
				DSSA-BW 0
Winthrop Mine	21	47N	27W	DSSA-W1 1.9
Witbeck	12	45N	30W	MILW-A 329.6
Witch Lake	23	45N	30W	MILW-A 326.6
Wolverine	28	44N	26W	E&LS-4 10.0
Yalmer	8	46N	23W	LS&I-M 37.1
Young	1	47N	27W	LS&I-S 69.8 –
				LS&I-SA 0

MENOMINEE COUNTY

Ames	24	36N	28W	W&M 40.9
#Anderson				CNW
Arnold	1?	36N	28W	W&M 44.7? –
				W&M-5 0
Bagley	36	37N	27W	CNW-A 82.2
#Ballous		37N	26W	CNW-A
Banat	13	36N	28W	W&M 42.7
#Berta				W&M
Birch Creek	3	32N	27W	CNW-A 57.6
Bird	3	37N	28W	W&M 51.9
#Blount				CNW
Blum	34	38N	28W	W&M 53.0
#Brooks		38N	28W	W&M 52
Camp 4	(now Vesper)			
#Camp 6				E&LS
Camp 31	31	38N	27W	SOO 308.2 + 4.1
Carbondale	3	33N	27W	CNW-A 62.8

Carney	19	37N	26W	CNW-A 84.7
Cedar	(now Camp 4)			
#Cedar		35N	28W	W&M 35
Cleeremans	18	39N	25W	CNW-E 18.6
Clytie	4	38N	27W	CNW-W 6.3
Coleman	27	32N	27W	CNW-A 52.7
#Comus				CNW-F 13
#Congo		36N	28W	W&M-5 0.8
Cunard	32	39N	27W	CNW-W 8.2
Daggett	2	35N	27W	CNW-A 75.7
Dougherty	11	38N	26W	CNW-A 94.2
Dryads	18	40N	25W	CNW-F 13.2
Eustis	24	39N	25W	SOO 325.1
Everett	25	37N	28W	W&M 46.2 – W&M-W 0
Faithorn	15	38N	28W	SOO 303.0
Faithorn Jct.	15	38N	28W	SPP 302.8 – S&M 55.2
#Farnham		39N	26W	SOO 318
Faunus	3	40N	26W	CNW-F 17.3
Ferry	(now Wilson)			
Fisher	36	35N	28W	W&M 32.8 – W&M-2 0
Gardner	12	36N	28W	W&M 43.9
Golden	13	40N	25W	E&LS-2 8.7
Gravel Pit	(now Talbot)			
Hammond	24	37N	28W	W&M 47.9 – W&M-4 0
Hansen	22	33N	27W	CNW-A 60.4
#Hansons Spur		39N	26W	SOO 318
Harris	11	38N	25W	CNW-A 101.6
#Hawley		36N	28W	W&M 40
Helps	19	41N	26W	CNW-F 22.6
Hermansville	11	38N	27W	CNW-W 4.3 – SOO 310.7
Houles	9	38N	25W	CNW-A 98.3
Houte	10	37N	28W	W&M 50.0
Indian Town	10	38N	25W	CNW-A 99.7
Ingalls	35	35N	27W	CNW-A 69.8 – W&M-2 5
#Johnsons Spur	21	38N	28W	SOO 302

Kells	11	35N	28W	W&M 36.7
Kew	15	32N	27W	CNW-A 54.6
Kirbys Spur	16	39N	25W	CNW-E 16.3
Kloman	32	38N	26W	CNW-A 89.0
Koss	36	35N	28W	W&M 32.9
LaBranch(e)	11	40N	26W	CNW-F 15.4
#Larsons Spur		39N	25W	SOO 323
#Lauris				W&M
Leapers	7	39N	27W	CNW-E 31.9
Longrie	26	35N	28W	W&M 34.3
Malacca	18	38N	27W	SOO 306.3
#Marl		38N	28W	W&M 57
Menominee	2	31N	27W	MILW-M 22.4
Menominee	3	31N	27W	CNW-A 50.7
Menominee Jct.	(now Powers)			
Meyer	9	38N	27W	SOO 308.2
#Mumfords		37N	26W	CNW-A
Nadeau	7	37N	26W	CNW-A 86.4
Nathan	24	37N	28W	W&M 47.0
#Newton				W&M
Oro	15	39N	26W	CNW-E 21.7
#Osborn				CNW
#Parsons Spur		39N	25W	SOO 324
Perronville	2	39N	25W	CNW-F 7.5
Phee	32	37N	28W	W&M-W 3.8
Porter	(now Powers)			
Powers	16	38N	26W	CNW-A 92.1 – CNW-W 0
#Radfords Spur		39N	25W	SOO 321
#Relay Station		35N	27W	W&M-2
Rondo	13	37N	28W	W&M-4 1.5
Rooney	7	38N	26W	CNW-W 2.1
#Sherlocks				CNW
Siding No. 2	13	39N	25W	CNW-E 14.0
Siding No. 3	15	39N	26W	CNW-E 22.2
Siding No. 4	9	39N	27W	CNW-E 30.1
Spalding	16	38N	26W	CNW-A 93.0; SOO 314.6 + 2.2
Spur 21	(now Stephenson)			
#Spur 308				SOO 308

Spur 309	10	38N	27W	SOO 309.5
Spur 315	4	38N	26W	SOO 314.6
Stephenson	23	35N	27W	CNW-A 72.4
Swanson	36	36N	28W	W&M 39.5
Talbot	14	36N	27W	CNW-A 79.1
#Vega	?11	39N	27W	CNW-E 28
Vesper	(now Cunard)			
Wallace	23	34N	27W	CNW-A 66.3
Whitney	34	40N	25W	CNW-F 9.6
Wilson	7	38N	25W	CNW-A 96.7

ONTONAGON COUNTY

Adventure	36	51N	38W	CR-G 1.1;
				MR-S2 0.8
Agate	16	47N	38W	DSSA-B 242.1
Baltimore	19	48N	39W	DSSA-B 252.5
#B. and B. Spur				MILW-0
Barclay	13	46N	39W	CNW-C 12.0
Belt	(now Lake Mine)			
Bergland	4	48N	42W	DSSA-C 269.5 −
				DSSA-CW 0
#Bergland Mills				DSSA
Bowles Spur	34	52N	40W	ONT 3.0
Brady	14	50N	39W	MILW-O 393.5
#Brauns				DSSA
Bruces Crossing	22	48N	39W	DSSA-B 250.0
#Camp No. 5		51N	41W	ONT 10.0
#Camp Tolfree	?6	50N	41W	ONT
Choate	27	46N	40W	CNW-C 23.1
#Cousin		51N	41W	ONT 10.8
Craigsmere	36	47N	40W	CNW-C 17.9 −
				CNW-C3 17.9
Cranberry Jct.	6	51N	40W	ONT 6.3
Evergreen	35	51N	38W	MR-S2 1.8
Ewen	27	48N	40W	DSSA-B 255.3 −
				DSSA-C 255.3
Falls	8	47N	38W	DSSA-B 243.2

Floodwood River	4	51N	40W	ONT 4.7
#Francis Siding				MR-S
#Gale				DSSA-C
Gem	24	48N	39W	DSSA-B 247.4
#Gilson				MR-S
Green	1	51N	41W	ONT 7.0
Greenland	35	51N	38W	CR-G 2.3
Greenland Jct.	31	51N	37W	CR-A 2.1 – CR-G 0
Groesbeck	(now Topaz)			
#Halpin		51N	41W	ONT 12.0
#Hannah		51N	41W	ONT 8.4
Haskins	17	48N	43W	DSSA-C 276.8
Hubbells Mill	(now Rousseau)			
Indiana	27	51N	37W	CR-A 5.8
#Interior		46N	38W	CNW-C2 9
#Interior Jct.		46N	38W	CNW-C 8 –
				CNW-C2 8
Iron River Jct.	12	51N	41W	ONT 7.5
#Iron River Spur				MILW-O
#Jensen				DSSA
#Jumbo				DSSA-B
Lake Gogebic	7	48N	42W	DSSA-C 272.4
Lake Mine	31	51N	37W	CR-A 2.6
#Lindstedt				DSSA-C
#Maki				MR-S
Mass	5	50N	38W	MR-S 32.8
Mass	9	50N	38W	MILW-O 388.9
#Mass Mine	6	50N	38W	MR-S2 2.8
Matchwood	14	48N	41W	DSSA-C 261.0
McKeever	9	50N	38W	CR-A 0 –
				MILW-O 388.2
Merriweather	12	48N	43W	DSSA-C 273.1
#Michigan Mine		50N	39W	MR-S3 3.4
#Miners Spur				MILW-O
#Nester				DSSA
#North Lake				CR
#Norton				MILW-O
O'Brien	(now Nester)			
Ontonagon	25	52N	40W	MILW-O 407.8 –
				ONT 0
Paynesville	25	48N	39W	DSSA-B 246.4

Paulding	10	46N	39W	CNW-C 14.6
Peppard	4	50N	38W	CR-A 1.4 — MR-S 32.0 — MR-S2 0
Radford	19	47N	40W	CNW-C 23.7
Range Jct.		(now McKeever)		
Riddle Jct.	18	50N	38W	MILW-O 391.2 — MR-S 35.6 — MR-S3 0
Robbins	18	46N	39W	CNW-C3 21.3
Rockland	16	50N	39W	MILW-O 396.2
Rogers	17	48N	43W	DSSA-C 277.2
Rousseau	30	50N	37W	MILW-O 384.2
#Rubicon				MR-S
#St. Collins	21	48N	39W	DSSA-B 251
Sandhurst	27	47N	40W	CNW-C 21.1 — CNW-C4 21.1
#Schriver				DSSA
Seager	11	51N	37W	CR-A 9.5
#Senecal				CR
Simar	35	51N	37W	MR-S 27.0
#South Lake Mine				CR
#Spies-Thompson		51N	41W	ONT 9.5
Spur 267	2	48N	42W	DSSA-C 267.2
Spur 274	11	48N	43W	DSSA-C 274.0
Spur 275	16	48N	43W	DSSA-C 275.5
Spur 276		(now Haskins)		
Spur 277		(now Rogers)		
#Spur 307				MILW-O
#Spur 314				MILW-O 397
Spur 318		(now Wood Spur)		
#Stevenson				MILW-O
Stratton	2	51N	37W	CR-A 10.5
Topaz	8	48N	41W	DSSA-C 264.5
#Tolfree				MILW
Trout Creek	12	47N	38W	DSSA-B 239.1
Wainola	15	50N	38W	MILW-O 387.7
#Ward Spur				?
Wasas	23	50N	38W	MILW-O 386.5
White Pine	4	50N	42W	DSSA-CW 14.0
Wood Spur	16	51N	39W	MILW-O 402.1

SCHOOLCRAFT COUNTY

Ackley	11	44N	13W	MAN-B 41.3
Bear Creek	16	43N	13W	B&S 6.8
Beesons (Spur)	16	43N	16W	M&LS 13.4
Blaney	21	43N	13W	B&S 6.1
Blaney Jct.	22	42N	13W	B&S 0 — SOO 404.1
#Camp Seven Hill	33	47N	13W	MAN-A 26
Camp 10	3	47N	13W	MAN-A 19.6
#Camp 14				B&S
Camp 34	25	44N	18W	M&LS-2 3.5
#Camp 35				M&LS
Camp 65	(now Scotts)			
#Camp 74				SOO
Camp 85	(now Hovey)			
Camp 86	(now Spur 15)			
#Casemore				M&LS
Cherry Valley	6	41N	15W	SOO 387.4
Cooks	30	41N	17W	GB 0 — SOO 375.0
Cooks Mill	(now Cooks)			
Cooper	21	45N	18W	M&LS-3 5.5 — M&LS-3A 0
Creighton	35	46N	16W	DSSA-A 95.0
Curson	35	46N	13W	DSSA-A 76.7
Cusino	30	47N	16W	LS&I-E 23.2
Delta (Jct.)	24	41N	17W	SOO 380.6
#Doyles				M&LS-3B 5
Doyles Wye	20	45N	18W	M&LS-3 6.6 — M&LS-3B 0
Driggs	(now Spur 88)			
East Branch Jct.	8	46N	13W	MAN-A 27.2
#Eastlake				SOO 379
#Fordville				B&S
Germfask	34	45N	13W	MAN-B 38.4
Goodson	35	46N	13W	DSSA-A 77.5
Gravel Pit	17	44N	17W	M&LS 23
Gridley	(now Blaney Jct.)			

Gulliver	35	42N	14W	SOO 398.5
Gulliver Lake	(now Gulliver)			
#Haco		41N	17W	SOO 376
#Hartman		42N	16W	M&LS 7
Hartman	6	44N	17W	M&LS 26.0
Hiawatha	27	43N	16W	M&LS 11.1 −
				M&LS-5 0
#Hiawatha Mill		43N	16W	M&LS-5 3
#Hovey				M&LS-3A 6
Inland Jct.	13	42N	13W	SOO 406.2
Klondike	7	44N	17W	M&LS 24.7
#Lilley Lake				M&LS
Limestone	3	42N	17W	B&S 2.7
Liston	23	47N	13W	MAN-A 22.2
#Maki				M&LS-3A 2
Manistique	12	41N	16W	M&LS 1.4; SOO
				386.7
Manistique River	36	42N	16W	M&LS 3.7
Manistique Wharf	13	41N	16W	M&LS 0
Marblehead				
Quarry	36	42N	15W	SOO 393.1 + 1.4
Marblehead Spur	1	42N	15W	SOO 393.1
McDonald Lake	30	42N	13W	SOO 400.5
#McInnes		44N	17W	M&LS
#McNeils		45N	18W	M&LS-3 8
Mooreville	28	43N	13W	B&S 5.1
#Moran		45N	18W	M&LS-3 6
#Myers				LS&I-E
Nelsonville	(now Creighton)			
#New Kentucky				B&S
#New Seney				DSSA-A
#Nicholsville				B&S
#Parker				M&LS-3A 3
Parkington	29	42N	13W	SOO 401.8
Puillions	(see Spur 28)			
Richardson	18	45N	17W	M&LS 31.0
#Riddles Spur				SOO
#St. Thomas				B&S
Scotts	31	45N	17W	M&LS 26.9 −
				M&LS-3 0
Scotts Camp	(now Scotts)			

Seney	32	46N	13W	DSSA-A 79.5 — MAN-A 31.6
Siding 378	26	41N	17W	SOO 378.5
Smiths Creek	8	43N	16W	M&LS 14.4
South Manistique		41N	16W	M&LS 2; SOO 385
Springer	(now Siding 378)			
#Spruceville		42N	16W	M&LS 8
#Spur 4		42N	16W	M&LS 4
#Spur 8		42N	16W	M&LS 8
#Spur 13		43N	16W	M&LS 13
#Spur 15		43N	16W	M&LS 15
#Spur 20				M&LS 20
#Spur 24		44N	17W	M&LS 24
#Spur 25		44N	17W	M&LS 25
#Spur 28				M&LS 28
Spur 80	32	46N	13W	DSSA-A 80.3
Spur 81	36	46N	14W	DSSA-A 81.7
#Spur 84				DSSA-A 84
Spur 88	36	46N	15W	DSSA-A 87.9
Spur 91	33	46N	15W	DSSA-A 91.1
Spur 97	33	46N	16W	DSSA-A 97.3
#Spur 392				SOO 392
#Spur 402				SOO 402
Starr Wye	11	47N	13W	MAN-A 20.5
State Road	4	47N	13W	MAN-A 18.3
Station Nine	2	42N	16W	M&LS 8.6
Steuben	20	44N	17W	M&LS 21.3
Walsh	34	46N	15W	DSSA-A 90.5
#Wards				MAN
White Dale	(now Gulliver Lake)			

SOURCES

The data for this compilation was obtained largely from railroad sources: public timetables and employee timetables issued between 1890 and 1970, and company directories of stations and agents. The mileage data then was transferred onto county maps to determine site locations more precisely. In some cases United States Geographic Survey topographical maps were also used. In a few cases railroad mileages have been corrected to place a station in its proper section of land. Added data was obtained from the *Official Guide of the Railways* (National Railway Publishing Co., New York) using random dates between 1868 and 1976. About three-quarters of the data herein came from these sources.

Abandoned lines for which satisfactorily accurate mileage data was not available were measured from topographical maps and checked against available sources.

The following sources were used, at random dates, to develop additional entries: *Bullinger's Postal and Shippers Guide* (Bullinger's Monitor Guides, Inc., New York), *Official List of Open and Prepay Stations* (Railroad Station Guide Publishing Co., St. Louis), and Rand McNally & Company *Commercial Atlas of the United States*. Non-railroad sources used were Walter Romig's *Michigan Place Names* (Grosse Pointe, n.d.), Roy Dodge's *Michigan Ghost Towns* (3 vols., Troy, 1970–1973), and the state legislature's *Michigan Manual* (Lansing, 1868–1900). A number of county atlases, published between 1870 and 1900, were used to clarify some of the entries.